Frantz Fanon for the 21st Century Volume 2

Frantz Fanon's Discourse of Decolonisation and Violence, the Nature of Power and Power Relations of Neo-colonial African States, the Neo-colonial Condition and the Impact of the Anti-colonial War of Algeria on the Psyche of Algerians Deconstructed.

Daurius Figueira

Table of Contents

Introduction 1

Chapter One | The Discourse of Decolonisation and Violence 3

Chapter Two | The Revolutionary Agents of Change 43

Chapter Three | The Neo-Colonial Condition 69

Chapter Four | War of Liberation, National Culture and National Consciousness 99

Chapter Five | French Torture and Algerian Mental Disorders 125

Chapter Six | Selections from "Toward the African Revolution" 183

Epilogue | The Neo-Colonial Condition of the 21st Century Illustrated 205

References 207

Introduction

The work that follows is a deconstruction of the discourse of Frantz Fanon contained in the final book he wrote before his death in December 1961 titled "The Wretched of the Earth." In this deconstruction the text is gleaned of its major discursive concepts and each discursive concept is stretched to the limits of its logical coherence to extract the maximum meaning from them towards their relevance to understanding 21st century reality. The final text consists then of the major discursive concepts of Fanon that are of potent relevance to the understanding of 21st century reality all named, cited from the text and deconstructed where its analytical potency and relevance to the 21st century is articulated. What results at the end of the process is a collection of tools and instruments that are vitally necessary to generating a liberationary knowledge contained within a liberationary discourse.

Frantz Fanon in "The Wretched of the Earth" wasted none of his limited time by pursuing the futile rocky road of dealing with the symptoms and outcomes of the neo-colonial subservience of the newly independent former colonies of Africa. Fanon dealt with the power relations and the actors enmeshed in these power relations that ensured we moved from colony to independence to neo-colonialism in one swift move laterally. Fanon then points to the mechanism of domination and the means of servility and subservience present to this day in the 21st century where he points to a psychological basis of servility and subservience. Fanon insists that colonial power pursued and ensured the constituting of personality types that with independence willingly worked for, sought, accepted, demanded and defended neo-colonial domination at the hands of the white North Atlantic. This is then for Fanon the essence of the neo-colonial condition and he insists that there will be **no** end to human suffering and underdevelopment under neo-colonial domination, for there can be no end for the simple reason that these subservient personality types are incapable of anything other than barbarity, suffering and underdevelopment. This is why Fanon unapologetically insists that decolonisation must be purchased through violent encounters with and against the colonial overlord for its only through anticolonial violence that the deeply ingrained depersonalisation, its inferiority complexes and the internal structure to constitute us into replicants will be dismantled and purged from our psyches. The gift of independence from the colonial massa is **not** decolonisation and **can never be** as it left all of these assets in place and in play, which flowed unhindered into the independence stage, which soon became the neo-colonial stage. Fanon in his discourse points to the colonial/neo-colonial continuum where the colonial power relations and the colonial personality simply flowed into the neo-colonial stage unhindered and unchanged giving rise to the neo-colonial personality and the condition. When you fail to decolonise via violent revolution then prepare to fail. In the 21st century the signs of failure are legion as they have not diminished with time, hence the need to now assault us with the white myth of Wakanda now monetised by Hollywood for we neo-colonials are shameless, which is simply one outcome of our servility. Steven, Chicken George, Gunga Din and Hop Sing all in a row.

This then is a deconstruction of Frantz Fanon's discourse of decolonisation and violence, the nature of power and the power relations of the neo-colonial African states, the neo-colonial condition and the impact of the anti-colonial war of Algeria on the psyche of the Algerians, where profound discursive concepts of strategic relevance to the 21st century are unearthed. In this exercise of deconstruction Fanon gestures repeatedly in the text to the operational existence of the colonial/neo-colonial continuum which is a most potent concept that must be fully articulated towards articulating the neo-colonial condition in all its nakedness. This concept insists that we must now seek out the evidence to articulate the enslavement/colonial domination continuum which is of special relevance to articulating the central role enslavement and colonial domination in the Caribbean played in the evolution of North Atlantic white supremacist discourse over the centuries.

Chapter One
The Discourse of Decolonisation and Violence

This first chapter deconstructs Fanon's discourse of decolonisation presented as the first portion of his work "Wretched of the Earth." There has been an emphasis on Fanon's position on violence and decolonisation in the decades of the 1960s and the 1970s following the publication of this work in French then English. This emphasis has attempted to silenced the potency of Fanon's analysis and insights expressed via his discourse of decolonisation, especially its relevance as an analytic tool for those neo-colonial social orders where the colonial overlord simply granted independence, choosing not to wage a war for retention of the colony, heralding in the new era of neo-colonial domination. The potency of Fanon's analysis is revealed via the deconstruction that follows.

Decolonisation

Fanon states as follows: "decolonisation is always a violent phenomenon." "decolonisation is quite simply the replacing of a certain 'species' of men by another 'species' of men. Without any period of transition, there is a total, complete, and absolute substitution." "But we have precisely chosen to speak of that kind of *tabula rasa* which characterises at the outset all decolonisation." "To tell the truth, the proof of success lies in a whole social structure being changed from the bottom up." (Fanon 1963 pg. 35). To focus on decolonisation as being always violent masks the reality that Fanon insists that there is decolonisation without the war of liberation. This is most apparent in his definition of decolonisation where he insists that the focus must be on the reality that obtained regardless of the process used to attain independence from colonial rule. That is the abrupt break in the nature of the power relations of the social order which occurred without transition, where the colonial power mechanism was rendered in time and space immediately illegitimate and the vacuum created must be filled by a new order of power immediately where the colonial operatives on the ground were now absent, illegitimate as was colonial law, manifest destiny and right of conquest. There is then this recognition by Fanon that both forms of decolonisation by war of liberation or by the gift of independence generated change in the social order without transition where a specific species of men disappeared, replaced by another species of men in the power structure. Fanon is not then extolling violence as the ideal, what he is positing is that there must be a criterion applied to discern the differences wrought by the application of both methodologies, wars of liberation or the gift of independence, which Fanon insists is the proof of success where the entire social order of the decolonised nation must be changed from the bottom up. Fanon is then insisting that a successfully decolonised social order is one where the victims of colonial domination, racism and underdevelopment are now wielding power in and over this social order. This is the criterion Fanon applies throughout his discourse of decolonisation towards explaining the failure to create a decolonised social order, in spite of decolonisation, in the majority of the former colonies of the world. This failure then constitutes us as underdeveloped and the Third World where we have failed miserably, for Fanon is affixing the blame on us as he flagellates our servile beings and the legacy we have foisted on our future generations. Fanon continues: "Decolonisation, which sets out to change the order of the world, is, obviously, a program of complete disorder." "Decolonisation, as we know, is a historical process." (Fanon 1963 pg. 36). Fanon is now in his text embracing the process of presenting the power relations of decolonisation in all its diversity, hence the variety of outcomes as it is a historical process. Therefore, each colony and the methodology applied has its specificity hence the quest for a new world order generates complete disorder. The reasons for this diversity and disorder generated by a historical process are as follows: "Decolonisation is the meeting of two forces, opposed to each other by their very nature, which in fact owe their originality to that sort of substantification which results from and is nourished by the situation in the colonies. Their first encounter was marked by violence and their existence together-that is to say the exploitation of the native by the settler-was carried on by dint of a great array of bayonets and cannons." "For it is the settler who has brought the native into existence and who perpetuates his existence." (Fanon 1963 pg. 36). The force/power relations of colonisation are those of decolonisation where the two social order entities wielding power in a power relation substantify each other, for there can be no settler without the native and vice versa. Decolonisation then constitutes a crisis of being, of transcendence of identity and the destruction of the material basis of a historical process of power which raises the potent question of how do you write decolonisation on the ground, on the micro engagements of power, hence its inherent disorder and instability. What arises to replace the settler-native configuration at the point of complete change without transition endemic to decolonisation, regardless of instrument utilised, is then the grave reality that must be focused on not Fanon's supposed embrace of violence as the idyllic. For in the absence of a mechanism to erase the legacy of colonial domination the entire apparatus of power that constituted the settler, colonial overlord/native, colonised complex will survive the transitionless substitution and replicate itself on a new terrain of power, thereby constituting the neo-colonial condition. Fanon was then presenting the nature of two social orders arising from decolonisation and in this comparison of postcolonial social orders he arrives at the mechanism of power that makes the difference between the neo-colonial condition driven by the white-black complex and the liberated postcolonial condition. For Fanon this mechanism of power is violence exercised within the parameters of a war of liberation from colonial domination. Fanon insists that colonial domination is premised on violence as it was attained by and maintained by violence where violence then permeated the power relations of the social order. Colonial domination is premised on violence, which ensures that decolonisation must also be violent, and the social order formed through decolonisation carries that taint and proclivity including and especially those where independence was a gift from the colonial overlord. For without the war of liberation the transitionless substitution was effected in a social order denied catharsis riddled with the tensions of the colonial order. Fanon continues: "Decolonisation never takes place unnoticed, for it influences individuals and modifies them fundamentally. It transforms spectators crushed with their inessentiality into privileged actors," "Decolonisation is the veritable creation of new men." "the thing which has been colonised becomes man during the same process by which it frees itself." "In decolonisation, there is therefore the need of a complete calling in question of the colonial situation." "That is why, if we try to describe it, all decolonisation is successful." (Fanon 1963 pgs. 36-37). Juxtaposed against colonisation and supposedly contrary to colonisation is decolonisation, where new human beings, free human beings are created by the process of decolonisation which is why the decolonisation process is and must be palpable for it banishes the inessentiality of being colonised, replacing it with privileged citizens. But does it? For the mere existence in the 21st century of the Third World indicates that decolonisation has in fact produced a tortured, fractured, underprivileged, servile, dominated and violent neo-colonial Third World where the North Atlantic retained and heightened its colonial hegemony during the post-colonial period. Hence the need for the interrogation of the colonial situation, for decolonisation in all its forms was successful, which illustrates the tenacity of the hegemonic power of the North Atlantic over the postcolonial world. The hegemonic power of the North Atlantic constitutes the Third World whilst the Third World affirms, enables and heightens the hegemonic power of the North Atlantic. They then substantify each other, potently indicating that the mechanism of power devised under colonial domination has survived, evolved and acquired a globalised basis in the 21st century which states potently that the colonial situation devised a mechanism of decolonisation that served its quest for sustainable hegemony with the full complicity of the colonised.

Violence

Fanon insists that given the violent nature of colonial domination and the violent and compartmentalised colonial social order, decolonisation should reflect this underlying reality and when it is not it is because of the complicity of the colonised. Fanon states: "For if the last shall be first, this will only come to pass after a murderous and decisive struggle between the two protagonists." "The native is ready for violence at all times. From birth it is clear to him that this narrow world, strewn with prohibitions, can only be called in question by absolute violence." (Fanon 1963 pg. 37). To overturn the order of colonial domination with this transitionless substitution, the colonial order teaches that the violence it embodies must be used against it and the colonised is convinced of this certainty. For the very spatial structure of the colonial order is premised on exclusion and the rigid policing of this exclusion which confirms a hierarchy where race, privilege, power and the wielding of the instruments of power, the primary being violence, merge, embrace and are exercised. The lesson of the need to match and exceed the endemic violence of the colonial order by the colonised in order to effect the transitionless substitution is afforded by the colonial order to every one of

the colonised on a daily existential basis and this lesson is in the 21st century part of the globalised neo-colonial order. Fanon states: "The colonial world is a world divided into compartments." "Yet, if we examine closely this system of compartments we will at least be able to reveal the lines of force it implies. This approach to the colonial world, its ordering and its geographical layout will allow us to make out the lines on which a decolonised society will be reorganised." (Fanon 1963 pgs. 37-38). Fanon is insisting that the lines of force/the power relations in the colonial society must be deconstructed in order to expose the relationship between the colonial order and the postcolonial order for in all instances, whether decolonisation by war of liberation or gift of independence, the power relations of the colonial order will impact the power relations of the postcolonial order. This impact is the product of the racist hierarchical structures of the colonial order reflected in its spatial organisation and the ferocity of its instruments of power. Fanon continues on the nature of the lines of force and the compartmentalisation of the colonial order as follows: "the policeman and the soldier, by their immediate presence and their frequent and direct action maintain contact with the native and advise him by means of rifle butts and napalm not to budge. It is obvious here that the agents of government speak the language of pure force. The intermediary does not lighten the oppression, nor seek to hide the domination; he shows them up and puts them into practice with the clear conscience of an upholder of the peace, yet he is the bringer of violence into the home and into the mind of the native." (Fanon 1963 pg. 38). In the colonial order the lines of force are made present, expressive and exercised to etch on the perceptions of the colonised the ever present reality of the ability and willingness of the coloniser to unleash violence on us. This is a strategy to impact the behaviour of the colonised where we police ourselves in a relentless futile bid to avoid violence that is a goal in itself devoid of cause and effect. And this order of violence continues in the postcolonial order where the lines of force are now demarcated and exercised by the policing agencies of the State and insurgent criminal groups and individuals. Fanon now deals with the spatial hierarchisation of the colonial social order as follows: "The zone where the natives live is not complementary to the zone inhabited by the settlers. The two zones are opposed, but not in the service of a higher unity." "No conciliation is possible, for of the two terms, one is superfluous. The settlers' town is a strongly built town, all made of stone and steel." "The settlers' town is a town of white people, of foreigners." "The town belonging to the colonised people, or at least the native town, the Negro village, the medina, the reservation, is a place of ill fame, peopled by men of evil repute." "It is a world without spaciousness" "The native town is a hungry town" "It is a town of niggers and dirty Arabs." "The colonised man is an envious man." (Fanon 1963 pgs. 38-39). The fact of and the strategic imperative of/for domination constitutes the rigidly defined boundaries of native town/settler town which ensures that the two spatial expressions are mutually irreconcilable, hence they can never be operationalised within a unified overarching order in search of unity of designated spaces. There can be no concept of nation and nationalism. There is then a mortal constant battle constituted hence the centrality of violence, for only one space so designated can have specificity expressed with dominance whilst the other is superfluous at best. Out of this cauldron of violence driven human interaction the native desires all the settler has and enjoys and the settler recognised this as a grave threat to her/his personal security and that of the sustainability of the colonial enterprise. In this driving desire and the paranoid fear the settler has, the power relations that impact the path chosen for decolonisation, namely defining of the choice between colonial resistance to the demand for decolonisation where colonial violence begets the war of liberation and the gift of independence where the coloniser simply walks away from the colony. The thin edge of the wedge, of the colonial power making any one of two possible choices, that is fully exploited is the desire of the native for all that the settler enjoys and possesses. For through the exploitation of this desire the neo colonial hegemony of the former colonial overlord is constituted. Fanon's position on violence is then a product of the centrality of violence to the colonial social order and faced with a colonial overlord choosing to wage war to defeat the movement for decolonisation violence is now the only means to realising decolonisation. Fanon continues: "When you examine at close quarters the colonial context, it is evident that what parcels out the world is to begin with the fact of belonging to or not belonging to a given race, a given species. In the colonies the economic substructure is also a superstructure. The cause is the consequence; you are rich because you are white, you are white because you are rich. This why Marxist analysis should always be slightly stretched every time we have to do with the colonial problem." (Fanon 1963 pg. 40). The violence of the colonial order which begets the violence of decolonisation is the product of the discourse of white supremacy that orders the society into a race based, racist hierarchy where the white minority dehumanises the non-white majority as the justification for the graphic violence unleashed to ensure white hegemony. White supremacy in a minority hegemonic position combines racism and violence, thereby constituting a racist endemically violent social order, where violence is racialized targeting the majority non-white race who responds to this daily reality in a number of ways, which includes the quest to eliminate the white minority to attain freedom from white supremacist domination. Violence then becomes a cleansing force bequeathed to the colonised by white supremacist colonial domination and the waging of war to deny the longing for freedom. Fanon states: "The violence which has ruled over the ordering of the colonial world," "that same violence will be claimed and taken over by the native at the moment when, deciding to embody history in his own person, he surges into the forbidden quarters." "The destruction of the colonial world is no more and no less that the abolition of one zone, its burial in the depths of the earth or its expulsion from the country." (Fanon 1963 pgs. 40-41). The white supremacist colonial enterprise then constitutes the need for violence to dismantle and uproot its power, presence and impact upon the colonised and the terrain of the colony for it's this racist enterprise that constitutes the colonised and the colony. Failure to affect this purge ensures the continuity of the white supremacist enterprise under a new guise of neo colonial hegemony, where the miseries of colonial domination multiply and become entrenched from generation to generation demeaning us to be the wretched of the Earth, to be Third

World rather than First World. Fanon in 1961, recognises the problematic involved in applying the Historical Materialist paradigm of Marx and Engels to colonial and postcolonial realities, a paradigm that throws up false realities when applied to the colonial and postcolonial existence. In the 21st century not even stretching this failed paradigm can render it relevant to our reality as it is addressed to North Atlantic realities, not ours, with all its connections to the Enlightenment.

Fanon continues his analysis of violence in the text as follows: "The uprising of the new nation and the breaking down of colonial structures are the result of one or two causes: either of a violent struggle of the people in their own right, or of actions on the part of surrounding colonised peoples which acts as a brake on the colonial regime in question." (Fanon 1963 pg. 70). There is then a multifaceted fight that is effective against colonial domination: a war of liberation in a specific colony and the impact of a war of liberation in a specific colony on the international strategy of a colonial metropolitan country. Fanon continues: "This encompassing violence does not work upon the colonised people only; it modifies the attitude of the colonialists who become aware of manifold Dien Bien Phus. This is why a veritable panic takes hold of the colonialist government in turn. Their purpose is to capture the vanguard, to turn the movement of liberation toward the right, and to disarm the people: quick, quick, let's decolonise." (Fanon 1963 pg. 70). Violence expressed in a war of colonial liberation not only impacts the colonised but the strategy of the metropolitan based coloniser, where in a bid to avert further escalation towards wars of liberation breaking out in other colonies the gift of independence is dispersed as Santa Claus on Christmas Eve in a concerted attempt to ensure the hegemony of the neo-colonial project. Which indicates that the neo-colonial project is the instrument formulated by the metropoles to exert hegemony over their colonies in the postcolonial phase of engagement between the North Atlantic and the Third World, and it is gravely threatened only by wars of liberation. Violence only can destroy the colonial Manichean duality and pre-empt the hegemony of the neo-colonial enterprise. Fanon continues: "To the strategy of Dien Bien Phu, defined by the colonised peoples, the colonialist replies by the strategy of encirclement-based on the respect of the sovereignty of states." (Fanon 1963 pgs. 70-71). The failure to defeat the Vietnamese and the Algerians in their respective wars of liberation necessitates the strategy of encirclement, where the infection is quarantined by a string of servile neo-colonial states thereby ensuring North Atlantic hegemony over that artifice of North Atlantic domination: The Third World. The North Atlantic/Third World duality is the expression of the Manichean duality that is the neo-colonial order, for under colonial domination there was no Third World only colonies as they constitute and condition each other's existence, for there can be a North Atlantic only with the existence of the Third World/colonies, for we of the Third World create the Third World in order to affirm our belief in and need for the North Atlantic for we are unable to build our world as free individuals without North Atlantic definition and affirmation. We then take base, mediocre human material and turn them into Supermen exerting hegemony over our daily lives such is the extent of our wretchedness.

Atmosphere of Violence/Violence in Action

Fanon turns to his concept of the atmosphere of violence and its evolution into violence in action as follows: "But let us return to that atmosphere of violence, that violence that is just under the skin." "Yet in spite of the metamorphoses which the colonial regime imposes upon it in the way of tribal and regional quarrels, that violence makes it way forward, and the native identifies his enemy and recognises all his misfortunes, throwing all the exacerbated might of his hate and anger into this new channel." (Fanon 1963 pg. 71). The atmosphere of violence comprises the power relation between the native and the coloniser, where the anger and hate generated by colonial domination is acted upon by colonial instruments of power to turn that anger inwards expressed as tribal and regional wars which grant the coloniser space in which to exercise power and dominion on a sustainable basis i.e. hegemony. The atmosphere of violence evolves in spite of these diversions when the native fully understands and focuses anger and hate on the enemy: the coloniser. With this evolving atmosphere of violence Fanon posits the question: "But how do we pass from the atmosphere of violence to violence in action? What makes the lid blow off?" (Fanon 1963 pg. 71).

Fanon in answering the question insists that the atmosphere of violence intensifies and explodes into violence in action spontaneously in response to actions launched by the coloniser against the nationalist movement. The masses then enter into a violent engagement with the coloniser seeking to protect a political entity and its leadership who are opposed to their mass action and willing agents of the metropolitan neo-colonial agenda. The spontaneous outpouring of mass action does not then trigger a war of liberation what it does is release fierce, punishing military assaults and at best a gift of independence with the agents of neo-colonialism in control. In fact, spontaneous mass action works to the ultimate benefit of the neo-colonial agenda and its local agents and to the detriment of the masses. Fanon states: "As a general rule, colonialism welcomes this godsend with open arms, transforms these 'blind mouths' into spokesmen, and in two minutes endows them with independence, on condition that they restore order. So we see that all parties are aware of the power of such violence and that the question is not always to reply to it by a greater violence, but see how to relax the tension." (Fanon 1963 pg. 73). Spontaneous mass action/violence is an intervention by the masses into the process of decolonisation in their image and likeness, which is skilfully utilised by the metropolitan agents of the neo-colonial agenda and their local supplicants to embark on decolonisation towards neo-colonial domination, which targets this spontaneous mass action to ensure that it never impacts the neo-colonial order as an agent of change. For Fanon, independence brings no change for the better for the masses as the colonial social order is replicated under neo-colonial domination with cosmetic changes to suit the new relationship between dominator/the North Atlantic and the supplicant dominated/the agents of neo-colonialism. The endemic violence of colonial domination persists and grows in intensity for now we are free, raising the investment made by the dominated and the dominator in deflecting mass action/violence inwardly, internally by designating potent enemies in need of elimination because of the threat posed to "Us." Fanon states: "Already we see that violence used in specific ways at the moment of the struggle for freedom does not magically disappear after the ceremony of trooping the national colours. It has all the less reason to disappear..." (Fanon 1963 pg. 75). The primary concern is the control of the masses under the neo-colonial order as there is no agenda of fundamental change possible and forth coming under the servile leaders of the neo-colonial order, for they are convinced that such an agenda poses a potent threat to their sustainable political domination of the independent nation. They then choose to deceive, to divide and to repress on a scale that outshines colonial domination, whilst they loot and plunder the assets of the State, which ultimately serves the interests of the North Atlantic and they are supported and propped up for a job well done. Fanon states: "the atmosphere of violence, after having coloured all the colonial phase, continues to dominate national life," (Fanon 1963 pg. 76). This is illustrated by the resort to social upheaval and internecine violence in the early years of the life of the newly independent neo-colonial social orders signalling the move to violence in response to power relations formed under colonial domination surviving the transition to independence and intensifying their acute, oppressive impact on the dominated. In the neo-colonial order violence is understood and endemic. Fanon persists in his analysis of the impact of wars of liberation from colonial domination and anticolonial insurgencies as Mau Mau have on colonialism and capitalism on an international scale. Fanon states: "From then on we understand why the violence of the native is only hopeless if we compare it in the abstract to the military machine of the oppressor. On the other hand, if we situate that violence in the dynamics of the international situation, we see at once that it constitutes a terrible menace for the oppressor." "Thus capitalism realises that its military strategy has everything to lose by the outbreak of nationalist wars. Again, within the framework of peaceful co-existence, all colonies are destined to disappear, and in the long run neutralism is destined to be respected by capitalism. What must at all costs be avoided is strategic insecurity:" (Fanon 1963 pgs. 79-80). Wars of liberation and insurgencies impact the international North Atlantic capitalist order which accelerates the demise of colonies through the widespread application of the instrument of neo-colonial domination, for the grave concern in the era of neo-colonialism is North Atlantic insecurity

in the face of international threats. In the 21st century that grave threat is posed by China, when Fanon wrote in 1961 it was the Soviet Union. The threat has evolved and the threat source has changed but the North Atlantic discourse of the duality of security/insecurity is unchanged. Today

China is viewed as posing the most concerted threat to the security of the neo-colonial project since its inception, a threat the nature of which the Soviet Union never posed, which has raised the question of the efficacy of peaceful co-existence to USA's hegemonic interests. Fanon is then insisting that contrary to the attacks on violence and human rights, international politics is premised on universal violence. Fanon then in the text points to a reality that is a most potent issue today in North Atlantic politics as follows: "Tomorrow, perhaps we shall see the shifting of that violence after the complete liberation of the colonial territories. Perhaps we will see the question of minorities cropping up." (Fanon 1963 pg. 80). With the liberation of the colonies minority race groups present in Europe as a result of the colonial legacy became a pressing political and social issue, which is driving today the reaction to the 21st century migration flows seen in the rise of neo Nazi and Fascist mainstream political parties in Europe contesting national elections and forming governments or commanding rising number of seats in national parliaments. From the 1950s to the present the issue of non-white minorities in the USA remains a current social and political issue that impacts US electoral politics, this is especially so as the race demography of the USA is evolving to one where the white race in the 21st century will become a minority race releasing the paranoia of fear of a black planet. But the neo-colonial nations have repeatedly shown the potency of the minority issue and the willingness to apply Final Solution methodology to end the problem permanently. What the white race of the North Atlantic desires, its neo-colonial supplicants show no hesitation to apply with extreme prejudice. This drives Fanon to state as follows: "Between the violence of the colonies and that peaceful violence that the world is steeped in, there is a kind of complicit agreement, a sort of homogeneity." (Fanon 1963 pg. 81). When we slaughter each other on an industrial scale in the neo-colonial world this depravity flows with the peaceful violence of the world order, for we are doing to each other what the white race will do to us and desires to do to us and to those who look like us in their ancestral homelands. That is the complicit agreement why in spite of all the talk of human rights and rule of law, the slaughter is a given for the Third World by our hands.

Fanon presents his position that the settler community of the requisite size in a colony can exert pressure on the metropole to wage a war on the natives for the defeat of the native movement for decolonisation. The settler community and their agenda to retain the colony at all costs and by any means necessary for Fanon drives the need for a war of liberation, for the settler community unleashes violence on the most benign of decolonisation movements ratcheting up the engagement to a full blown war of independence. The case of Algeria, the strategy of the settler community there and the war of liberation that was the response is the basis of Fanon's model, a model fundamentally different from that of Indochina/Vietnam. There is also the instance where British colonialism intervened militarily to protect white settler and economic interests in the face of insurgencies then granted the gift of independence with the defeat of the insurgencies as in Kenya, Malaysia and British Guiana. Fanon states: "In fact, as always, the settler has shown him the way he should take if he is to become free. The argument the native chooses has been furnished by the settler, and by an iconic turning of the tables it is the natives who now affirm that the colonialist understands nothing but force." (Fanon 1963 pg. 84). The settler by his actions instructs the native on the nature of the only valid path to freedom in the colonial context: violence. For the settler insists that the only valid path to the retention of colonial domination is the use of superior military force of the requisite volume, intensity and expanse to bring the native into submission. Violence begets violence in the Manichean world of the colonial domination. Fanon continues: "To begin with, the affirmation of the principle 'It's them or us' does not constitute a paradox, since colonialism, as we have seen, is in fact the organisation of a Manichean world, a world divided up into compartments." (Fanon 1963 pg. 84). The settler faced with insurrection, with a movement for decolonisation views, perceives and reacts to native action via a Manichean worldview of all or nothing. The native masses view the threat posed by the settler and the war unleashed to preserve colonial domination via a Manichean worldview of all or nothing. In fact, the most potent, extreme indicator of the operationalisation of this Manichean worldview in an existential battle between massa and the former enslaved, are the actions of Dessalines during the Haitian Revolution to cleanse the white and mulattoes from the liberated Haiti. A colonial predilection repeated in postcolonial/neo-colonial history to this day. This product of Manichean duality, violence, is then understood when conjured up by the settlers and the colonial metropole and therapeutic for both warring factions, settler/native, for the Manichean duality presents and enables only violence and genocidal violence as the preferred method of conflict resolution. Hence the strategy of dispensing the gift of independence to evade the risk of derailing the neo-colonial agenda. In this colonial cauldron that impacts the psyche in multi-faceted ways, violence then is the outcome of the colonial cauldron that opens the door to dismantling the colonial psyche. Fanon states: "Violence is thus seen as comparable to a royal pardon. The colonised man finds his freedom in and through violence. This rule of conduct enlightens the agent because it indicates to him the means and ends." (Fanon 1963 pg. 86). Violent action by a native against a settler earns the native the forgiveness of all sins committed during his servility to colonial domination, envisioned as service to the settlers. Violent action, forgiveness of sins and the resulting state of consciousness of the native liberated, in persistent liberation that is sustainable resistance instructs the native that violent action is both the means and the ends. Fanon then presents his position that settler and native violence are part of a nexus formed with the colonial Manichean duality as follows: "It is understandable that in this atmosphere, daily life becomes quite simply impossible. You can no longer be a fellah, a pimp, or an alcoholic as before. The violence of the colonial regime and the counter-violence of the native balance each other and respond to each other in an extraordinary reciprocal homogeneity." "The development of violence among the colonised people will be proportionate to the violence exercised by the threatened colonial regime." (Fanon 1963 pg. 88). The power relation between coloniser and colonised has now been usurped by mutual violence exercised, creating the dynamic of a violence relationship where the daily life of the coloniser and the colonised is fundamentally changed compared to the daily life predicated on and permitted by violence. Colonial normality is now dead as the ebb and flow of battle now determines dominance and the white/black complex is challenged to its core hence the effects of which is palpable in daily life. For violence is also applied inwardly within the native population, where those who are not in support of the insurgency or the war of liberation are targets of violence. The change in the perceptions, attitudes and actions of the natives as a result of these relationships of violence is readily apparent and further impacts the relationships of violence. The attacks then take on a life of their own where strike and counterstrike dance in a terrain of tit for tat revenge and pre-emptive strikes to illustrate the willingness to carry out the most horrific assaults as an indicator of the resolution for victory. For this is a war where both sides agree it will be won on depravity that outstrips that of the enemy, a war of the Manichean duality. A war then that is driven by and is the product of this Manichean duality must exhibit this "extraordinary reciprocal homogeneity" for the single source origin with the specific nature of the Manichean duality generates the homogeneity as it does the reciprocal nature of the actions operationalised. This creates a terrain of violence that is in fact extraordinary, different and separate from that of the North Atlantic for it's a colonial reality. Both parties engaged in the struggle for dominance can only exist because of the existence of the other, hence the war is fratricidal, whilst presenting a grave existential threat to both parties for should one exterminate the other, then the survivor entity must constitute a new existential condition which excludes the other for the duality is now destroyed. Fanon believed that this war of colonial fratricide will free the native from the damage of colonial domination by exterminating the visible expression of colonial domination thereby freeing the native to return to the source as the mechanism to liberation. The neo-colonial agenda embraced those who refused to commit fratricide, thereby maintaining the Manichean duality, as North Atlantic domination never ceased and we embraced being the wretched of the earth whilst insisting we are free citizens of sovereign nations. Fanon continues: "The settler's logic is implacable and one is only staggered by the counter-logic visible in the behaviour of the native insofar as one has not clearly understood beforehand the mechanisms of the settler's ideas." (Fanon 1963 pg. 89). "The setter's work is to make even dreams of liberty impossible for the native. The native's work is to imagine all possible methods for destroying the settler. On the logical plane, the Manicheism of the settler produces a Manicheism of the native. To the theory of the 'absolute evil of the native' the theory of the absolute evil of the settler' replies." (Fanon 1963 pg. 93). The settler and the native are both constituted by the domination of the colonial, Manichean duality of irreconcilable good and evil locked in mortal combat for dominance. There can be no settler without native, no dominant settler without servile, subordinate native but because of the nature of the Manichean duality both sides of the duality must wage fratricidal war against each other which threatens the very survival of the Manichean duality. As the dominant party the settler resorts to fratricide instinctively for it is a minority race in a dominant position. The native responds in kind in keeping with the Manichean duality, which is a process in response to the threat posed by the fratricide of the settler, for the native has to overcome the psychoexistential complex of colonial domination that assaults her/his persona in the quest to render them servile. The settlers' paranoid racism coupled with its faith in its overwhelming military force and superiority unleashes the barbarity that triggers the native Manichean response of fratricidal war of elimination. This war of fratricide will then render the Manichean duality inoperable thereby opening the path to native liberation.

On violence and the opening of the path to liberation Fanon states: "But it so happens for the colonised people this violence, because it constitutes their only work, invests their characters with positive and creative qualities." (Fanon 1963 pg.93). The violence generated by the action of the colonial elite, especially the settler, a reaction then to settler violence, constitutes a change in the characters of the colonised by assaulting the outcome and legacy of the psychoexistential complex. The native has under this colonial reality only a single work to undertake: defensive violence that regenerates her/his being gravely impacted by colonial domination to render the native servile. Fanon continues: "The mobilisation of the masses, when it arises out of the war of liberation, introduces into each man's consciousness the ideas of a common cause, of a national destiny, and of a collective history. In the same way the second phase, that of the building-up of the nation, is helped on by the existence of this cement which has been mixed with blood and anger." (Fanon 1963 pg. 93). The mass mobilisation of the war of liberation then marries violence to nationalism, patriotism and a common destiny that assaults the divisions of the native population as tribe, ethnicity and race effected under colonial domination. Fanon is insisting that violence expressed via a war of liberation is the only effective mechanism of liberation available to the colonised. The alternative choice is neo-colonial domination where the psychoexistential complex of colonial domination survives, evolves and constitutes the Third World which is ever present in the 21st century. Fanon speaks of the "great organism of violence" with its power relations where through violence individuals are linked forming the great chain of violence that enmeshes the entire social order. All individuals are linked in a chain to this great organism of violence where individual power relations are impacted by violence, where social groups are fractured, redefined and recoalesce on the impact of violence at the personal level. The entire social order constituted to serve colonial domination is shredded at the individual level and no one can put the colonial Humpty Dumpty together again which poses the gravest threat to the neo-colonial agenda. Mau Mau was an insurgency in colonial Kenya undertaken by a specific ethnic group, the Kikuyu, that targeted the settlers, native allies of colonial domination and colonial officials. Mau Mau was defeated militarily but the settler agenda to defeat the movement for decolonisation failed as the great organism of violence, unleashed by the Mau Mau, destroyed the colonial Humpty Dumpty and the British settled for the gift of independence to ensure the success of the neo-colonial project rather than risk a national war of liberation.

In the text Fanon now explains the reason for the tribal, ethnic wars and the utilisation of genocide as a political weapon under the neo-colonial order of the Third World. Fanon states: "By its very structure, colonialism is separatist and regionalist. Colonialism does not simply state the existence of tribes, it also reinforces it and separates them." (Fanon 1963 pg. 94). Colonial domination requires the division of the dominated into mutually irreconcilable divisions, where the colonial official is in fact the power broker between groups separated by suspicion, mistrust, hate and aggression. There is then no coherent nation driven by nationalism there is only tribe, ethnicity and race definitions of self and identity. Under neo-colonial domination these divisions persist, evolve and become much more acute for the quest under neo-colonial domination is State capture and domination. Politics then drives this process as it is now the politics of tribe, ethnic and race hegemony which is embraced by the political actors, whether elected or having seized the State by coup d'état, placing ethnic cleansing and genocide on the agenda. The politics of neo-colonial domination illustrates the inability of neo-colonialism to destroy the psychoexistential complex and the legacy of colonial domination and forge a nation, a national identity and an individual who is liberated. Fanon has then presented his evidence that violence expressed as a war of national liberation is the only valid mechanism to destroy the colonial legacy and enable us to embrace the path of liberation.

All of us trapped in neo-colonial social orders today in the 21st century are then plagued with a grave illness for the neo-colonial psychoexistential complex continues to affirm our inferiority to ourselves and we continue to act upon this inferiority, which we deny with a body of delusions which amounts to lies we tell to ourselves. Fanon's message is then clearly stated as follows: "At the level of the individual violence is a cleansing force. It frees the native from his inferiority complex and from his despair and inaction; it makes him fearless and restores his self-respect." "When the people have taken violent part in the national liberation they will allow no one to set themselves up as 'liberators.'" (Fanon 1963 pg. 94). At the level of the individual the colonial and neo-colonial psychoexistential complexes impact the individual to ensure their servility. The failure to apply the cleansing force at the individual level assured the hegemony of the neo-colonial enterprise

and the constituting of the Third World across time/space to the 21st century. For Fanon liberation is only possible from the legacy of colonial domination by the prosecution of a war of liberation in which violence is understood. Only within the context of a war of liberation is violence against the colonial dominator a cleansing force. Violence of itself, by itself and for itself is simply colonial negation of the native self. This violence breeds genocide as a political instrument as is the case of the Nigerian civil war, Rwanda and Kampuchea.

Native Intellectuals and Politicians

Fanon in the text now deals with the strategies adopted by the colonial metropoles towards the movement for decolonisation in the colonies and strategies adopted by the native intellectuals and politicians. Fanon states: "As soon as the native begins to pull on his moorings, and to cause anxiety in the settler, he is handed over to well-meaning souls who in cultural congresses point out to him the specificity and wealth of Western values." "In the period of decolonisation, the colonised masses mock at these very values, insult them, and vomit them up." "This phenomenon is ordinarily masked because, during the period of decolonisation, certain colonised intellectuals have begun a dialogue with the bourgeoisie of the colonialist country." (Fanon 1963 pgs. 43-44). Fanon now presents the constituent agencies of the power relations of decolonisation: the colonial bourgeoisie of the metropole, the settlers, the native intellectuals and the natives. There is no Manichean divide in these power relations premised on the colonial racist divide for in the new politics of decolonisation the settler can find themselves locked in a power struggle with the colonial metropolitan powered elite. The strategy of the colonial metropolitan powered elite, then defines the terrain of engagement in the quest for a neo-colonial order post decolonisation, demands a strategic relationship with the new neo-colonial elite whose task is to control the masses in the interest of neo-colonial domination. The fact that the gift of independence was the dominant strategy adopted by the colonial powers, outstripping that of wars to defeat the anticolonial movement, illustrates the importance of understanding the power relation between native intellectuals and the metropolitan powered elites, framed by the instrument of the gift of independence towards realising the attainment of neo-colonial North Atlantic hegemony. Fanon states: "The intellectual who for his part has followed the colonialist with regard to the universal abstract will fight in order that the settler and the native may live together in peace in a new world. But the thing he does not see, precisely because he is permeated by colonialism and all its ways of thinking, is that the settler, from the moment the colonial context disappears, has no longer any interest in remaining or in co-existing." (Fanon 1963 pg. 45). Hence in post-apartheid South Africa the recognition and preservation of white settler privilege was enshrined in order to present the Mandela myth realised of interracial unity and the threat to this enshrined body of privilege as perceived by the white settlers is now finally raising the issue of decolonisation in South Africa in the 21st century. The grave lesson Fanon posits here is the role of the colonialized native intellectual in willingly being the instrument for the creation of the neo-colonial hegemony of the North Atlantic, by actively engaging with the masses to channel their demands for change to acceptance of the neo-colonial condition. This is not primarily a quest for power, wealth and glory by the native intellectuals, for they believe in and act on their North Atlantic worldview, which means that they favour the accolades of the metropolitan powered elites over those of the native masses. Fanon continues as follows: "We have said that the colonial context is characterised by the dichotomy which it imposes upon the whole people. Decolonisation unifies that people by the radical decision to remove from it its heterogeneity, and by unifying it on a national, sometimes a racial basis." (Fanon 1963 pgs. 45-46). Decolonisation fires up the search for a return to a civilisation that was theirs before colonial domination, which raises the issue of the continued presence of the white settlers in this rebirth and their loyalty to and willingness to recognise the hegemony of the last over the first. Under the leadership of the native intellectuals this quest can now be directed to naming and purging enemies among the mass of natives, where fractures now appear on the basis of ethnic differences defined and utilised under colonial domination which served the colonial state, as in the case of the Nigerian Civil War. This quest for cleansing and rebirth evolves into racism when an ethnic group, a tribe, now embodies the nation to the detriment of all others. Fanon continues on the native intellectuals as follows: "The colonialist bourgeoisie, in its narcissistic dialogue, expounded by its members of its universities, had in fact deeply embedded in the minds of the colonised intellectual that the essential qualities remain eternal in spite of all the blunders men may make: the essential qualities of the West, of course. The native intellectuals accepted the cogency of these ideas, and deep down in his brain you can always find a vigilant sentinel ready to defend the Greco-Roman pedestal." (Fanon 1963 pg. 46). The native intellectual is the most potent asset of the west in the quest for decolonisation in the colonies of the North Atlantic as they are imbued with, accept and act upon the core discursive constructs of the discourse of the west. An asset the hegemonic elites of the North Atlantic utilise during decolonisation and the condition of neo-colonial domination. Fanon continues: "Such a colonised intellectual, dusted over by colonial culture" (Fanon 1963 pg. 47). They are then colonised intellectuals, having failed to decolonise themselves they can only neo-colonialize not decolonise, for they are all are the product of colonial culture, mass produced dusted over and released to pursue their personal interests as defined by and facilitated by the hegemonic North Atlantic elites. Fanon points to a specific strategy of colonial domination that facilitates this elitist frustration of the desire of the masses as follows: "The colonialist bourgeoisie had hammered into the native's mind the idea of a society of individuals where each person shuts himself up in his own subjectivity, and whose only wealth is individual thought." (Fanon 1963 pg. 47). Colonial power relentlessly seeks to constitute servile individuals who are devoid of concepts of mass action, solidarity and movement, hence of power, where all reality is envisaged and acted upon via the perspective of the individual. The quest for decolonisation can then be redefined and managed in the interests of the North Atlantic elites in conjunction with their native allies thereby enabling the neo-colonial project. Fanon has now arrived at the point where he must distinguish between the conditions which enable liberation from colonial domination and neo-colonialism from those which deny liberation by enabling the neo-colonial project.

Fanon insists that there is decolonisation as the result of the "struggle for liberation" or a war of liberation as in Indochina/Vietnam and Algeria and there is decolonisation devoid of a war of liberation where there is the gift of independence. There is then a qualitative difference in the nature of the postcolonial social orders produced by these two distinct methodologies of decolonisation. Fanon states: "But it so happens sometimes that decolonisation occurs in areas which have not been sufficiently shaken by the struggle for liberation, and there may be found those same know-all, smart, wily intellectuals. We find intact in them the manners and forms of thought picked up during their association with the colonialist bourgeoisie. Spoilt children of yesterday's colonialism and of today's national governments, they organise the loot of whatever national resources exist." "In this arid phase of national life, the so-called period of austerity, the success of their depredations is swift to call forth the anger and violence of the people." (Fanon 1963 pgs. 49-49). Decolonisation in the absence of a war of liberation gives the un-regenerated native intellectuals and the North Atlantic elites the space in which to realise the neo-colonial project, which explains the dominance of the methodology of the gift of independence over that of the colonial war to suppress decolonisation as it best enabled the success of the neo-colonial project which constituted the Third World. The native intellectuals in the absence of a war of liberation carefully unleashed the nationalist agitation for the gift of independence, knowing fully well that it was there for the asking, utilising this manufactured nationalist movement to solidify their power over the masses and the postcolonial State which enabled their plundering of the State and their political hegemony. In order to satisfy the prime directive of servility to the North Atlantic and enabling the sustainable neo-colonial project to flourish, which are powerful instances of their gratitude to their massa. The operational reality of this neo-colonial social order is the continued operational hegemony of the mechanism of power unleashed under colonial domination, potently illustrated by the epidemic use of skin bleaching creams in Africa and India in the 21st century and the fixation with illicit migration to Europe as the panacea for their personal deprivation, regardless of the risks and costs involved which they are willing to pay even with their lives. Colonial domination never ended, it was simply redefined to attain a new end in the era of biopower in the North Atlantic. Fanon continues: "Objectively, the intellectual behaves in this phase as a common opportunist. In fact, he has not stopped manoeuvring." (Fanon 1963 pg. 49). The native intellectual is totally consumed with self-aggrandisement through defining and constraining the demands of the masses and showing her/his gratitude to the colonial/ postcolonial massa. In the context of decolonisation and a neo-colonial social order, the native intellectual must be an accomplished opportunist gifted in deception and willing to venture into grave zones of political activity which threaten the very survivability of the social order in the quest to retain political power, genocide being one of these areas. This reality must be viewed within the context of the embrace of genocide by the North Atlantic in its pursuit of the colonial and neo-colonial enterprises. This then describes the nature of postcolonial politics of the Third World.

The Masses and the Native Intellectual

Fanon must in his analysis of the native intellectual deal with the masses and mass action in the process of decolonisation. Fanon states: "For this same people, poverty-stricken yet independent, comes very quickly to possess a social conscience in the African and international context of today, and this the petty individualists will quickly learn." "Now the *fellah*, the unemployed man, the starving native do not lay a claim to the truth; they do not *say* that they represent the truth, for they *are* the truth." (Fanon 1963 pg. 49). The grave problem posed to the hegemony of the native intellectuals over decolonisation and the neo-colonial project is the very nature of the masses seen in the demands they are making driven by their expectations of what they will derive from decolonisation. Whilst the native intellectuals insist they are the truth, they say they represent the truth hence power is rightfully theirs, the very existence of the masses is the truth. The pressure the masses exert demands that they be made pliant, even servile, to a political order for failure to do so poses a grave threat to the sustainability of the neo-colonial enterprise. The masses are then ahead of the native intellectuals in the race to realise a decolonisation to serve specific interests of groups in the social order, for the masses have adopted an independent, internationalist, Pan-African social conscience which the native intellectual can never match. Hence the willingness to unleash on the postcolonial social order ethnic wars of cleansing, which are in fact race wars for tribe and ethnicity is redefined as race in the colonial context, which is an embrace of genocide. For destroying the cohesion of the masses is seen as the means to attain the hegemony of the native intellectuals and the postcolonial project. Since the existence of the masses is truth then you destroy the cohesion of the masses and splinter truth into a million disparate pieces where the social order becomes the captive of barbarism and banditry, whilst the postcolonial project remains robust. Fanon now deals with the issue of truth, the native and decolonisation which enables the process of understanding the dynamic that enables the neo-colonial enterprise. Fanon states: "The native replies to the living lie of the colonial situation by an equal falsehood. Truth is that which hurries on the break-up of the colonialist regime; it is that which promotes the emergence of the nation; it is all that protects the natives, and ruins the foreigners. In this colonialist context there is no truthful behaviour: and the good is quite simply that which is evil for 'them.'" (Fanon 1963 pg.

50). The native intellectuals in alliance with the North Atlantic elites simply keep redefining the context of "them" to insist that the government of the native intellectuals and all that they do is good, whilst evil only can come from "them." The battle for decolonisation is then never ended, finished and finalised with victory for there is always the threat of "them", which ultimately leads to the unleashing of genocide with all its graphic butchery where natives fall on natives with the hatred of the native/settler colonial dichotomy. Fanon in the text now presents the Manichean reality of decolonisation as follows: "Thus we see that the primary Manicheism which governed colonial society is preserved intact during the period of decolonisation; that is to say that the settler never ceases to be the enemy, the opponent, the foe that must be overthrown." "The immobility to which the native is condemned can only be called in question if the native decides to put an end to the history of colonisation-the history of pillage- and to bring into existence the history of the nation-history of decolonisation." (Fanon 1963 pgs. 50-51). In the process of decolonisation, the Manichean duality of native/settler, the duality that immobilized the native under colonial domination is preserved which means that under the instrument of the gift of independence the immobility is never removed as the Manichean dichotomy is not destroyed, simply reformulated; where replacements for the settlers must be rolled out by the native intellectuals on a continuing basis in order to maintain sustainably the immobilisation of the masses. Hence the need to reformulate ethnic and tribal differences as the colonial race dichotomy driven by racism defined by white supremacy. A situation of black on black racism where the instrument of race hate is white supremacist, hence the barbarity of the genocidal assaults for all warring factions are less than human in search of humanity and accolades attesting to their humanity through graphic slaughter of your fellow black race enemy. Decolonisation rewarded with the gift of independence retains the social order of, and the hegemonic order of, discourse of colonial domination simply refashioned and tinkered with to adapt to the order of biopower.

Colonial Manichean duality

Fanon describes this colonial Manichean reality which enables a comparison with postcolonial reality to discern if this colonial order has in fact been dismantled. Fanon states: "A world divided into compartments, a motionless Manicheistic world, a world of statutes" "The first thing which the native learns is to stay in his place and not go beyond certain limits." "When the native is confronted with the colonial order of things, he finds he is in a state of permanent tension." "The settler's world is a hostile world, which spurns the native, but at the same time it is a world of which he is envious." "the native never ceases to dream of putting himself in the place of the settler-not of becoming the settler but of substituting himself for the settler. This hostile world, ponderous and aggressive because it fends off the colonised masses with all the harshness it is capable of, represents not merely a hell from which the swiftest flight possible is desirable, but also a paradise close at hand which is guarded by terrible watchdogs." (Fanon 1963 pgs. 51-53). All natives are afflicted with this desire to replace the settler but this desire is the product of a Manichean duality of irreconcilable opposites where a living hell for all natives holds and beckons with a promise of paradise. You hate the settler but you desire the paradise of racial privilege in all its repressive splendour that the settler animates, deploys and most of all enjoys the fruits of thereof. This desire is the grave weakness of the decolonisation movement and it's especially potent in colonies where the instrument deployed was the gift of independence. The native intellectual insists that the paradise is theirs and theirs alone to possess across time and to deploy against the pressure of the masses for possession of the settlers' paradise/hell. The colonial overlord conspires with the native intellectuals to ensure that the hell/paradise is the inheritance solely of the native intellectuals with independence by writing a constitution and handing over the repressive state apparatus intact with continued military aid during independence which ensure the hegemony of the comprador native intellectuals. The neo-colonial condition is then rooted in the Manichean duality of colonial domination simply reconfigured for the era of independence and neo-colonialism under the hegemony of biopower in the North Atlantic. The hell of the Manichean duality outstrips that of the colonial hell as it is constantly evolving, there was no break in its evolution, especially in its barbarity, for now native is slaughtering native in the name of freedom. Whilst the paradise has embraced obscene depravity which even surpasses that of the barbarous looting of the Congo by the Belgians. Since independence we have earnestly strove to prove to massa that we can meet and surpass all the high points of his colonial enterprise, thereby ensuring that the neo-colonial enterprise surpasses the mountain of value extracted from the Third World and the level of underdevelopment that envelops the masses of the Third World. We have now finally proved ourselves worthy of massa's trust and affirmation as we surpass the model of *Steven* in Tarantino's *Django*. Fanon in his continued description of the condition of the native under colonial domination and in the phase of decolonisation enables the analysis of the Manichean duality that continues from colonial domination to neo-colonial domination. Fanon states: "The native is an oppressed person whose permanent dream is to be the persecutor." "The settler-native relationship is a mass relationship. The settler pits brute force against the weight of numbers. He is an exhibitionist." "The settler keeps alive in the native an anger which he deprives of outlet; the native is trapped in the tight links of the chain of colonialism. But we have seen that inwardly the settler can only achieve a pseudo petrification. The native's muscular tension finds outlet regularly in bloodthirsty explosions-in tribal warfare, in feuds between septs, and in quarrels between individuals." "Thus collective auto destruction in a very concrete form is one of the ways in which the native's muscular tension is set free. All these patterns of conduct are those of the death reflex when faced with a danger, a suicidal behaviour which proves to the settler (whose existence and domination is by them all the more justified) that these men are not reasonable human beings. In the same way the native manages to by-pass the settler." (Fanon 1963 pgs. 53-54). With this block of quotes from Fanon's text we simply replace settler with native intellectuals and a potent description of the neo-colonial condition emerges, where as in the colonial condition the native remains angry under the postcolonial condition for the longevity of the Manichean duality maintains the substantive reality of the colonial condition under the neo-colonial condition because the native is yet to be the persecutor. The native intellectual has effectively become the persecutor but not of the settler, of the native. The native responds with muscular tension and a death reflex that poses a grave threat to the native intellectuals and generates a paranoid fear of the masses in the mind of the native intellectuals. The native intellectuals then repeatedly move to channel and control this anger by formulating the device of the grave threat of the enemy by tribalising/ethnicising the State and unleashing the dogs of tribal/ethnic cleansing and genocide. But the base reality is the endemic deprivation that is made acute under neo-colonialism and the anger which has to be dealt with by the sufferers thereby survival strategies are constantly formulated and reformulated. But these survival strategies cannot be external of the terrain of the Manichean duality and the operational terrain it constitutes. Fanon states: "A belief in fatality removes all blame from the oppressor; the cause of misfortunes and of poverty is attributable to God: He is Fate. In this way the individual accepts the disintegration ordained by God, bow down before the settler and his lot, and by a kind of interior restabilisation acquires a stony calm. Meanwhile, however, life goes on, and the native will strengthen the inhibitions which contain his aggressiveness by drawing on the terrifying myths," (Fanon 1963 pgs. 54-55). The native faced with the real deprivation that is life has to cope, to survive which necessitates the acceptance of blame for her/his condition in life thereby diverting the gaze from the political structure and those elites that animate these structures. The native deflects from gazing on, understanding and exercising power in order to change their condition of life thereby absolving power exercised of all blame and assault. In this analysis what is missing of grave impact and importance is the role of politics and political mobilisation in exercising the influence of the native intellectuals in the terrain of the native response to the Manichean duality. For what the postcolonial condition adds to the mix is the politics of a free, sovereign State, the discourse of political mobilisation unleashed and the structure and nature of politics and government which were all alien to the colonial condition. It is politics and political mobilisation that enables the unleashing, acceptance and operationalisation of tribal/ethnic hegemony, tribal/ethnic cleansing and genocide which was not a colonial instrument as this is black on black genocide.

The Nationalist Political parties

At this point in the text Fanon asks himself very hard questions which arise from the text that preceded. Fanon states: "when can one affirm that the situation is ripe for a movement of national liberation? In what form should it first be manifested? Because the various means whereby decolonisation has been carried out have appeared in many different aspects, reason hesitates and refuses to say which is a true decolonisation, and which a false." "What are the forces which in the colonial period open up new outlets and engender new aims for the violence of colonised peoples?" (Fanon 1963 pg. 59). Fanon now has to analyse the terrain of colonial domination to uncover which aspects of the terrain of domination actually empowers the violence of the colonised to be the basis of a war of liberation or those that mute this violence that feeds a movement of decolonisation that is not rooted in a war of liberation. Which means that the end results of both processes must be fully understood. Fanon in the text in keeping with the agenda deals with the nationalist political parties as follows: "The national political parties never lay stress upon the necessity of a trial of armed strength, for the grave reason that their objective is not the radical overthrowing of the system. Pacifists and legalists, they are in fact partisans of order, the new order-but to the colonialist bourgeoisie they put bluntly enough the demand which to them is the main one: 'Give us more power.'" (Fanon 1963 pg. 59). The national political parties deny the need for armed struggle, for the war of liberation as they are pacifists and legalists engaged in a power relation with the colonial elite towards attaining the gift of independence enmeshed in the neo-colonial order. For their servility the national politicians want power as they and the neo-colonial elites share a common enemy in the masses committed to their quest to replace the settler. There is then a power relation embracing the masses, the native intellectuals, the national politicians and the neo-colonial elites where the masses in their quest to replace the settler poses the grave threat to all three. Fanon now deals with violence and the national politicians: "On the specific question of violence, the elite are ambiguous. They are violent in their words and reformist in their attitudes. When the nationalist leaders *say* something, they make quite clear that they do not *really* think it." (Fanon 1963 pgs. 59-60). The national politicians are not committed to a war of liberation and violence in spite of the violence generated by the colonial Manichean duality. They have then a problem of legitimacy with the masses which results in their use of violent political language as a means of political mobilisation which raises the temperature of the engagement, which is used by the national politicians to place pressure on the neo-colonial elite to speed up the time table for the gift of independence. The national politicians and the native intellectuals by their actions and worldview replicate the Manichean duality of the colonial enterprise in the neo-colonial enterprise as they have no commitment to deal with the Manichean duality, hence they are unable to deal with this personally destructive duality. Fanon continues: "This characteristic on the part of the nationalist political parties should be interpreted in the light of both the make-up of their leaders and the nature of their followings." (Fanon 1963 pg. 60). Fanon deals with the leaders as follows: "The native intellectual has clothed his aggressiveness in his barely veiled desire to assimilate himself to the colonial world. He has used his aggressiveness to serve his own individual interests. Thus there is very easily brought into being a kind of class of affranchised slaves, or slaves who are individually free. What the intellectual demands is the right to multiply the emancipated, and the opportunity to organise a genuine class of emancipated citizens." (Fanon 1963 pg. 60). The leaders of the nationalist parties want above all to be functioning, accepted wielders of power in the neo-colonial enterprise for the neo-colonial elite has indicated that the neo-colonial enterprise is the future they desire not the prolongation of the colonial enterprise. The leaders of the nationalist parties want it now under the colonial dispensation necessary to ensure their hegemony in the neo-colonial order to follow. To attain this position of sustainable power the leaders have embraced the task of masking their aggressiveness through the formulation and unleashing of a political discourse which speaks to nationalist redemption through the end of colonial domination. This is decolonisation without a war of liberation, with a disparaging of violence accomplished through the constituting of legions of slaves who are citizens, voters, bearers of rights, free. A contradiction in terms which can only be the product of the Manichean duality where we are free, citizens, voters emancipated from colonial domination but chained to, slaves of North Atlantic neo-colonial hegemony. A hegemony which is demanded by and acceptable to us, the emancipated slaves, where the chains that bind us are invisible even appealing for they are not perceived as chains but ties that bind for the white man loves us, yes we know for they tell us so! Under neo-colonial domination we then police ourselves to ensure we remain slaves with human rights. This entire postcolonial reality expressed in the social order can only be the product of the Manichean duality.

In dealing with the power relation between the nationalist parties and the North Atlantic elite Fanon deals with the instruments devised by this power relation to channel and defuse the violence of the masses namely: non-violence and compromise. Fanon states: "Non-violence is an attempt to settle the colonial problem around a green baize table, before any regrettable act has been performed or irreparable gesture made, before any blood has been shed. But if the masses, without waiting for the chairs to be arranged around the baize table listen to their own voice and begin committing outrages and setting fire to buildings, the elite and the nationalist bourgeois parties will be seen rushing to the colonialists to exclaim, 'This is very serious!' We do not know how it will end; we must find a solution-some sort of compromise." (Fanon 1963 pgs. 61-62). The nationalist parties, the native intellectuals and the colonial elite are engaging with the North Atlantic elite for the grant of independence under terms and conditions favourable to the parties locked in the power relation. The discourse of a non-violent path to independence is being pushed to the masses seeking their compliance and acceptance of their marginalisation from the process, the outcome and their continued marginalisation in the neo-colonial social order that emerges. Whenever the masses respond with their violence against the colonial order the entire process is now effectively challenged which drives the Stevens of the colony into a state of panic where they call for compromise. But what is the nature of this compromise? Fanon states: "The idea of compromise is very important in the phenomenon of decolonisation, for it is very far from being a simple one. Compromise involves the colonial system and the young nationalist bourgeoisie at one and the same time. The partisans of the colonial system discover that the masses may destroy everything." "Compromise is equally attractive to the nationalist bourgeoisie," "At best, he shuts himself off in a no man's land between the terrorists and the settlers and willingly offers his services as go-between;" "find themselves somersaulted into the van of negotiations and compromise-precisely because that party has taken very good care never to break contact with colonialism." (Fanon 1963 pg. 62). Compromise in decolonisation in effect targets the masses for they are the villains of the piece posing a common threat to the interests of the political and national elites and the neo-colonial project of the North Atlantic elite. The native intellectuals, the nationalist politicians and the national bourgeoisie are separated and segregated from the masses where the threat posed by the masses intensify the need to marginalise them further under the neo-colonial order. This group of colonial elites have no affinity with the masses as they are all servile to North Atlantic hegemony and its discourse of the west, the masses are then alien to this group even though they share common genetic and cultural origins. Fanon continues: "For in fact they are not at all convinced that this impatient violence of the masses is the most efficient means of defending their own interests. Moreover, there are some individuals who are convinced of the ineffectiveness of violent methods; for them, there is no doubt about it, every attempt to break colonial oppression by force is a hopeless effort, an attempt at suicide, because in the innermost recesses of their brains the settler's tanks and airplanes occupy a huge place." "They are beaten from the start." (Fanon 1963 pg. 63). This elite group of the colony driven by the desire to replace the settler and the foreign colonial state functionary is convinced and driven by the belief that the west is best, disparages violence as a grave threat to its interests and those of the masses. They can only believe that violence against the colonial massa is futile as they expect that their embrace of anticolonial violence will decimate their ranks and deny them their manifest destiny to rule, for servile Chicken George and Steven can never envisage engaging and defeating the white man in battle. From the outset the colonial overlord/massa is in the ascendency in this decolonisation project for servile Steven is literally incapable of resistance, much less a war of liberation, and massa knows this, for all Stevens repeatedly inundate massa with their pleading for compromise as they shuck and jive their way to a servile independence rooted in the neo-colonial project dragging the nation behind them. Servile around the green table they must overcompensate in the eyes of the masses where they become liberators from colonial domination perpetually identifying the enemies within, thereby commencing the process of identifying the State with a tribe/ethnic group and /or a race to fracture the masses and set them at each other's throats which drives the blood lust of the neo-colonial project.

Fanon continues his assault on the nationalist parties by dealing with the reformist tendency that drives their agitation against colonialism. Fanon states: "All these forms of action serve at one and the same time to bring pressure to bear on the forces of colonialism and allow the people to work off their energy. This practice of therapy by hibernation, this sleep-cure used on the people, may sometimes be successful; thus out of the conference around the green baize table comes the political selectiveness which enables Monsieur M'ba, the president of the Republic of Gabon, to state in all seriousness on his arrival in Paris for an official visit: 'Gabon is independent, but between Gabon and France nothing has changed, everything goes on as before.' In fact, the only change is that Monsieur M'ba is president of the Gabonese Republic and that he is received by the president of the French Republic." (Fanon 1963 pgs. 66-67). The engagement with the colonial state by the nationalist parties is a strategic instrument designed to control the masses by feeding them small doses of anticolonial action which do not and cannot in effect challenge the power of the colonial state. This then is therapy applied to the masses to exhaust their desire to replace the settler through hibernation produced by the sleep-cure. This sleep-cure is premised on having the masses surrender the attainment of their desire to the nationalist maximum leader thereby placing their destiny in the hands of the asset of the neo-colonial agenda rather than themselves. With this surrender of the power of self-determination the masses are now in hibernation thereby empowering the hegemony of the neo-colonial enterprise. We have made ourselves the wretched of the earth by our complicity with the North Atlantic agenda and Fanon illustrates this with the president of Gabon, a recipient of the gift of independence and the statement of fact that with independence the power relation between France and Gabon remains one of North Atlantic domination. Fanon in the text now presents another strategy utilised by the nationalist parties towards ensuring the ambivalence of the masses and their hegemony over the political process of decolonisation to ensure the success of the neo-colonial project by providing space to the revolutionary political movement then at the opportune time eliminating them as a political force with the full support of the colonial state. Fanon states: "Obviously there are to be found at the core of the political parties and among their leaders certain revolutionaries who deliberately turn their backs upon the farce of national independence. But very quickly their questionings, their energy, and their anger obstruct the party machine, and these elements are gradually isolated, and then quite simply brushed aside. At this moment, as if there existed a dialectical concomitance, the colonialist police will fall upon them." (Fanon 1963 pg. 67). The purge is necessary because of the threat posed but the purge deepens the commitment to neo-colonial domination. Fanon now insists that the nationalist parties and their maximum leaders are play-acting at an anti-colonial conflict, where this conflict is an ersatz conflict or an inferior substitute for an anti-colonial conflict, which can only lead to domination and underdevelopment under the hegemony of the neo-colonial enterprise. Fanon states: "On the other hand, the elite of the colonial countries, those slaves set free, when at the head of the movement inevitably end up by producing ersatz conflict." "The truth is that they never make any real appeal to the aforesaid slaves; they never mobilise them in concrete terms. On the contrary, at the decisive moment (that is to say, from their point of view the moment of indecision) they brandish the danger of a 'mass mobilisation' as the crucial weapon which would bring about as if by magic the 'end of the colonial regime.'" (Fanon 1963 pg67). Shucking and jiving passing for anti-colonial conflict, constituting an ersatz conflict, for the leadership of the anti-colonial forces are working in complicity with the metropolitan elite to entrench and exercise the hegemony of the neo-colonial enterprise with these leaders dominating the social orders of the ex-colonies. This ersatz conflict formulated, released and managed by the nationalist parties in alliance with the North Atlantic neo-colonialists involves the use of the language with its attendant symbolism of anti-colonialism married to a neo-colonial agenda thereby perpetuating the Manichean duality and the propensity to violence in the social order. Fanon states: "The politicians who make speeches and who write in the nationalist newspapers make the people who dream dreams. They avoid the actual overthrowing of the state, but in fact they introduce into their readers' or hearers' consciousness the terrible ferment of subversion." "The nationalist politicians are playing with fire." "When a political leader calls a mass meeting, we may say that there is blood in the air. Yet the same leader very often is above all anxious to 'make a show' of force, so that he need not use it. But the agitation which ensues, the coming and going...all this hubbub makes the people think that the moment has come for them to take action." (Fanon 1963 pgs. 68-69). The agenda to implement the neo-colonial order is driven by an ersatz conflict in the public domain where the nationalist politicians are relentlessly seeking to establish their credentials as the premier anti-colonial political agitators of the colony. These credentials are perceived as being vitally necessary to the nationalist politicians exerting leadership control of the masses of the colony as the masses are seen as the potent threat to the agenda given their propensity to violence. These politicians are in fact generating ferment amongst the masses in a bid to control the masses which with the granting of independence is expressed publicly in various forms as wars of succession, popular revolts against the nationalist politicians and tribal, ethnic cleansing and genocide. Fanon terms this the "ripening process" (Fanon 1963 pg. 69) which is frustrated by the grant of independence and the implementation of the neo-colonial process where there is no material change in the quality of the daily life of the masses. The static deprivation of colonial domination continues and evolves under neo-colonialism, thereby breathing new life into the Manichean mechanism for violence under colonialism transplanted to neo-colonialism.

The Peasantry/Revolutionary Agent

Fanon in keeping with his stated analytic agenda deals with the membership and followers of the nationalist parties which uncovers the appeal of these political parties to the population of the colony. Fanon states: "The rank-and-file of a nationalist party is urban. The workers, primary schoolteachers, artisans, and small shopkeepers who have begun to profit-at a discount, to be sure-from the colonial setup, have special interests at heart. What this sort of following demands is the betterment of their particular lot: increased salaries, for example. The dialogue between these political parties and colonialism is never broken off." (Fanon 1963 pg. 60). The embrace of colonialism by nationalist political parties is reflected in it leadership and the nature of its membership and followers. Fanon insists that the followers/membership is rooted in the urban colonial expanse comprising the workers, the small traders, petty capitalists and those in the service of the colonial

State. As the leadership the followers/membership are averse to any war of liberation, to violence, to the masses and to a discourse of self-reliance and rejection of the west. The profile of these parties is best described as enablers of the neo-colonial enterprise. Fanon in keeping with his adherence to the basic tenets of historical materialism must seek out and find a revolutionary class whose existence provides some hope towards the possibility of revolutionary change. Fanon in his discourse of decolonisation now posits the peasantry as the revolutionary class in the colonial political context he is describing. Fanon states: "The peasantry is systematically disregarded for the most part by the propaganda put out by the nationalist parties. And it is clear that in the colonial countries the peasants alone are revolutionary, for they have nothing to lose and everything to gain. The starving peasant, outside the class system, is the first among the exploited to discover that only violence pays. For him there is no compromise, no possible coming to terms; colonisation and decolonisation are simply a question of relative strength." (Fanon 1963 pg. 61). Fanon in his quest for the revolutionary agent is searching amongst the most marginalised of the colonial social order to identify and present the revolutionary agent which suggests that revolutionary potential exists and is attainable. In this instance in his text Fanon insists that this agent is the peasantry where their marginalisation in the colonial social order is acute as they are excluded from the class structure, largely discarded by the political mobilisation of the nationalist parties and their grinding poverty teaches them quickly that they have nothing to lose by embracing violence. What drives the peasantry is the desire to replace the settlers as the peasants are the victims of the colonial land grab where in a plainly visible hierarchy where race, land ownership and starvation coincide. To replace the settler is then to end land starvation and restore the African peasants and the countryside to stability. The case of Kenya, the Mau Mau insurgency and land starvation is a prime case in point, as well as the case of South Africa where the matter is yet to be resolved as the Mandela neo-colonial plaster over the weeping sore is now in collapse. Fanon's designation of the peasantry as the only revolutionary agent will change in this text of his as when his methodology is applied to other colonial social orders a different revolutionary agent emerges: the lumpen proletariat. Fanon has now stretched Marx's schema well past its breaking point and at this point he is simply adding as he goes along, for the schema is in itself gravely flawed when applied to the North Atlantic and glaucomic when applied to Third world reality. What has to be accepted and acted upon in analysis is that the revolutionary agent is simply idyllic for the complexity of violence and a war of liberation outstrips the futile attempt to reduce it to the existence or absence of a revolutionary agent. The focus must then be on power relations. Fanon is insisting that those at the bottom of the social order, the gravely marginalised can and do understand and express it in their daily lives that: "Colonialism. It is violence in its natural state, and it will only yield when confronted with greater violence." (Fanon 1963 pg. 61). But what happens when the neo-colonial project grants the gift of independence, forms the alliance with leaders of the nationalist parties, the native intellectuals and the colonial elites, and fully supports and finances the suppression of all opposition to this alliance for a speedy independence? Clearly, the strategy to ensure the postcolonial hegemony of the neo-colonial enterprise was driven by the gift of independence, hence its hegemony as the favoured instrument applied. Fanon's search for the revolutionary agent then applies only to colonies where a war of liberation was unleashed as Algeria, Vietnam, Angola, Mozambique and Guinea-Bissau with this dichotomy in his work being the product of addressing two distinct realities which must be distinguished and differentiated.

Independence and A Dependent Social Order

Fanon in closing his treatment of the gift of independence and the neo-colonial enterprise states: "It is true to say that independence has brought moral compensation to colonised peoples, and has established their dignity. But they have not yet had time to elaborate a society, or to build up and affirm values. The warming, light-giving center where man and citizen develop and enrich their experience in wider and still wider fields does not yet exist. Set in a kind of irresolution, such men persuade themselves fairly easily that everything is going to be decided elsewhere, for everybody at the same time. As for the political leaders, when faced with this situation, they first hesitate then choose neutralism." (Fanon 1963 pg. 81). Independence has bestowed moral compensation only, for there is no other compensation forthcoming, thereby establishing the dignity of the independent but a hollow dignity lacking in substance as there is no social order buttressed by common values affirmed through its hegemony. This failure to create a social order is rooted in the absence of an indigenous hegemonic discourse through its mechanism of power that drives the constituting of members of the social order who find definition, purpose and safety in the social order. There is a social order that is under the hegemony of a discourse that is alien to independence and the dignity of the independent, intent on exerting hegemony over this social order to realise the neo-colonial project. This discourse, anathema to independence, exerting hegemony over the social order has constituted independent, free individuals devoid of resolute action, they are vacillators and hand wringers incapable of action to remedy the grave defects of independence as they expect the solution will be coming from an external source, the neo-colonial solution. This is the hegemonic discourse of the Manichean duality which only allows us to seek solutions cobbled together in realities external of ours for we are the captives of our denial. They then and can only choose neutralism, which is simply neo-colonial domination as usual, but their lack of resolution leaves them no other choice. The social order Fanon describes never evolves as an independent entity constituting free people for it cannot given its dependence on hegemonic North Atlantic discourse and its fear to act, to be resolute, herein lies the genesis of the wretched of the earth alive and kicking from the 1940s to the 21st century.

Monopoly Capitalism and Neo-colonialism

Fanon now recognises that the utility of the colonies has changed as capitalism has evolved, but there is a tension between the old colonialism of the conquest and the new order demanded by monopoly capitalism out of which emerges neo-colonialism and the gift of independence. Fanon states: "The colonies have become a market." "The monopolistic group within this bourgeoisie does not support a government whose policy is solely that of the sword. What the factory owners and finance magnates of the mother country expect from their government is not that it should decimate the colonial peoples, but that it should safeguard with the help of economic conventions their 'legitimate interests.' Thus there is a sort of detached complicity between capitalism and violent forces which blaze up in colonial territory." (Fanon 1963 pg. 65). There is then a power relation between those who view the colonial enterprise as an operational framework that is limiting the efficient extraction of value from the colonies. This faction and its allies in the colonies are adherents of the model of neo-colonial domination. Then there are those who insist retention of the colonies at all costs is a necessity as it projects the power of the colonial nation, its international power and image and most of all it is their right as white people through manifest destiny to hold non-white races in subjection by any means necessary. Then there are the politicians who vacillate as they contemplate the impact of every political decision on their political careers and constantly react to actions already taken in defence of and propagation of their political careers. This constantly evolving terrain of power relations produce a range of decisions taken on the colonial question which flowed between two poles: the wars for colonial survival to the gift of independence. Fanon recognises that the ally of monopoly capitalism and its neo-colonial agenda in the colonies are those spontaneous outbursts of mass action/violence which are utilised by the nationalist parties and the political allies of monopoly capitalism to agitate for the speedy implementation of the gift of independence.

Underdevelopment, Colonialism and Neo-colonialism

In the final section of the text Fanon deals with the power relations of underdevelopment in its nexus with neo-colonial domination. Fanon insists that the manner in which the reality of underdevelopment is addressed is deeply flawed if not totally inaccurate. What is then needed is a discourse of underdevelopment rooted in its reality formulated and released by us, for us of the Third World. Fanon states: "This manner of setting out the problem of the evolution of underdeveloped countries seems to us to be neither correct nor reasonable." (Fanon 1963 pg. 95). Fanon has rejected the pro-capitalist discourse of evolutionary development of Third World countries premised upon neo-colonial capitalist dependency as its engine of growth. This discourse presents a model of European capitalist development that is mythic, if not base lies. Fanon commences his discourse by describing what is the condition of the underdeveloped world who all have a long history of colonial domination or being subject to the imperial power of Europe, if not formally colonised, as follows: "It is an underdeveloped world, a world inhuman in its poverty; but also it is a world without doctors, without engineers, and without administrators. Confronting this world, the European nations sprawl, ostentatiously opulent. This European opulence is literally scandalous, for it has been founded on slavery, it has been nourished with the blood of slaves and it comes directly from the soil and the subsoil of that underdeveloped world. The well-being and progress of Europe have been built up with the sweat and the dead bodies of Negroes, Arabs, Indians and the yellow races. We have decided not to overlook this any longer." (Fanon 1963 pg. 96). That Europe attained developed status by dint of their hard work, entrepreneurial skills and all the other special characteristics of the white man which we don't have is fundamentally a lie. Development was attained through violent domination of non-white races in the colonies where value was extracted from these dominated non-white races and exported to Europe where it generated wealth for the white man and chronic pain for us the dominated. For us to attain developed status with capitalism we have then to repeat the white model of violent domination towards the extraction of and export of value to generate wealth and wealth maximisation governed by a hierarchy of race privilege. The white discourse of development is formulated to blame us continuously and repeatedly for our pain and suffering, whilst masking the power relations of exploitation rooted in a hierarchy of race privilege and ultimately constituting our servility to the hegemony of the neo-colonial enterprise. Fanon continues: "The former dominated country becomes an economically dependent country. The ex-colonial power, which has kept intact and sometimes even reinforced its colonialist trade channels, agrees to provision the budget of the independent nation by small injections. Thus we see that the accession to independence of the colonial countries places an important question before the world, for the national liberation of colonised countries unveils their true economic state and makes it seem even more unendurable." "What counts today, the question which is looming on the horizon, is the need for a redistribution of wealth." (Fanon 1963 pg. 98). The end of colonial domination then reveals two realities: the grave underdevelopment wrought by colonial domination, which is effectively the product of the violence unleashed by white domination and the continued power relation of domination that exists in the post-independence era. Freedom then masks continued domination towards exploitation, which must place on the agenda the issue of the distribution and redistribution of wealth in the world, as freedom is not sufficient to address and transform the chronic underdevelopment of the ex-colonial states. Freedom as the mask of continued exploitation raises the issue of the methodology we must adopt to deal with the hegemonic discourse of neo-colonial domination. Fanon states: "The Third World ought not to be content to define itself in terms of values which have preceded it. On the contrary, the underdeveloped countries ought to do their utmost to find their own particular values and methods and a style which shall be peculiar to them." (Fanon 1963 pg. 99). "The country finds itself in the hands of new managers; but the fact is that everything needs to be reformed and everything thought out anew." (Fanon 1963 pg. 100). Liberation begins at the level of the idea for servility begins at the level of the idea. To be liberated it is necessary to formulate new ideas that constitute a new individual driven by a new worldview, that is anathema to the discourse and worldview of domination and servility. Our acceptance of and action constituted by the discourse of domination render us and our social orders underdeveloped, we are therefore culpable in our suffering for we are not passive bystanders to our domination, servility and suffering for we police ourselves to the benefit of the North Atlantic and the pliant elites of the Third World and to the detriment and suffering of ourselves and successive generations. Decolonisation is expressed by the operational reality of business as usual from colonial domination to independence, where the entire State apparatus of the independent nation is rooted in European colonial models for there is no reform, nothing thought out anew, no new values, methods and style. The retention of the operationalised colonial worldview under independence potently illustrates the power relations of neo-colonialism, ensures that we remain servile to the white power structure, whilst insisting that we are now free and sovereign. We remain caught in the Manichean duality.

Chapter Two
The Revolutionary Agents of Change

In Section 1 of the "Wretched of the Earth" Fanon presents his discourse of decolonisation and violence. In Section Two of the work Fanon presents his analysis of the discursive concept presented in his discourse of decolonisation and violence of the revolutionary agent of change in the colonial context. As analysed in Chapter One Fanon presents the peasant as the sole revolutionary agent of change dismissing the proletariat as the revolutionary class. In this chapter Fanon's analysis of this position will be presented.

The Proletariat

Fanon has grave problems with the political party forms and organisation simply lifted from colonial metropolitan reality and applied to colonial reality. Fanon states: "The elite will attach a fundamental importance to organisation, so much so that the fetish of organisation will often take precedence over a reasoned study of colonial society." (Fanon 1963 pg. 108). The native intellectuals inevitably act upon their worldview which insists that all things of western origin are ultimately relevant to colonial reality which trumps the need to do the studies of the colonial world vitally necessary to understand the colonial reality, which still obtains in the 21st century. But it's not only an uncritical importation and application of institutional forms and organisation but also an uncritical importation and application of the discourse that formulates and drives these forms and organisations. This is the product of the inferiority complex which refuses to/can never accept that we are fundamentally different from the white colonial and neo-colonial metropole, for to do so cracks the façade of hallucinatory whiteness of Steven. Fanon states that this delusional embrace of all things white results in the expectation in the colony that the proletariat is the revolutionary agent when it is not and can never be, which is a serious political strategic mistake. Fanon states: "It cannot be too highly stressed that in the colonial territories the proletariat is the nucleus of the colonised population which has been most pampered by the colonial regime." (Fanon 1963 pg. 108). The proletariat formed by colonial domination is an instrument of colonial domination not the revolutionary agent of change necessary to liberation. Hence the attachment of the colonial proletariat to the nationalist parties and the neo-colonial agenda. The proletariat is the core of those constituted by racist colonial discourse to affirm colonial domination, enable colonial domination and act as a buffer between the colonial administrators, the settlers and the marginalised natives. The proletariat then belongs to the group of compradors who will inherit the gift of independence to the detriment of the marginalised natives. Fanon continues: "In the colonial countries the working class has everything to lose, in reality it represents that fraction of the colonised nation which is necessary and irreplaceable if the colonial machine is to run smoothly" (Fanon 1963 pg. 109). Constituted by colonial domination the proletariat has a vested interest in colonial domination which it transfers to neo-colonial domination thereby affirming its strategic importance to both the sustainability of the colonial enterprise and that of its replacement: the neo-colonial enterprise. Fanon is at this instance of his discourse literally ripping asunder Marxist orthodoxy, especially that propagated by the native intellectuals educated in the colonial metropoles who adhered mechanistically to this orthodoxy. In fact, Fanon's position questions the relevance of historical materialism to the task of unravelling the nature of the colonial and neo-colonial social orders. Fanon insists that the proletariat is part of the "bourgeois" faction of the colonised people, not in what they own and control of the means of production, but the modern white ideas they embrace and act upon which assaults the cultural values, traditions and discourses of pre-colonial native civilisation. Fanon states: "Here 'modern ideas reign.' It is these classes that will struggle against obscurantist traditions, that will change old customs, and that will thus enter into open conflict with the old granite block upon which the nation rests." (Fanon 1963 pg. 109). The proletariat and this bourgeois faction are then an instrument of colonial power where they police and employ themselves in the task of deepening the colonial dominance of the native terrain by assaulting native discourse towards the hegemony of white racist colonial discourse. This bourgeois faction will be assigned the same said task under neo-colonial domination, but with a changed discourse and ensuing power relations.

The Peasantry

Fanon now expands on his discourse of the peasantry as revolutionary agent which we analysed in Chapter One. Fanon states: "The overwhelming majority of nationalist parties show a deep distrust toward the people of the rural areas. The fact is that as a body these people appear to them to be bogged down in fruitless inertia." "we must remember that colonialism has often strengthened or established its domination by organising the petrification of the country districts." (Fanon 1963 pg.109). "the feudal leaders form a screen between the young Westernised nationalists and the bulk of the people." (Fanon 1963 pg. 110). The young westernised nationalists must view the masses of the countryside as backward, trapped in a pre-colonial netherworld, which they cannot and must not understand for fear of contamination as they share a common genetic origin. This is where race, tribe and ethnic classifications of division arise to distinguish between friend/modern/western/white and enemy/backward, feudal, non-white or the Manichean duality redefined for the neo-colonial order. The bourgeois faction of the colonised people encumbered with hallucinatory whiteness must then harbour and act upon a deep distrust of such rural natives for they are the inhabitants of a Manichean compartment they know nothing of, which by its nature poses a grave threat to the bourgeois faction. The coloniser has deliberately constructed this Manichean compartment for the rural native thereby seeking to fossilise native culture in this compartment, rendering its threat to the colonial State mute, but this has resulted in spawning a monster posing a grave threat to decolonisation seeking to implant the neo-colonial order. For the attempt at the fossilisation and petrification of rural native culture has not diminished the resistance to colonial domination whilst insulating the compartment from actions of the bourgeois faction to infect the compartment with white, modern ideas of servility. The racist arrogance of the colonial massa and his servile, racist, bourgeois faction blinded them to the reality that effective and destructive resistance is not solely the product of modern, white, western ideas, for violence is violence under a diversity of discourses especially pre-colonial discourses. The peasantry that remains in the countryside emerges from this colonial crucible the revolutionary agent of change. Fanon states: "The peasant who stays put defends his traditions stubbornly, and in a colonised society stands for the disciplined element whose interests lie in maintaining the social structure." "But in their spontaneous movements the country people as a whole remain disciplined and altruistic. The individual stands aside in favour of the community." "Here, we are not dealing with the old antagonism between town and country; it is the antagonism which exists between the native who is excluded from the advantages of colonialism and his counterpart who manages to turn colonial exploitation to his account." (Fanon 1963 pgs. 111-112). Fanon distinguishes between those who stay in the countryside and those who leave for the colonial city. Those who stay are rooted in a pre-colonial order with its independent discourse and worldview that constitutes peasants who are in a power relation with the colonial State and its comprador natives. The peasants resist the attempt to dominate them by seducing them to be servile to the colonial massa which places them in a violent power relation with the colonial State and its native compradors and these peasants in battle show individual characteristics of resistance which are the product of resistance generated by pre-colonial civilisation. Resistance to North Atlantic colonial "modernity" is then successfully mounted by what colonial "modernity" describes as traditionalist backwardness, superstition and worst of all Islamic inertia. This is a reality that was operative in Algeria, Vietnam, the Mau Mau insurgency of colonial Kenya, Guinea-Bissau, Angola and Mozambique. On the peasants that migrate from the countryside to the urban colonial compartment Fanon states: "The landless peasants, who make up the *lumpenproletariat*, leave the country districts, where vital statistics are just so many insoluble problems, rush towards the towns, crowd into tin shack settlements, and try to make their way into the ports and cities founded by colonial domination. "(Fanon 1963 pg. 111). Fanon now introduces into his discourse the discursive concept of the lumpenproletariat which is a product of the colonial assault on the traditional structure of the countryside, where the landless peasants are forced to migrate to the colonial urban compartment as the impact of the colonial economy and the settlers on the economy of the countryside displaces the most vulnerable of this economy. Fanon is insisting that the urban lumpenproletariat is of rural, peasant origin therefore they are bearers of the traditional values of the colonial rural compartment, the culture of resistance in the colonial urban compartment.

Urban Lumpenproletariat

The effective resistance of the peasants is not only the product of traditional rural culture but also the dismal failure of the nationalist parties to politically mobilise the countryside by integrating the traditional worldview and social order into its political discourse. Fanon states: "The political parties do not manage to organise the country districts. Instead of using existing structures and giving them a nationalist or progressive character, they mean to try and destroy living tradition in the colonial framework." (Fanon 1963 pgs. 112-113). The native politicians are intent to embrace only those compradors as themselves within their political orbit for they are convinced that only those embracing and acting upon white values can in fact engage successfully with the colonial overlord for the gift of independence and ensure the modern future of the independent nation. All those inhabitants of the colony who refuse to embrace the white man's modernity are the grave threats to the independence/neo-colonial project. This is why with independence the assault on the countryside is heightened as the land grab intensifies but now with black and white overlords. The drift from rural to urban intensifies and the size and scale of the urban lumpenproletariat explodes, housed in huge squatter settlements devoid of the basic necessities of life where successive generations are born and live in squalor and deprivation with no memory of the rural lifestyle and traditional values but yet to be immersed by modern/postmodern white values. They then inhabit a neo-colonial netherworld where they are marginalised economically, physically, emotionally and discursively where the State is remote, cryptic and undecipherable in their daily survival strategy. But this lumpenproletariat is a strategic political asset utilised by first the colonial massa and then the neo-colonial compradors. Fanon states: "Colonialism, in order to reach its ends, used the most traditional methods: frequent arrests, racist propaganda between tribes, and the creation of party out of the unorganised elements of the *lumpenproletariat.*" (Fanon 1963 pg. 115). The colonial State was not then averse to politicising elements of the lumpenproletariat as an instrument of colonial power to exert social control over the colonised and this instrument took various forms and was applied strategically to a variety of situations. Informers, enforcers, hitmen, militia mercenaries were some of the forms applied, but the overarching reality is that the very existence of the lumpenproletariat and the discourse of their inherently criminogenic nature justified policing as social control from colonial domination to 21st century neo-colonial domination. The lumpenproletariat is then the most strategically important human grouping to the exercise of power from the colonial to the neo-colonial social orders as reserve army of cheap labour, political shock troops, the inhabitants of the prime landscape of the economy of crime which caters to all desires, both legal and illegal, and most important the living, breathing repository of all things evil and malevolent that generates the moral panic that demands social control of a specific type and nature that exposes the reality that the Constitution is a grave lie. The most potent gift of neo-colonial domination to the world is the lumpenproletariat and all that it exposes as to the nature of man/woman and power.

Fanon continues his analysis of the urban *lumpenproletariat* by recognising its place in the colonial social order and the impact on the social order this marginalised social group exerts. Fanon states: "The men whom the growing population of the country districts and colonial expropriations have brought to desert their family holdings circle tirelessly around the different towns, hoping that one day or another they will be allowed inside. It is within this mass of humanity, this people of the shanty towns, at the core of the *lumpenproletariat,* that the rebellion will find the urban spearhead. For the *lumpenproletariat,* that horde of starving men, uprooted from their tribe and from their clan, constitutes one of the most spontaneous and the most radically revolutionary forces of a colonised people." (Fanon 1963 pg. 129). The uprooted, marginalised people of the rural areas, the displaced peasantry have migrated to the urban areas and are now forced to inhabit a colonial compartment where they are locked out of all compartments previously created by colonial domination to enable sustainable colonial hegemony. This new compartment is the direct product of colonial power relations operationalised which generates a throw away population, which is marginalised to the fringes of the urban, colonial social order left up to their own survival devices where their only contact with the colonial State is with the policeman. All the basic amenities as pipe borne water, sewage disposal, roads, electrification, education, health care and housing are denied these marginal areas. There is simply no attempt to plan, manage and integrate these spaces into the colonial state, there is only a strategy for social control and subordination of select elements of the marginalised population as it serves the interests of the colonial overlord. In these zones of human deprivation and suffering revolutionary forces sprout, grow and evolve, but they are faced with two grave impediments that enhance the power of the colonial State to break the back of the revolutionary forces: the lumpen in the employ of the colonial massa as the informers, criminal groups and their leaders and the lumpen mercenaries of the colonial massa and then there are the native colonised who view the revolutionary force from the ghettoes as a grave threat to their political ascendency. Unless this lumpenproletariat revolutionary force integrates itself with the rural revolution they face extinction in the city as was clearly illustrated by the case of Mau Mau in colonial Kenya. This disciplined lumpenproletariat in the service of the colonial State was the greatest gift the colonial massa made to the Stevens of independence and the neo-colonial project. Fanon continues his analysis of the lumpenproletariat as follows: "This lumpenproletariat is as a horde of rats; you may kick them and throw stones at them, but despite your efforts they'll go on gnawing at the roots of the tree." "The lumpenproletariat once it is constituted, brings all its forces to endanger the 'security' of the town, and is the sign of the irrevocable decay, the gangrene ever present at the heart of colonial domination." (Fanon 1963 pg. 130). The lumpenproletariat effectively marginalised from the social order and interacting with the colonial State is left in a state of personal deprivation which is supposed to discipline them and render them servile, but the very survival strategies they formulate and execute on a daily basis continually assault the legitimacy and order of the colonial State. Daily survival is then premised on a daily state of rebellion to the hegemonic order which the colonial State must deal with if it is to ensure that this lifestyle does not engender social chaos. The colonial order then moves to co-opt specific sections of the lumpenproletariat to ensure control over elements of the lumpenproletariat that post a grave threat to the colonial State. Those most willing to serve the colonial State which intensifies their power and wealth generation capacity in the ghettoes at first are the criminals: pimps, prostitutes, break-in artists, bar owners, brothel owners, gamblers etc. evolve into the colonial militia of the ghettoes and in return they become rich, powerful and leaders of organised crime. With independence this legacy is handed over to the native politicians and the ghettoes multiply in size and scale by geometric progression and their sociology changes as tribal/race war is now political mobilisation; organised crime of the ghettoes becomes national and then international organised crime and persons employed in the neo-colonial economic order with expectations of living in the suburbs are now the new entrants to ghetto life given the land hunger that grips the nation as the native colonial elite has now transformed itself into the native landed gentry. What has not changed is the colonial strategy for marginalising and controlling the population so marginalised within these ghettoes, there is then a continuity from the colonial condition to the neo-colonial condition as the hierarchical social order is maintained dominated by white supremacist North Atlantic discourse and its mechanism of power. Fanon is then insisting that this throw away population of colonial domination which potently illustrates all that is destructive with colonial domination has the capacity to destroy colonial domination because of its marginalised nature. But whilst having this capacity only when constituted the lumpenproletariat remains a sustainable social entity under colonial and neo-colonial domination, the potent indicator of the grave and extreme dysfunctionality of the colonial and neo-colonial social orders and most of all of the evolutionary line of descent that links colonial domination to neo-colonial domination as they share a common DNA profile which generated the lumpenproletariat and made it sustainable from colonialism to neo-colonialism. The lumpenproletariat, then and now in the 21st century, is the most potent evidence to convict white supremacist North Atlantic imperialism of crimes against humanity along with their compradors, Stevens, Chicken Georges, Gunga Dins and Hop Sings.

Fanon deals with the power relation between the lumpenproletariat and the colonial massa as follows: "Colonialism will also find in the lumpenproletariat a considerable space for manoeuvring. For this reason, any movement for freedom ought to give its fullest attention to this lumpenproletariat. The peasant masses will always answer the call to rebellion, but if the rebellion's leaders think it will be available to develop without taking the masses into consideration, the lumpenproletariat will throw itself into the battle and will take part in the conflict-but this time on the side of the oppressor. And the oppressor, who never loses a chance of setting the niggers against each other, will be extremely skilful in using that ignorance and incomprehension which are the weaknesses of the lumpenproletariat. If this available reserve of human effort is not immediately organised by the forces of rebellion, it will find itself fighting as hired soldiers side by side with the colonial troops." (Fanon 1963 pgs. 136-137). The lumpenproletariat, the product of colonial domination by its very nature, is an instrument of colonial power that surpasses the utility of the colonised elite as the lumpenproletariat stands as an effective, available resource to be utilised by the colonial massa towards ensuring sustainable colonial domination. By way of a pre-emptive strike those intent on rebellion against colonial domination must organise the lumpenproletariat thereby quarantining it from colonial incursion and adding its spontaneous, violent quality to the forces of the rebellion. Failing to do this the colonial massa will induct the lumpenproletariat into its common front of natives dedicated to defeating the rebellion. The colonial massa is well disposed to recruit the lumpenproletariat to its agenda given the rewards that the colonial massa can dispense in the present, here and now for it is only select sections of the group the colonial massa will seek to recruit, the rest will be simply repressed into compliance; whilst the rebellion is an uncertain outcome in the future, where they are called upon to trust persons and make sacrifices for in the here and now which presents grave danger to life and limb. This choice scenario presents a complex terrain for a struggler to traverse who is immersed in a grinding daily survival strategy with limited resources. The lumpenproletariat has ignorance and incomprehension of the lifestyle of the peasants and what motivates their rebellion as the peasants have of theirs, and their overarching drive for self-survival and the divisions that divide the colonial social order also impact their relationship as tribe/ethnicity/race and class hatred which makes joint action very difficult. The colonial massa is then well placed to select groups and manipulate them to his own ends from within the lumpenproletariat, as he does with all colonised groups, for this is not a specific, unique propensity of the lumpenproletariat. This is a specially demarcated group in the colonial order where evil, malevolence and criminality reside and thrive, the designated scapegoats of the colonial social order, which is the reserve army of the colonial massa and the justification for repression and the compartmentalisation of the social order as social control. With independence the structure survives, evolves as the lumpenproletariat adopts the persona of the criminal insurgent driving moral panic in the social order which demands the heightening of compartmentalisation, repression and militarised policing in a "free," "democratic" society. Whilst the politicians employ the colonial strategy to politicise the lumpenproletariat and utilise chosen sections of its composition to exert political control over the spaces and the people who inhabit these spaces in the compartment assigned to the lumpenproletariat to fill the void created by a State that has abrogated its right and duty to exert hegemony over these spaces. To fill this, void the politicians use their political followers, the criminal groups in their orbit backed up with infrequent search and seizure operations of the police. The foundation laid under colonial domination has then changed little, if at all qualitatively, barring the transition from colony to free, sovereign State. Eventually the politicians lose what little control they exercised on the ground as the criminal insurgency driven by organised and transnational organised crime breaks the shackle of dependence on the politicians for the benefits of State patronage, thereby constituting an effective challenge to the hegemony of the State in the compartment of the lumpenproletariat

in the 21st century. This criminal insurgency spreads to the prisons, to the education system, to policing and impacts the quality of daily life in the other compartments of the social order other than that dominated by the lumpenproletariat which contributes to a crisis of legitimacy of the neo-colonial project in the 21st century. Fanon continues his analysis of the lumpenproletariat as follows: "The enemy discovers the existence, side by side with the disciplined and well organised advance guard of rebellion, of a mass of men whose participation is constantly at the mercy of their being for too long accustomed to physiological wretchedness, humiliation, and irresponsibility. The enemy is ready to pay a high price for the services of this mass. He will create spontaneity with bayonets and exemplary floggings." (Fanon 1963 pg. 137). The product of colonial domination operationalised is then a resource and asset of colonial domination, an instrument of colonial power which the colonial massa will mobilise to defeat the anti-colonial movement. Fanon is attesting to the existence of a complex duality within the native population where you have the colonised elite and the colonised natives, but both overarching groups are not homogeneous as you have colonised natives outside of the colonised elite and in this group there is the duality of the lumpenproletariat and the advanced guard of the rebellion. The key to this operational terrain is the impact of colonisation and its psychoexistential complex on the native and the native groups constituted in the social order. Fanon is clear in his position that the discourse of marginalisation allied to the psychoexistential complex has constituted a unique native in the colonial social order, the lumpenproletariat which will be utilised by the colonial massa with the complicity of the lumpenproletariat against the organised advanced guard of the rebellion. The lumpenproletariat, as is the case of the colonial elite and other natives are all complicit with colonial domination. This lumpenproletariat's complicity which continues under neo-colonial domination, a legacy of colonial domination, then impacts the evolution of the neo-colonial social order. Fanon recognises that the sections of the lumpenproletariat recruited by the colonial massa in the war against rebellion have little choice in the matter as the mechanism of power applied against the lumpenproletariat has created an apparatus of marginalisation where the lumpenproletariat is constituted to serve power as the reserve army of power. Fanon therefore speaks of the wretchedness of the life of the lumpenproletariat as a result where the lumpenproletariat in the service of the colonial massa spreads and deepens the application of colonial brutality, which will generate spontaneous rebellion even among the mass of the lumpenproletariat, for only a minority are inducted into the service of the colonial massa. This then is the potential of the lumpenproletariat as a revolutionary agent of change. But the colonial massa clearly visualised this danger and nipped it in the bud with the gift of independence, where under neo-colonialism the marginalisation continued and was heightened and sections of the lumpenproletariat became the shock troops for the nationalist political parties in their wars for control of the State, thereby forming operational bonds between politicians and the lumpenproletariat that politicised the ghettoes and granted impunity to their political militias. When politically expedient these political militias will be the shock troops to commence the pogroms, ethnic cleansing and genocide against political enemies. Fanon at this point has now returned to the issue of the impact of colonial domination on the psychology of the colonised.

Peasants, Workers and Trade Unions

Fanon returns to his analysis of the peasants as follows: "The peasantry spontaneously gives concrete form to the general insecurity; and colonialism takes fright and either continues the war of negotiates." (Fanon 1963 pg. 116). The peasant spontaneously engages the colonial overlord with a challenge to his domination of the colony, a challenge so spontaneous in origin and violent in intent the colonial overlord has option of choosing only one of two possible choices: wage war or negotiate. The key here is spontaneous violent action by the peasants which presents a potent challenge to the colonial order as it was unable to pre-empt this violent action, which forces a decision to be only made by the metropolitan elite which will impact various agendas especially that of the neo-colonial project. It is spontaneous violent action that delays the implementation of the neo-colonial project or worse yet it precipitates a war of liberation where the neo-colonial project is waylaid by the interruption of the timetable for the granting of independence. Or ultimately it precipitates the response of a colonial war against the anti-colonial movement. A range of choices that impact the future of the colony in relation to the possible actions of the colonial metropole. Fanon now presents his analysis of another transplanted North

Atlantic institution to the colonies and its relation with the peasants: the trade unions. Fanon states: "Suddenly the unions discover that the back-country too ought to be enlightened and organised. But since at no time have they taken care to establish working links between themselves and the mass of the peasants, and since this peasantry precisely constitutes the only spontaneously revolutionary force in the country, the trade unions will give proof of their inefficiency and find out for themselves the anachronistic nature of their programs." (Fanon 1963 pg. 123). The workers, the most pampered faction of the colonised, cannot be the spontaneous revolutionary force of the colony and the institution transplanted uncritically from the colonial metropole, can only see the need to serve the colonisers, the harbingers of modernity and progress in the colony. The trade unions see no need to organise the peasants, what they do see is the need to civilise the peasants in order to free them from the backwardness of tradition, superstition and magic that inhibits them from embracing modernity and progress. The trade unions are then just another instrument of colonial domination and with independence an instrument of power of the discourse of neo-colonial domination. Fanon is then identifying all the agents of colonial domination, the compradors plagued with hallucinatory whiteness and the institutions they utilise to ensure colonial domination then the hegemony of the neo-colonial project. Fanon now deals with the nationalist parties as follows: "We have seen that inside the nationalist parties, the will to break colonialism is linked with quite another different will: that of coming to a friendly agreement with it. Within these parties, the two processes will sometimes continue side by side." (Fanon 1963 pg. 124). The ambivalence at best, the schizophrenia at worst, of the nationalist parties is the product of the fact that its leadership and prime, active membership are dominated by the colonised of the native population of the colony all burdened by the psychoexistential complex and its hallucinatory whiteness. This colonised elite must act as they do when they are faced with the movement for decolonisation by desiring and actively pursuing the gift of independence towards the implementation of the neo-colonial project with this elite in ascendancy.

Spontaneity

Fanon's position on the spontaneity of the anti-colonial movement and the nature of the native constituted by colonial power must now be dealt with in this deconstruction. Fanon repeatedly insists that the brutality of colonial domination elicits the native spontaneous action of rebellion, but the issue is the efficacy of spontaneous action when faced with the resources and strategy of the colonial massa. On the spontaneity of the masses Fanon states: "They feel a positive hatred for the 'politics' of demagogy, and that is why in the beginning we observe a veritable triumph for the cult of spontaneity." "There is no program; there are no speeches or resolutions, and no political trends. The problem is clear: the foreigners must go; so let us form a common front against the oppressor and let us strengthen our hands by armed combat." (Fanon 1963 pg. 131). There is a cult of spontaneity where the reality is reduced to a single duality with a single, simple solution. The problem is the foreigner, the settler, the colonial massa and the solution is expelling the foreigner with spontaneous mass action that is the product of, the reaction to stimuli applied by the colonial massa. The cult of spontaneity is the product of the Manichean duality where there is no need to strategize, to assess the enemy and to take the initiative with mass action. For as dualities that condition, constitute and create each other, all that is required to reverse the power relation where dominator becomes dominated is simple, spontaneous mass action. But the grave problem arises when faced with an intractable enemy spontaneous mass action soon wanes and melts away into the shadows. Fanon continues: "We are dealing with a strategy of immediacy which is both radical and totalitarian: the aim and the program of each locally constituted group is local liberation." "Tactics are mistaken for strategy. The art of politics is simply transformed into the art of war; the political militant is the rebel. To fight the war and to take part in politics; the two things become one and the same." (Fanon 1963 pg. 132). Spontaneity does not and cannot envisage a prolonged war of liberation which requires longevity of mass action and the development of a military strategy and command separate and apart from colonial politics. Spontaneity can only view politics as mass action, even as war which results in tactics mistaken for strategy and the opening of mass action to assault by the colonial massa by unleashing the gift of independence which immediately destroys mass action and puts in play neo-colonial domination as at a specific time and date the foreigner will be gone and we will all be free and sovereign. Spontaneous mass action ensured the success of the neo-colonial project when the colonial massa granted all that the masses wanted: the colonial massa gone and they now filling the spaces created to be the new massa for massa day done! This is what happens when you mistake politics for war and tactics for strategy going up against an enemy that is your twin joined at the hips constituted by the Manichean duality. The salient difference between the twins was that one was the dominator and the other the dominated, and in this power relation the dominator never intended to simply surrender her/his position of power and all the benefits derived thereof simply because of your threat of mass action or mass action launched. The colonial massa devised a strategy to ensure sustainable domination into the 21st century and beyond whilst we deployed a tactic, not a counter strategy, for we were incapable of visualising the strategy of the colonial massa much less to formulate a counter strategy. Because we are enamoured by thoughts of whiteness, of being finally accepted in the white league of free nations, of finally being granted access to the Great House of massa so we accepted the neo-colonial project from colonised elite to the masses in rebellion, for all we had was a tactic to get rid of massa and replace her/him with ourselves for we want to be white animating all the structures she/he utilised under colonial domination and left for us as her/his legacy. We then are in control of our free, sovereign states but willingly accept the terms and conditions of North Atlantic domination. Spontaneity and its mistakes is then the product of the Manichean duality and the impact of its mechanism of power on our psychology to this day for spontaneity was never invested with the ability to destroy the Manichean duality and its mechanism of power which now drives the process of constituting the neo-colonial non-white individual. Fanon continues on the product of spontaneity and its weakness as follows: "That spectacular volunteer movement which meant to lead the colonised people to supreme sovereignty at one fell swoop, that certainty which you had that all portions of the nation would be carried along with you at the same speed and led onwards, that strength which gave you hope: all are now seen in the light of experience to be symptoms of a very great weakness." (Fanon 1963 pg. 138). The grave weakness of spontaneity spawned the delusion that politics is in fact an anti-colonial war, which generated the denial that fostered the belief that tactic was strategy and all that was needed was anti-colonial action of any kind which will effectively sweep the foreigner, unify the disparate segments of the nation as they march onwards to victory and liberty. Political sloganeering then passing for reality which Fanon says was easily falsified by experience. Fanon continues: "While the native thought that he could pass without transition from the status of a colonised person to that of a self-governing citizen of an independent nation, while he grasped at the mirage of his muscles' own immediacy, he made no real progress along the road to knowledge. His consciousness remains rudimentary." (Fanon 1963 pg. 138). Fanon insists that there must be a stage of transition between colonised and free which is the state of revolution utilising the instrument of the war of liberation. Those who believe and act upon this belief that there is no state of transition between these two extreme existential conditions are trapped in the world constituted by the Manichean duality, where the colonised are afflicted by the mirage of their personal power to effect personal liberation, an affliction which views liberation as local and personal, tactical rather than strategic and political rather than war of liberation. This mirage of personal liberationary power is the affliction of the psyche of the colonised constituted by the Manichean duality and its mechanism of power which shunts the colonised from the necessity to make war, preparing them to readily, gladly and willingly accept the gift of independence and the neo-colonial condition as the realisation and expression of being free without the necessity of a state of transition. For the process embraced as being adequate for liberation cannot add to knowledge nor raise the consciousness of the colonised, thereby enabling the great neo-colonial deception for the process and the liberation derived are all the products of a mirage, illusory without concrete expression in reality.

Colonial Strategy

Fanon now deals with the multifaceted strategy launched by the colonial massa to compromise the native rebellion by first analysing the psychological need of the native, the launching of the psychological assault where the colonial massa is playing the native need for white affirmation. Fanon states: "The native is made to feel that things are changing. The native, who did not take up arms simply because he was dying of hunger and because he saw his own social forms disintegrating before his eyes, but also because the settler considered him to be an animal, and treated him as such, reacts very favourably to such measures. Hatred is disarmed by these psychological windfalls." (Fanon 1963 pg. 140). There are then specific native types who respond to the psychological assault of the colonial instrument of power, these are those who chose not to embrace the movement to assault the colonial occupation, they remained passive offering various rationales for their inactivity. These are the natives who then fall prey to the psychological assault, insist that colonialism isn't all that bad look how massa is changing for the better and then willingly and lovingly embrace the gift of independence. Any hatred these groups harboured for the colonial massa is then easily muted by the psychological assault of an instrument of power that is maintained and perfected under neo-colonial domination, potently

illustrated by the widespread use of skin bleaching creams in the 21st century. Fanon continues: "The native is promoted; they try to disarm him with their psychology, and of course they throw in a few shillings too." "The native is so starved for anything, anything that will turn him into a human being, any bone of humanity flung to him, that his hunger is incoercible, and these poor scraps of charity may, here and there overwhelm him. His consciousness is so precarious and dim that it is affected by the slightest spark of kindness." (Fanon 1963 pg. 140). The impact of the colonial Manichean duality through the psychoexistential complex on the psyche of the native is illustrated by the impelling desire of the native for white affirmation, where when faced with a simple change in the manner the colonial massa treats with the native she/he becomes overwhelmed with perceptions of acceptance, embrace, the granting of humanity, access to compartments previously denied therefore finally affirmation of the humanity of the native. The native complies, surrenders and rewards the colonial massa with her/his acquiescence, surrender and ambivalence toward the anti-colonial movement. The gift of independence and the neo-colonial project ensures this craving for white affirmation continues and evolves enabling North Atlantic domination through the craving for whiteness.

War of Liberation

Fanon now deals with the lessons learned by those involved in a war against colonial domination, lessons which testify to the specific and unique nature of the power relations of the colonial social order and are not forthcoming to those who are acquiescent. Fanon states: "The peasant's pride, his hesitation to go down into the towns and mingle with the world that the foreigner had built, his perpetual shrinking back at the approach of the colonial administration: all these reactions signified that to the dual world of the settler he opposed his own duality." (Fanon 1963 pg. 139). To reject the colonial world and its hierarchical Manichean order, to purposively evade interaction with and integration into this colonial Manichean order is for the native to reject his duality imposed on him by the colonial Manichean order. To challenge your duality in this manner is not sustainable for liberation from the grasp of the Manichean duality requires the smashing of the duality and its dual power relationships with the violent seizure of power from the colonial dominator. Fanon then deals with the realisation of the nature of the native when faced with the assault of the colonial massa and its impact on the liberation movement as follows: "The discovery of this instability in the native is a frightening experience for the leaders of the rebellion." (Fanon 1963 pg. 140). Those waging war on the colonial duality receive a rude awakening that there are members of the native population who pose a noted threat to the success of the rebellion, the war of liberation. This threat is the product of the failure to engage with the duality of colonial domination and its impact on the psyche of the native. There must then be a strategic response to this reality which Fanon presents as follows: "Colonialism has greater and wealthier resources than the native." "for the truth is that the settlement was begun on the very first day of the war, and it will be ended not because there are no more enemies left to kill, but quite simply because the enemy for various reasons, will come to realise that his interest lies in ending the struggle and in recognising the sovereignty of the colonised people." (Fanon 1963 pg. 141). The colonial State is engaged in a war where the resources at its command when properly strategized ensures that the colonial State defines and sets the agenda of this engagement. The colonial elite will end the engagement when it is strategic for them to do so, for prolonged war is not in the interests of the colonial elite and North Atlantic domination of the Third World. It is then strategically necessary for the North Atlantic to maintain its domination of the colonial world sustainably and to achieve this it is necessary to end colonial domination thereby erecting a new social order in the former colonies which engenders North Atlantic domination. This domination must be expressed on the local and international levels which requires the replication of colonial power relations into a new operational context where locally and internationally the persons dominated are free and sovereign, this then is the neo-colonial order. Fanon now deals with the impact of colonial domination on the mind of the native and the threat it poses as follows: "The native must realise that colonialism never gives anything away for nothing." "The colonised peoples, the peoples who have been robbed, must lose the habits of mind which have characterised them up to now." (Fanon 1963 pgs. 142-143). These colonial habits of mind which constitute the worldview of the colonised is the thin edge of the wedge that enables the success of the neo-colonial project for it not only seduces natives to reject rebellion and a war of liberation or at least to be ambivalent, it also impacts the actions of those involved in rebellion and a war of liberation towards compromising principles which redound in the favour of the colonial and neo-colonial dominator. The liberationary instrument of power to break the back of the colonial instrument of power must be formulated and applied for failure to do so prohibits liberation and propagates neo-colonial domination, the effects of which we have viewed from the 1940s to the 21st century. Fanon continues: "The people will thus come to understand that national independence sheds light upon many facts which are sometimes divergent and antagonistic. Such a taking of stock of the situation at this precise moment of the struggle is decisive, for it allows the people to pass from total, indiscriminating nationalism to social and economic awareness." (Fanon 1963 pg. 144). The nationalist politicians do everything in their power to ensure that the masses do not attain the condition of social and economic awareness as this condition constitutes discerning masses who are very difficult to lead by the nose through promised paths that are inimical to the interests of the masses. These politicians want to banish the masses to a condition of analytical blindness where they sacrifice their own interests on the altar of neo-colonial expediency by immersing themselves in a permanent state of indiscriminating nationalism. Politicians wary of the masses slipping away from the hold of indiscriminate nationalism then are not averse to unleashing the discourse of grave internal and even external threats to the nation where tribal/ethnic differences are redefined as race and prosecuted as race wars. The nationalist politicians formulate and unleash a discourse of fervent nationalism centred on the anti-colonial fight led by the nationalist politicians where great sacrifices were made to realise the free sovereign nation confirmed by a pantheon of national heroes who all embody the values of indiscriminating nationalism. This discourse has the enemy within defined from the outset as a vital and necessary tool of political mobilisation to be animated when the politics of the day demands. This discourse of ultra-nationalism strenuously seeks to mask all the contradictory realities of the anti-colonial period, especially the dance with the colonial massa made by the political strongman and his minions who led the masses out of colonial domination to freedom. Most strategic is the use of a mythic, uncritical, revisionist discourse of history and the cult of the maximum political leader to strenuously mask the realities of the neo-colonial condition. The elites of this postcolonial order then police the terrain of hegemonic discourse with a paranoid fervour, especially seen in the universities of the postcolonial nation, ever cognisant of the need to banish alternative discourses to the periphery if not to silence them. From its first hour of existence the independent nation in its neo-colonial configuration was imbued with the operational mechanism of an acutely fascist order of power which the North Atlantic dreams of and desires to be made the order of things. Fanon continues as follows: "The people who at the beginning of the struggle had adopted the primitive Manicheism of the settler-Blacks and Whites, Arabs and Christians-realise as they go along that it sometimes happens that you get Blacks who are whiter than the Whites and that the fact of having a national flag and the hope of an independent nation does not always tempt certain strata of the population to give up their interests or privilege." (Fanon 1963 pg. 144). This penetration of the mental fog of the Manichean duality where the masses then understand that there are fellow natives who are whiter than white thereby posing a grave threat to the freedom of the nation. At this point the masses are liberated from the colonial worldview where they can now discern enemies by their action not by their skin colour. This then enables the discerning of the threats posed by the elite who will seek their interests to the detriment of the masses, including and especially the politicians. The masses then can discern power relations and understand actions taken and actions expected to be taken as a result of this ability, which throws the discourse of ultra-nationalism into a crisis of hegemony which unleashes the colonial massa response which in a free, sovereign democratic state is the fascist response. The politicians, the elites and their North Atlantic overlords at all costs must ensure the sustainable hegemony of the Manichean duality to pre-empt the appearance, growth and development of race, social and economic awareness in the postcolonial State. To accomplish this task, the politicians, the elites and all those buying into the discourse of total, indiscriminating nationalism must embrace, wallow in, internalise and act upon the Manichean duality and its psychoexistential complex. The neo-colonial condition is then premised on and is an aggregation of Stevens, Chicken Georges, Gunga Dins and Hop Sings to form a social order proving that massa day never done yet! Fanon continues his analysis of realities that present themselves in an anti-colonial war of liberation as follows: "The militant who faces the colonialist war machine with the bare minimum of arms realises that while he is breaking down colonial oppression he is building up automatically yet another system of exploitation." "The people find out that the iniquitous fact of exploitation can wear a black face, or an Arab one, and they raise the cry of 'Treason.' But the cry is mistaken; and the mistake must be corrected. The treason is not national, it is social. The people must be taught to cry 'Stop thief!' In their weary road toward rational knowledge the people must also give up their too-simple conception of their overlords." (Fanon 1963 pg. 145). There is then no idyllic of violence, for whilst great sacrifices are being made on the ground to defeat the colonial war mechanism there are power relations driving to attain the strategic end of simply replacing the colonial oligarchy with a new native oligarchy thereby replicating the structure of the colonial social order under the neo-colonial order. Exploitation, domination, privilege and a hierarchical social order are not the invention and preserve of the white colonial massa under neo-colonial domination, but the intent and the creation of the non-white neo-colonial massa. This intent and worldview of those driving the power relation to replace the colonial massa and replicate the colonial social order is not then national treason but social treason for they are intent on replicating the colonial social order under a neo-colonial operational terrain. The issue then is the desire for sustainable hegemony over the postcolonial nation by a new oligarchy whose worldview only sees this being accomplished with the replication of the colonial order and the continued domination of the North Atlantic. What is noteworthy in this neo-colonial enterprise is the composition of the neo-colonial oligarchy where minority races maintained their position in the neo-colonial oligarchy, which was a continuation of the reality of the colonial oligarchy, whilst new minority groups rapidly rise to enter the oligarchy whilst the majority race group is underrepresented or absent from the neo-colonial oligarchy. This then is the most powerful indicator of the social treason which is premised on the looting of the wealth of the nation by the oligarchy and their political allies to the detriment of the interests of the majority race. In spite of the nationalist and ultra-nationalist discourse of the native politicians, in private spaces the racist colonial hierarchy of colonial domination is maintained and expanded where the majority race is either excluded or underrepresented in the ranks of the oligarchy and the representatives of North Atlantic transnational corporations dominate the oligarchy. The issue then is the need for systematic, organised education of those engaged in the war with the colonial massa and of the masses to dispel the flawed perceptions and the knowledge base formulated and exercised by the Manichean duality on the minds of the colonised. Overlords must be seen in terms of power, power relations and the strategies of power exercised rather than via the Manichean duality where you focus on the enemy as white and the ally, friend as non-white. This duality prepares us for the acceptance of the neo-colonial condition under the rule of neo-colonial non-white politicians. To accept the colour of the skin as enemy or friend enables the strategy to mask the power relations between the elites and the North Atlantic overlords and their common, mutually beneficial agenda. In this movement for decolonisation through a war of liberation there is the tendency to brutality which is the product of the colonial order. Fanon states: "There exists a brutality of thought and a mistrust of subtlety which are typical of revolutions; but there also exists another kind of brutality which is astonishingly like the first and which is typically anti-revolutionary, hazardous and anarchist. This unmixed and total brutality, if not immediately combated, invariably leads to the defeat of the movement within a few weeks." (Fanon 1963 pg. 147). In the colonial order a duality of brutality exists where there is a total, unmixed brutality exercised by the colonial massa which is challenged by the rise of revolutionary brutality in a death match as the totality of colonial brutality is anti-revolutionary, anarchist and poses grave threats hence its hazardous impact on the social order. This colonial brutality has the power to defeat a revolutionary movement as it is the product of colonial Manicheism and inevitably embraced by the colonial elites intent on creating and ensuring the sustainability of the neo-colonial project. Total, unmixed brutality is an instrument of colonial power and will be unleashed to defeat a war of liberation as expected, but much more importantly it is an instrument of power in the hands of the elite the colonial massa handed the colonial State to with the gift of independence. This instrument of power will be unhesitatingly unleashed to preserve the hegemony of the oligarchy and the politicians of the neo-colonial social order. In States founded upon a successful war of liberation, the brutality of the colonial order this revolutionary state emerged from is transformed into a revolutionary brutality, which continues to evolve along the genetic lines of colonial brutality, which is the result of revolutionary nation building utilising discourses from the North Atlantic such as historical materialism. There can be an entire collapse of the revolutionary process where there are contending factions for power where the colonial brutality is regenerated and unleashed, primarily because the contending factions for power are all the products of colonial domination whether secular or atheist revolutionary or pre-colonial traditional forces. For a revolution does not inoculate against infection from the colonial legacy, when you utilise a North Atlantic Enlightenment discourse that cannot address the specifics of colonial domination and formulate a strategy to dismantle this impact on the colonised: the best example of this being historical materialism. There is then revolution the colonial dominator is defeated but the definition and worldview of the revolution remains North Atlantic which enables the operationalisation of the colonial/neo-colonial continuum which inevitably leads to assaults on the revolution internally and externally deeply impacting the human condition within the revolution as it turns inwards on itself and its citizens for survival. In fact, no discourse of the North Atlantic Enlightenment can dismantle the impact of North Atlantic colonial domination on the colonised. You embrace North Atlantic discourse/knowledge you then embrace and propagate neo-colonial domination, the discourse of our inherent inferiority and white supremacy and total, unmixed brutality that is normalised.

Violence

Fanon now ends this second section of his work with his position that the only path by which we will evade the neo-colonial condition is the embrace of revolutionary violence. Fanon states: "Violence alone, violence committed by the people, violence organised and educated by its leaders, makes it possible for the masses to understand social truths and gives the key to them. Without that struggle, without that knowledge of the practice of action, there's nothing but a fancy dress parade and the blare of the trumpets. There's nothing save a minimum of re-adaptation, a few reforms at the top, a flag waving: and down there at the bottom an undivided mass, still living in the middle ages, endlessly marking time." (Fanon 1963 pg. 147). It is not violence per se, but the struggle against domination, the knowledge that develops and evolves with the power relations of war, especially the necessity of strategizing, the definition of action and the terrain of action which forms the knowledge of the necessity of a correct practice of action which is vitally necessary to liberation from the burden of colonial domination. We can lose the battle and win the war for in the process of losing the battle we release the process of liberation which with the inevitable gift of independence that follows we are in a different operational terrain where the neo-colonial project is not the only and absolute choice, for we now have a viable, palpable choice of liberation with a momentum necessary to exercise hegemony over the course of postcolonial history. Without this liberation only attained through a war of liberation, whether won or lost, then neo-colonial domination is the only course for there are no alternative paths presenting a choice to be made. The course of meaningless, soulless ritual, stagnation, business as usual and the immersion of the masses in a neo-colonial netherworld of black on black race hate and racist action, which is a continuation of the colonial netherworld. Change is then illusory where cosmetic change, change in response to new technology and evolving power relations are portrayed and mistaken for the promise of fundamental change that supposedly underpinned the independence project. Massa day ain't done yet!

Chapter Three
The Neo-Colonial Condition

National Consciousness and the Middle Class

In the third section of "Wretched of the Earth" Fanon is dealing with a specific instance of the embrace of the neo-colonial project by the nationalist politicians and the colonial elite and its impact on the neo-colonial social order. In this section Fanon is specifically dealing with the specific instance of the national consciousness that is the product of the neo-colonial project and its nature and impact on the neo-colonial social order. Fanon states: "National consciousness, instead of being the all-embracing crystallisation of the innermost hopes of the whole people, instead of being the immediate and most obvious result of the mobilisation of the people, will be in any case only an empty shell, a crude and fragile travesty of what it might have been." (Fanon 1963 pg. 148). National consciousness is the condition where the deepest hopes of all citizens of the newly independent nation are solidified into a national palpable entity of reference which can only be attained and accomplished with the mobilisation of the masses towards liberation from colonial subjugation. The embrace of the gift of independence by the elite, the masses and the nationalist politicians ensured that there was no mass mobilisation for liberation. This refusal to mobilise the masses for a war of liberation has now resulted in a national consciousness that is an empty shell, a cruel parody, a Frankenstein monster and a schizophrenic entity with the propensity for total brutality. Fanon continues: "The faults that we find in it are quite sufficient explanation of the facility with which, when dealing with young and independent nations, the nation is passed over for the race, and the tribe is preferred to the state. These are the cracks in the edifice which show the progress of retrogression, that is so harmful and prejudicial to national effort and national unity." (Fanon 1963 pgs. 148-149). The birth and evolution of the nation and national consciousness which spawn national unity and effort are effectively sabotaged by the strategy applied at independence where the nation is defined as a race and the state is captured by a tribe. What in fact happens is the nation being defined as the preserve of a race thereafter defined as the race, the absolute and inviolable right of the race and the tribe is adhered to and binds to a common worldview whilst the state is utilised as an instrument to exercise the power of the tribe, not as the sole expression of the nation. This then is a condition of retrogression where total, unmixed brutality even before independence or soon after the date of independence expresses the hegemony of race and tribe over nation and state. In a nation and a state showing this predilection to unlimited brutality the divisions wrought by colonial domination are embraced, redefined and unleashed as an instrument of power where black on black racism, race hate and the quest for racist hegemony is in fact a political instrument utilised to ensure the hegemony of the oligarchy, their political allies and the neo-colonial enterprise. With the unleashing of this unlimited brutality, the repressive agencies of the State constituted by the colonial overlord before their departure and within the warm embrace of the neo-colonial metropole following independence, become overdetermined in the politics of the nation. Hence the rise of the military to state power given the unleashing of unlimited brutality by the politicians of these independent nations. Fanon continues: "We shall see that such retrograde steps will all the weaknesses and serious dangers that they entail are the historical result of the incapacity of the national middle class to rationalise popular action, that it is to say their incapacity to see into the reasons for their action." (Fanon 1963 pg. 149). The national middle class was handed the legacy of the colonial state at the point of independence and it is this middle class, sometimes even before the handover, that commences the process of subverting national consciousness with tribal, ethnic and race solidarity and hegemony. This middle class can only view the world in terms of narrow, particularistic, racist aggregates as they are the product of, the inheritors and executors of the legacy of white colonial domination. This middle class is incapable of mass mobilisation, much less popular action, and a war of liberation is not seen in their worldview, in fact this discourse of Fanon being deconstructed will not resonate with their worldview for it is all gobbledygook to them. All this middle class is then capable of is replicating the colonial model, which means that it is incapable of being the facilitator of national consciousness, thereby condemning all of us who embraced the gift of independence to neo-colonial domination and total, unlimited brutality. This national middle class is incapable of an epiphany, of finally understanding their incapacity to understand what was required of them for they are the expressions of the Manichean duality, for the neo-colonial order constituting the insurmountable burden we bear in the Third World nation rendering us the Sisyphus of the world, the wretched of the earth. Fanon states: "This traditional weakness, which is almost congenital to national consciousness of underdeveloped countries, is not solely the result of the mutilation of the colonised people by the colonial regime. It is also the result of the intellectual laziness of the national middle class, of its spiritual penury, and of the profoundly cosmopolitan mould that its mind is set in. The national middle class which takes over power at the end of the colonial regime is an underdeveloped middle class." (Fanon 1963 pg. 149). The national middle class was never a bourgeois class as the domination of the colonial economy was in the hands of the white colonial oligarchy which included the agents of monopoly capital of the colonial metropole. This middle class was a political class or a faction of political operatives of the national middle class intent on serving colonial domination and inheriting the neo-colonial state's political apparatus with independence. This political faction targeted national politics in the pre-independence ferment to make themselves of strategic importance to the colonial metropole towards the realisation of the neo-colonial project, specifically by seizing control of the mass movement and defining it as an independence movement not as an insurgency and never a war of liberation. From the outset this political faction formed a working alliance with the metropolitan elites: political, economic and the deep state which jointly rolled out the agenda for the neo-colonial project hinged on the gift of independence. These political operatives of the colonial and neo-colonial overlords were and are driven by the desire for power and amassing personal wealth through their political careers. This political elite's desire for power encompasses, accepts and acts on subservience to the colonial overlord, the neo-colonial overlord and the national and international oligarchy. Being a functional bitch, this political faction accepts and acts on subservience whilst it preaches nationalism and when required politically according to their political perceptions race, tribe and ethnicity exclusiveness encapsulated in hegemonist discourse. This political faction is the repository of North

Atlantic fascist discourse in the Third World for this strain of North Atlantic discourse is what constitutes them, what they embrace and what frames and populates their worldview. The national middle class' political faction is then the most potent legacy of colonial domination, the gift that keeps on giving to all of us in the Third World. This faction of the national middle class is more than traditionally weak, lazy and underdeveloped for it is the product of metropolitan fascist discourse which immersed them during their education, their sojourn in the cosmopolitan colonial metropole, as the case of Pol Pot potently illustrates. This colonial/neo-colonial middle class is a lumpen middle class framed and constituted by metropolitan, fascist discourse to ensure white supremacy/non-white inferiority, underdevelopment, powerlessness and arrested development which is encapsulated by non-white genocide. The lumpen middle class is the double to the white dominator which means that the lumpen middle class can only destroy the non-white masses, the lumpen middle class is non-white genocide. The Manicheism of the colonial/neo-colonial world demands the operational existence of the lumpen middle class, therefore we bequeath unto ourselves and successive generations arrested development and genocide by embracing the agenda of this lumpen middle class and the gift of independence. What we needed in order to emancipate ourselves from colonial domination we refused to sacrifice and struggle for by settling for a gift of being the wretched of the earth. We then choose total brutality and denial to cope with the reality we chose and continue to choose. Fanon continues on this political faction of the national middle class: "It so happens that the unpreparedness of the educated classes, the lack of practical links between them and the mass of the people, their laziness, and, let it be said, their cowardice at the decisive moment of the struggle will give rise to tragic mishaps." (Fanon 1963 pg. 148). The formula is then filled to unleash tragic mishaps on all of us in the postcolonial nations of the Third World, the wretched of the earth as the educated classes can only unleash mishaps on us for they are constituted to serve the neo-colonial massa, not us, they are therefore well prepared even over-prepared to attain the neo-colonial end. For this accomplishment they must be divorced from the masses, lazy and cowards they are, as they are not here to serve us and our well-being for they are not allied with us they are joined to the neo-colonial massa systematically engaged with the strategy of dominating us, sustainably content with the crumbs falling from massa's mouth, whilst relishing the power that they exert over us and our daily lives, satisfied in their servitude as Steven to the neo-colonial overlord. A human who will settle for subservience in order to wield power over his kind and to steal from his kind to the point of national destitution can only be the product of colonial domination whose ancestral line was founded by the slavers of West Africa. The national middle class of the Third World is in the 21st century the living expression of the slavers constituted by Europe in its pursuit of the African slave trade. The neo-colonial project then reconstituted the slavers of West Africa and placed our independent states in their hands at that fateful moment when they said we were now independent, free and sovereign.

Fanon insists that the national middle class is incapable of constituting itself as a national bourgeoisie which means that the colonial oligarchy inherited from colonial domination is segregated from this middle class which the political faction serves. Fanon states: "Neither financiers nor industrial magnates are to be found within this national middle class. The national bourgeoisie of underdeveloped countries is not engaged in production, nor in invention, nor building, nor labour; it is completely canalised into activities of the intermediary type. Its innermost vocation seems to be to keep in the running and to be part of the racket." (Fanon 1963 pgs. 149-150). A class that is drawn to political action in the run up to independence in its quest for personal power and wealth, totally committed to being always an intermediary never proactive, never innovative, incapable of being a visionary. White supremacy's greatest creation to ensure sustainable North Atlantic domination to the 21st century. Fanon continues: "But unhappily we shall see that very often the national middle class does not follow this heroic, positive, fruitful, and just path; rather, it disappears with its soul at peace into the shocking ways-shocking because anti-national-of a traditional bourgeoisie, of a bourgeoisie which is stupidly, contemptibly, cynically bourgeois." (Fanon 1963 pg. 150). The national bourgeoisie of the postcolonial world has the worldview of the slaver where all their actions are to benefit themselves, for they are the intermediary of the local oligarchy and the North Atlantic overlord, they are therefore incapable of actions driven by nationalism and the need to make your nation which you control politically, great for they are not in control, they are not hegemonic over the postcolonial nation. Fanon uses the reference of the European shopkeeper in reference to them but in reality they cannot have the worldview of a European shopkeeper for they are the product of colonial domination, they are the reformulated model of the African slaver. Their role is to exercise control over the masses thereby facilitating the neo-colonial enterprise by any means necessary whilst enabling exploitation of the resources and markets of the postcolonial nation, they therefore are a dependent bourgeoisie, unlike the North Atlantic bourgeoisie, constituting them a lumpen bourgeoisie, the specific creation of colonial/neo-colonial North Atlantic domination. Fanon continues on the mission of the national middle class as follows: "The national middle class discovers its historic mission: that of intermediary. Seen through its eyes, its mission has nothing to do with transforming the nation; it consists, prosaically, of being the transmission line between the nation and a capitalism, rampant though camouflaged, which today puts on the mask of neo-colonialism." (Fanon 1963 pg. 152). The national middle class is the intermediary for monopoly capitalism operating in the postcolonial world via its strategy of domination and exploitation of independent states through neo-colonialism. This new class of slavers are vital to the success of the neo-colonial strategy as it is being operationalised, not under colonial power relations, but under an order premised on free, sovereign nations encapsulating free, sovereign citizens where domination and exploitation by the North Atlantic is sustainable and the underdevelopment of colonial domination is exacerbated by a much more organic and efficient order of domination and exploitation under neo-colonialism. Without the active complicity of the class of slavers this project would have failed miserably, which points to the inextricably organic connections of this slaver class to the North Atlantic deep state which repeatedly intervenes into these neo-colonial states to ensure the integrity and hegemony of the neo-colonial order. On the nature of this conjoining of the slaver class with the North Atlantic oligarchy Fanon states: "For a very long time the native devotes his energies to ending certain definite abuses: forced labour, corporal punishment, inequality of salaries, limitations of political rights, etc. This fight for democracy against the oppression of mankind will slowly leave the confusion of neo-liberal universalism to emerge, sometimes laboriously, as a claim of nationhood." (Fanon 1963 pg. 148). The struggle for decolonisation will create the space for not liberal universalism to emerge in the postcolonial order but for a neo-colonial, neo liberal universalism noted for its total, unlimited brutality to become hegemonic for this is the order of democracy of the slavers. This is then a new liberal democratic order rooted in liberal universal North Atlantic values where unlimited brutality is made manifest on a daily basis thereby constituting slaver fascism. The laboratory for the formulation and evolution of the North Atlantic discourse of neo-liberalism is the colonies of colonial domination and the neo-colonial order of being free yet enslaved of the former colonies.

Nationalisation and the Slaver Class

Fanon uses the fixation of the slaver class with nationalisation to illustrate the nature of governance practised by this new ruling class as follows: "from their point of view, nationalisation does not mean placing the whole economy at the service of the nation and deciding to satisfy the needs of the nation. For them, nationalisation does not mean governing the state with regard to the new social relations it has been decided to encourage. To them, nationalisation quite simply means the transfer into native hands of those unfair advantages which are a legacy of the colonial period." (Fanon 1963 pg. 152). There is but one strategy behind the slaver fixation with nationalisation which is to transfer the unfair advantage enjoyed by the colonial elite to the hands of the slavers, their minions, family, tribe, clan, ethnic group and race. This instrument is strictly for personal slaver gain, there is no concept of nation, national development, wealth creation to the benefit of the broad based citizenry and placing the destiny of the nation in the hands of the masses. To criticise the slavers for these shortcomings/failures is comparing mangoes to ganja for the slavers are not wired to see and act upon this discourse, they only act on and are motivated solely by self-interest, they thus see no merit in this criticism as it simply cannot resonate with their worldview. Fanon recognises this reality of an amoral even an asocial or sociopathic slaver class wielding political power when he states as follows: "The national bourgeoisie will be quite content with the role of the Western bourgeoisie's business agent, and it will play its part without any complexes in a most dignified manner. But this same lucrative role, this cheap-Jack's function, this meanness of outlook and this absence of all ambition symbolises the incapacity of the national middle class to fulfil its historic role of bourgeoisie." (Fanon 1963 pgs. 152-153). The slaver class has no historic role to be the bourgeoisie of the postcolonial world as the power relations of neo-colonial has furnished the role of intermediary, the hawker of cheap, inferior overpriced goods, the cheap-Jack for all that is substantive, valuable, desired and capable of generating wealth are in the hands of the metropolitan and local oligarchs. The slavers are constituted to be exactly what they are and love doing what they do, they can be nothing else and to criticise them for what they are is to impute that they have a historic potential to attain a historic destiny which is totally wrong for it is the product of flawed historic materialist reasoning. The slavers are exactly what they have been constituted to be: the deadliest plague unleashed by the white supremacist North Atlantic on the Third World to-date. Lumpen capitalism, lumpen bourgeois, lumpen proletariat, comprador working class – all constructs that mirror the influence of historical materialism, however stretched but still inadequate to the task of explaining the power relations of our colonial and postcolonial worlds. The key then is sustainable domination and the power relations that are spawned under this regime. Fanon continues his analysis of the national middle class as follows: "Because it is bereft of ideas, because it lives to itself and cuts itself off from the people, undermined by its Hereditary incapacity to think in terms of all the problems of the nation as seen from the point of view of the whole of that nation, the national middle class will have nothing better to do than to take on the role of manager for Western enterprises, and it will in practice set up its country as the brothel of Europe." (Fanon 1963 pg. 154). In these brothels of the North Atlantic everything and everyone is for sale to the most powerful bidders with the proceeds going to the political elite of the national middle class. In this neo-colonial enterprise citizenship is for sale via Citizenship by Investment Programmes (CIP), the vote of the neo-colonial state in multilateral institutions is for sale, diplomatic recognition is for sale, as is the case of the recognition of the Republic of Taiwan, and the new overlord being aggressively courted to exploit the brothel is China. In the 21st century the plunder of the resources and wealth of the neo-colonial world continues as there are always willing Johns paying to exploit the resources of the brothel, with no benefit to the inmates of the brothel.

National Middle Class, Race, Tribe and Ethnic Group

Fanon deals now with the tribal, ethnic and race tensions that escalate into ethnic cleansing and genocide in the neo-colonial context under the hegemony of the political elite of the national middle class. Fanon states: "It waves aloft the notion of the nationalisation and Africanisation of the ruling classes. The fact is that such action will become more and more tinged by racism," (Fanon 1963 pg. 155). "From nationalism we have passed to ultra-nationalism, to chauvinism, and finally to racism." (Fanon 1963 pg. 156). "we observe a falling back toward old tribal attitudes, and, furious and sick at heart, we perceive that race feeling, in its most exacerbated form is triumphing." (Fanon 1963 pg. 158). The national middle class in pursuing its quest for hegemony launches the movement to purge those identified as being undesirables holding posts they desire. This purge is replicated throughout the social order driven by the resurgence of colonial antagonism and hatred between tribal and ethnic groups, but it now evolves to black on black racism in search of the Final Solution as the national middle class now exercises political power without the need nor the means to arrest the slide to civil war prosecuted via the instrument of genocide. For under neo-colonial domination the national middle class views genocide as a viable political instrument of power fully supported by their North Atlantic overlords. This reality is most potently illustrated by the case of Nigeria, its oil reserves and the war of seccession of the state of Biafra from Nigeria and the use of genocide as a political and military weapon against Biafra and the majority Igbo ethnic group of the state of Biafra. In 1963 the Republic of Nigeria was proclaimed free and sovereign from British colonisation and by 1967 the war broke out and ended in 1970. The salient issue for the North Atlantic was the control of the vast oil resources of the Niger Delta which were under the hegemony of North Atlantic transnational energy companies, particularly

Shell and BP. Biafra annexed territory of the Niger Delta which now split the Delta into portions controlled by two states and since France backed Biafra the threat of Total of France entering the Delta now rang alarm bells. For this temerity of the national middle class of Biafra, the masses of Biafra were the recipients of an assault intent on the Final Solution, the eradication of the Igbo ethnic minority. To-date no one has been able to put together again the colonial creation of Nigeria. The national middle class in the spaces of the neo-colonial order with the input and complicity of the North Atlantic overlords has formulated, germinated, unleashed and it continues to evolve black on black racism of the neo-colonial variety. This is the most potent gift of the national middle class to the humans of the Third World. Fanon states: "The nationalist bourgeoisie of each of these two great regions, which has totally assimilated colonialist thought in its most corrupt form, takes over from the Europeans and establishes in the continent a racial philosophy which is extremely harmful for the future of Africa. By its laziness and its will to imitation, it promotes the ingrafting and stiffening of racism which was characteristic of the colonial era." (Fanon 1963 pgs. 161-162). Fanon is referring to the arbitrary, racist designation of North Africa and Africa South of the Sahara or South Africa, where in both regions the national middle class immersed in whiteness creates and unleashes this black on black racism where non-whites, fellow Africans are the prime potent enemies of the national middle class and by extension the nation. Being constituted by white supremacist discourse the national middle class is besieged and driven by the will to imitation of massa, but all that they can and choose to imitate is the depravity and barbarity of North Atlantic discourse. There is no will to innovation, only imitation, which results in intellectual paralysis where all solutions to local problems must be imported from the North Atlantic and all true, worthy and relevant expertise must and can only come from North Atlantic white people. The national middle class is then incapable of producing organic intellectuals from within its ranks and can only stymie such attempts by the masses. This is the living expression of dependence, servility and the embrace of inferiority at the level of the idea, which is the necessary and most potent enabler of North Atlantic white supremacist domination. Under the neo-colonial order this national middle class is now wielding political power which enables the depravity to germinate, grow, fester and continuously evolve. For the limitations placed on the colonial overlord simply do not apply to a free, sovereign state, hence the choice of the neo-colonial project as the vitally necessary successor to colonial domination. In a free, sovereign state comprising free, sovereign citizens the national middle class turns the nation into the premier laboratory of fascism in the modern/postmodern world and in so doing moulds the Third World into the image and likeness of North Atlantic white supremacist discourse. Fanon continues on the racism of the national middle class as follows: "As we see it, the bankruptcy of the bourgeoisie is not apparent in the economic field only. They have come to power in the name of a narrow nationalism and representing a race;" "Western bourgeois racial prejudice as regards the nigger and the Arab is a racism of contempt; it is a racism which minimises what it hates." "The racial prejudice of the young national bourgeoisie is a racism of defence, based on fear. Essentially it is no different from vulgar tribalism, or the difference between septs and confraternities." (Fanon 1963 pgs. 163-164). The black on black racism of the national middle class is one where the antagonisms, fears and hatred engendered and magnified by colonial domination are now magnified and redefined under the neo-colonial order into an instrument of power, separate and apart from white supremacy, but deeply impacted by and influenced by the discourse of white supremacy. The race that the national middle class/national bourgeoisie represents is then the white race in spite of its nationalist rhetoric, whilst it engages in the vulgar tribalism of black on black racism in response to the threats perceived being posed by black enemies to their position of power in the neo-colonial social order. Neo-colonial black on black racism is the product of the will to imitation, hence its propensity for total, unlimited brutality and its fixation with genocide, never forget Rwanda!

Fanon continues his analysis of the national middle class/national bourgeoisie and its role in the neo-colonial enterprise as follows: "In fact, the bourgeoisie phase in the history of underdeveloped countries is a completely useless phase. When this caste has vanished devoured by its own contradictions, it will be seen that nothing new has happened since independence was proclaimed, and that everything must be started again from scratch. The changeover will not take place at the level of the structures set up by the bourgeoisie during its reign, since that caste has done nothing more than take over unchanged the legacy of the economy, the thought, and the institutions left by the colonialists." (Fanon 1963 pg. 176). The hegemony of the bourgeoisie over the politics of the newly independent former colonies has benefited the bourgeoisie, their allies as the local oligarchy and most of all enabled the neo-colonial enterprise. But this hegemony is built on the foundation of colonial domination, which has ensured that organic change is absent and in fact impossible in this neo-colonial State that remains dominated by and dependent on the North Atlantic. But this condition does not ensure the collapse of the neo-colonial enterprise, even though it can generate violent political and social instability which works to the detriment of the hegemony of the bourgeoisie. The neo-colonial world has shown repeatedly from the 1940s to the 21st century the unique ability to maintain the neo-colonial enterprise in the midst of sustainable political and social upheaval with the Democratic Republic of Congo being a most potent example of this reality today. In fact, in the midst of the political and social upheaval the exploitation of the strategic resources of these nations intensify to the level of banditry and brigandage as the case of coltan and its strategic importance to digital devices. The neo-colonial enterprise is only concerned with exploitation via sustainable hegemony and a political, geo-political and social order is necessary to effect this. The issue of change, decolonisation, liberation and development is of no concern to and is not part of the strategic order of the neo-colonial project and it can never be, for they are constructs of a discourse of lies ever seeking to seduce the masses to accept subservience and servility. The bourgeoisie and its allies can, because of their embrace of the neo-colonial project, never be agents of change, decolonisation, liberation and development and the crumbs they collect from the mouths of the North Atlantic oligarchy are the rewards they expected from their participation in the neo-colonial enterprise. The neo-colonial enterprise will shred the hegemony of the bourgeoisie when required in order to replace an ineffective elite whose incompetence is posing problems to the hegemony of the neo-colonial enterprise. This is done by mobilising whatever assets of the North Atlantic deep state are available on the event horizon such as the armed forces, tribal, ethnic and race based insurgencies and organised crime groups posing as insurgencies regardless of the destruction levied on the political and social orders. Human life in the neo-colonial enterprise is summed up in terms of a cost benefit analysis to determine what is the best course of action for the North Atlantic, where we of the Third World are the collateral damage. The North Atlantic oligarchy, the political elite and the deep state will do all that is necessary to ensure its hegemony over the neo-colonial world to the point of destroying it, as plainly illustrated by the case of Yemen today. Fanon continues as follows: "This native bourgeoisie, which has adopted unreservedly and with enthusiasm the ways of thinking characteristic of the mother country, which has become wonderfully detached from its own thought and has based its consciousness upon foundations which are typically foreign, will realise, with its mouth-watering, that it lacks something essential to a bourgeoisie: money." (Fanon 1963 pg. 178). The bourgeoisie is desirous of hegemonic political power to ensure its strategic importance and centrality to the neo-colonial enterprise for this political hegemony is necessary to address the salient issue: its relative poverty compared to the local colonial oligarchy. To the victor belongs the spoils and the bourgeoisie embraces the North Atlantic neo-colonial elite from the outset to ensure its political dominance and its unrestricted access to the state coffers vitally necessary to accumulating their personal wealth. This local elite will never desert the neo-colonial enterprise and its North Atlantic overlords as they are servile and subservient to massa and the reward of wealth stolen and amassed overseas in the North Atlantic justifies their subservience and servility. This satisfaction gained through servility is bolstered by the impunity granted by servile action to the North Atlantic, which stimulates soaring flights of self-importance as Icarus, as emperors and dictators for life which litter the Third World landscape. Fanon now deals with the structure of patronage that develops through the expansion of the reach of the State in the economy as a result of political action as follows: "Every time such a procedure has been adopted it has been seen that the government has in fact contributed to the triumph of a dictatorship of civil servants who had been set in the mould of the former mother country, and who quickly showed themselves incapable of thinking in terms of the nation as a whole. These civil servants very soon began to sabotage the national economy and to throw its structure out of joint; under them, corruption, prevarication, the diversion of stocks, and the black market came to stay." (Fanon 1963 pg. 180). The colonial civil service was a servile cog in the wheel of colonial domination taking pride in their service to massa. They then became ardent followers of the maximum leader of the nationalist movement and his brand of decolonisation. They bought into the gift of independence with passion longing for the day of independence where they will now replace the colonial foreigners and become massa in their own right. To achieve this end of becoming the new massa the civil service was now re-politicised in the image and likeness of the dominant maximum leader who now formed the new government of the independent nation. The civil service and the political elite then danced together in a very tight embrace where the effective power and impunity of the civil service grew and multiplied paralleling that of the political elite, the local oligarchy and the local operatives of North Atlantic monopoly capitalism. The civil service established its utility to North Atlantic domination during the period leading up to the gift of independence and proved its worth during independence as the fifth columnist within the neo-colonial State. The civil service proved its worth by being the expertise on the ground in government in support of the North Atlantic strategy and its willingness to serve the interests of the North Atlantic especially its deep state agencies. By its operational relationships with the elites of neo-colonial domination the civil service evolves into a body that is now massa in its own right, actively seeking its hegemony by which to amass personal wealth thereby facilitating the hollowness of the neo-colonial State, its plunder and servility and subservience to an elite with multiple factions in contention for power and dominance. This then constitutes the final constituent element of the great procession of corruption of the neo-colonial State rooted in an operational terrain characterised by the exercise of extreme brutality and its fragility, hence the 20th century concept of the failed state.

Maximum Leader, Political Party and the Army

Fanon now presents his analysis of the political instruments under the control of the political elite of the independent nations and the legacy bequeathed to the citizens of these newly independent former colonies. Fanon addresses the instrument of the single political party or the one party state as follows: "The single party is the modern form of the dictatorship of the bourgeoisie, unmasked, unpainted, unscrupulous, and cynical." "It is true that such a dictatorship does not go very far. It cannot halt the processes of its own contradiction." "moreover, it is preoccupied with filling its pockets as rapidly as possible but also as prosaically as possible." (Fanon 1963 pg. 165). The political faction of the national middle class formulates the instrument of the single political party legally sanctioned, with all others being illegal, to constitute the one party state where this single party becomes one with the state thereby instituting the dictatorship of a maximum leader, the followers and the oligarchs they serve. This single party becomes identified with a tribe, an ethnic group dominated by specific elite interests which writes on the terrain of the nation the dictatorship of this elite, summed up in the figure of the maximum leader who is the head of government. This is the political instrument devised to control the masses, to dominate the politics of the nation, to politicise and dominate the state especially the repressive agencies of the state as the armed forces, the public service and the quasi-state sector as the nationalised entities, to marginalise the perceived enemies of the political elite and most importantly to facilitate the looting of the state and its agencies. This is then an instrument devised to exert sustainable hegemony over the politics of the nation and the state necessary to creating sustainable hegemony for the political elite, the maximum leader and the neo-colonial enterprise. This strategy has the full support of the neo-colonial overlords and the agencies of their deep state, which creates an abiding power relation of neo-colonial domination which impacts local power relations and at times relegates local power relations to a secondary role. This power relation is the basis of the geopolitical strategies that are unleashed on the neo-colonial nation which is the basis of neo-colonial North Atlantic imperialism. Given the driving need for the neo-colonial elite to ensure the security and sustainability of neo-colonial hegemony, the North Atlantic neo-colonial overlord from the day of independence commences the process of the application of dominance to ensure compliance. The political elite of the national bourgeoisie is then trapped by its inability to resolve the contradictions of its subordinate position in its favour, thereby opening the way for the application of extremism as genocide and blatant corruption so vulgar in its methodology it lacks all sophistication, invisibility and masking. The key to this strategy of hegemony is the maximum leader at the head of the single party and the government which the national bourgeoisie needs in order to attain this strategic end. On this reality Fanon states: "it will discover the need for a popular leader to whom will fall the dual role of stabilising the regime and of perpetuating the domination of the bourgeoisie. The bourgeois dictatorship of underdeveloped countries draws its strength from the existence of a leader." "In the underdeveloped countries on the contrary the leader stands for moral power, in whose shelter the thin and poverty-stricken bourgeoisie of the young nation decides to get rich." (Fanon 1963 pgs. 165-166). The maximum leader is the strategic necessity of the neo-colonial agenda that enmeshes and defines the actions of the national middle/bourgeois class. Both the North Atlantic neo-colonial elites and the local bourgeoisie invest in the creation of the maximum leader and when the one in use is of no further use or presents a threat to the neo-colonial order, there is removal and the insertion of a replacement, even courting a military maximum leader inserted via a coup d'état. The state and the constitution must serve the neo-colonial project even at their expense. The North Atlantic deep state is deeply involved in the neo-colonial project from its inception to the 21st century as it polices the neo-colonial terrain to ensure compliance and the unhindered extraction of wealth. The maximum leader has to ensure the compliance of the masses and the sustainability of political domination of the national middle class vitally necessary to the plunder, where the national middle class feeds off the crumbs falling from the mouth of the North Atlantic actors engaged in the plunder of the resources and markets of the independent former colony. In the neo-colonial enterprise the national middle class in its quest to enrich itself can only plunder the state. Fanon continues on the maximum leader as follows: "He acts as a braking power on the awakening consciousness of the people. He comes to the aid of the bourgeois caste and hides his manoeuvers from the people, thus becoming the most eager worker in the task of mystifying and bewildering the masses." (Fanon 1963 pg. 168). The maximum leader is the premier trump card played by the North Atlantic imperialists and the local national middle class for they both have the dire need to pacify and render the masses servile and compliant but cannot accomplish this task from the power relations that enmesh them. From the period of the run-up to the gift of independence the North Atlantic imperialists and their deep state were deeply committed to finding and grooming a maximum leader to cultivate, to enable and to support towards his singular domination of the nationalist movement. This maximum leader then begat the political elite of the national bourgeoisie as they rode his coattails to state power with independence. This maximum leader's utility and credibility to the North Atlantic imperialists and the national bourgeoisie was premised on the servility and culpability of the masses with the neo-colonial enterprise dominated by the North Atlantic imperialists and the national bourgeoisie. A contradiction of expectation and reality, as the masses are not designated beneficiaries of the neo-colonial enterprise as the national bourgeoisie and the local oligarchy it serves simply does not share what falls from the mouth of the North Atlantic imperialists. Fanon states: "The leader is all the more necessary in that there is no party." (Fanon 1963 pg. 169). "The living party, ...has been transformed into a trade union of individual interests." (Fanon 1963 pg. 170). "The party is becoming the means of private advancement." (Fanon 1963 pg. 171). The nationalist party formed around the persona of the maximum leader must collapse with the capture of state power with independence for the agenda of the North Atlantic imperialists, their deep state, the national middle class and the maximum leader will now be rolled out which stymies the organic growth and development of the party. The party was an artifice formulated to mobilise the masses towards the gift of independence and winning the initial general election, thereafter with state power in hand the maximum leader can determine that general elections are no longer necessary and the party is no longer vitally necessary to his power base as he appeals personally to the masses, whilst the party can harbour those desirous of removing him from power. With state power and the state trough to feed from, the national bourgeoisie no longer needs to invest in the party leaving the party to those seeking access to the state trough through ruling party activism. The outcome of these developments is the hardening of the social hierarchy inherited from colonial domination where the national bourgeoisie evolves rapidly into a caste, the colonial oligarchy grows in size but not in depth as it continues to be dominated by minority race groups and the peasants swell the ranks of the marginalised, especially in urban areas, forming an underclass that dwarfs that inherited from colonial domination. Fanon describes the outcome of independence as follows: "The peasant who goes on scratching out a living from the soil, and the unemployed man who never finds employment do not manage, in spite of public holidays and flags, new and brightly coloured though they be, to convince themselves that anything has really changed in their lives." (Fanon 1963 pg. 169). There is no qualitative change in the daily lives of the peasant and the unemployed in spite of freedom from colonial domination but there is qualitative change in the daily lives of the maximum leader, the national bourgeoisie and the oligarchy. For they now command and exercise state power and political power to their material benefit as they loot the state to maximise their personal wealth accumulation to the detriment of the losers of the neo-colonial enterprise: the masses. Fanon describes this personal wealth accumulation as follows: "By dint of yearly loans, concessions are snatched up by foreigners; scandals are numerous, ministers grow rich, their wives doll themselves up, the members of parliament feather their nests and there is not a soul down to a simple policeman or the customs officer who does not join in the great procession of corruption." (Fanon 1963 pg. 172). The state that gives the neo-colonial enterprise its operational acumen, harbours and enables the great procession of corruption, which testifies to the fact that the neo-colonial enterprise is premised on only looting the resources of the former colonies. The neo-colonial state and the great procession of corruption are then given for the neo-colonial enterprise and no matter what raft of anti-corruption legislation is placed on the statute books there will be and can be no fundamental change. For the neo-colonial enterprise demands the neo-colonial state and the great procession of corruption, therefore to end this great procession of corruption you must dismantle the neo-colonial enterprise. This operational reality masked by liberal universalism is but another expression of the Manicheism that drives the neo-colonial order where every single operational prerequisite of the neo-colonial order abrogates the liberal universalist values that underpin the Constitution and the State, constituting the great lie which we experience in our daily lives where independence does not constitute change for the better in our lives. This is a social order of extremism which is driven by the constant attempt to mask the lie whilst it cannot be masked. We are constantly bombarded with racist North Atlantic explanations for all our problems such as our endemic corruption, inequality and underdevelopment which are all crude, ineffective masks for the underlying reality that we are what we are because the operational condition of our social order is vitally necessary to the sustainable operation of the neo-colonial project as it loots our resources and exports our wealth to the North Atlantic leaving holes in the ground, a huge national debt and the wretched of the earth as their heirs to failed states. Fanon describes one aspect of this neo-colonial domination as follows: "In this way the former mother country practices indirect government, both by the bourgeoisie that it upholds and also by the national army led by its experts, an army that pins the people down, immobilising and terrorising them." (Fanon 1963 pg. 174). The North Atlantic neo-colonial overlords must ensure continuity of the neo-colonial enterprise by having a stream of servile rulers available and in the pursuit of this strategy the liberal universal values of the Constitution amount to nothing but platitudes for the fascist alternative is always the favoured response. Whenever the maximum leader proves ineffective in the face of mass unrest and challenges to the neo-colonial enterprise or he and his party are now off the North Atlantic reservation, then the prime trump card is played: the armed forces created by the colonial order, penetrated by the North Atlantic deep state and left as a legacy to the maximum leader who fails to break the link between the North Atlantic military complex and the deep state and pays for that. This indirect rule of the North Atlantic imperialists impacts the social order in such a telling manner as it moulds the terrain upon which power relations between the political elites, the national middle class, the local oligarchy and the State are operationalised on. Imperialist intervention at crucial instances frame the course of the social order much more tellingly than the power relations between the masses and the ruling elites. This establishes the order of brutal fascism over lengthy periods of time which determines the nature of politics and power relations, the hierarchical nature and the distribution of wealth seen in the social order and the nature of race, tribal and ethnic relations in the social order. Lengthy periods of fascism under the rule of military Juntas or dictators for life have then brutalised and afflicted the social orders of neo-colonial nations with acute arrested development and engrained within the power relations of the social order, especially political power relations, a fascist discourse of power and its social order. This fascist discourse is unleashed in the politics of these States to protect the oligarchs from the vast army of the seething masses who are viewed as grave threats to the fascist order, whilst embracing the neo-colonial order with great gusto.

National Party and Racist Hegemony

Fanon now deals with the national party and use of ethnicity to politically mobilise support and the consequent barbarity that flows from this strategy. Fanon states: "As far as national unity is concerned the party will also make many mistakes, as for example when the so-called national party behaves as a party based on ethnic differences. It becomes, in fact, the tribe which makes itself into a party. The party which of its own will proclaims that it is a national party, and which claims to speak in the name of the totality of the people, secretly, sometimes even openly, organises an authentic ethnic dictatorship. We no longer see the rise of a bourgeois dictatorship but a tribal dictatorship." (Fanon 1963 pg. 183). The instrument of the national party is an artifice to proclaim national unity under the leadership of the maximum leader towards decolonisation which comes to an end with the gift of independence. With independence the hatred and antagonism between native groups becomes redefined by a neo-colonial discourse of black on black racism driven by the impetus to dominate the State and wield hegemonic power over the enemy. This quest for racist hegemony by the ethnic and race groups of the social order is aided and abetted by the North Atlantic neo-colonial elite who views such internecine fighting as the weakening of the political elites and the State in their favour. The colonial massa in their run up to independence also showed a propensity to demand from and enable the colonial political elite on the brink of independence to commence the building of the ethnic hegemony desired in the neo-colonial era during the closing stage of the colonial era. Even before independence the political elite that the colonial massa handed power and the colonial State over to were already complicit with the North Atlantic neo-colonial elite. With independence day the icing on the cake was all that was missing to complete the neo-colonial wedding cake. In the run-up to independence the colonial massa utilised black on black racism to purge an undesirable political elite whose ability to win general elections was unassailable by fomenting a race war, military intervention, a change of the electoral system and the forming of a government of desirables with the undesirables condemned to opposition, with the local elites complicit in this deep state action granted the gift of independence soon after. Black on black racism is an artifice used in the run up to independence to impact the political process in the favour of North Atlantic neo-colonial hegemony and still used to this day to ensure North Atlantic neo-colonial hegemony. This artifice has been used, is used and will continue to be used without concern for the blowback, the pain, misery and suffering unleashed on the masses of these neo-colonial nations for we all of the no-colonial world allow it to be used.

Legitimacy and the Nature of Hegemony

In this neo-colonial scenario described by Fanon one lesson taught to the masses by the actions of the powered is the disconnect between the acquisition and accumulation of wealth and honest hard work. Liberal universalism and the Protestant Ethic have all been falsified in the cauldron of neo-colonial domination, as it was under colonial domination, exposing the sheer brutality of hegemonic power/force relations in the neo-colonial social order. Fanon states: "The people come to understand that wealth is not the fruit of labour but the result of organised protected robbery. Rich people are no longer respectable people; they are nothing more than flesh-eating animals, jackals, and vultures which wallow in the people's blood." (Fanon 1963 pg. 191). The hegemonic elites have no legitimacy for it is a social order held together by raw, naked force with a propensity for barbarity which potently illustrates that there is no hegemonic discourse in operation, as in the social order of the North Atlantic. There is a multiplicity of discourses in contention, constituting an extreme fluidity to hegemony which demands the use of violence and marginalisation in a bid to purchase compliance. Hence the continuous faith placed in techniques of marginalisation as tribe, ethnic group and race hierarchies characterised by extreme inequality. The result is a social order where corruption and crime become endemic throughout the social order where self, I, me is the prime, central concern of daily life and the attainment of my goals by any means necessary. In this neo-colonial order there is no rule of law, for law is the instrument of the powerful to stave off the continuous assaults of their enemies, which indicates the continuity between the colonial and neo-colonial social orders. Criminality is a given, even demanded by this social order, but it is also another excuse used by the powerful and justified by their camp followers to brand their enemies as being criminogenic, which justifies the application of the fascist solution of social cleansing under the guise of the rule of law which does not apply to the rich and powerful. Manicheism in an evolving neo-colonial social order is then under assault as a hegemonic discourse as the good fades into the bad and the bad emerges from the shadows to proclaim it is now the good. Neo-colonial universal relativism is now laying waste to Manichean absolutes and certainty thereby constituting schizoid personalities at the action level of human endeavour. In the neo-colonial world we have now surpassed colonial ambivalence having replaced it with neo-colonial nihilism, which is rampant at all levels of the social order where we even have neo-colonial narcissistic nihilism in action. This is a specific neo-colonial condition where in its specificity North Atlantic discourse is simply irrelevant.

The Nation and the National Bourgeoisie

In ending this section Fanon illustrates the threats posed by the failure to create a nation out of the colonial morass. Fanon continues to insist that the national bourgeoisie is not concerned with its vital task of survival of the nation nor is it capable of it. For Fanon this vital, strategic task will only be accomplished by inclusion of all of the marginalised in the social order bonded together by a single vision, backed up by action that brought deep seated change to the daily life of the masses. Fanon was then insisting that the structure of the neo-colonial order was incapable of accomplishing this strategic task and the masses will ultimately pay the price. Today in the 21st century the masses continue to pay the price and sadly we are yet to prove Fanon wrong. As long as Fanon writing in 1961 is right in his assessment we are paying the price, we are suffering! Fanon states: "But, we must repeat, it is absolutely necessary to oppose vigorously and definitively the birth of a national bourgeoisie and a privileged caste. To educate the masses politically is to make the totality of the nation a reality to each citizen. It is to make the history of the nation part of the personal experience of each of the citizens." (Fanon 1963 pg. 200). The national bourgeoisie has been long formed and has failed miserably, but neo-colonial domination remains sustainable in spite of this as every neo-colonial nation and economy remain locked into a power relation of domination and dependence with the North Atlantic where geopolitical power is applied to ensure compliance with the neo-colonial rules of the game. In the 21st century the power reality exceeds that of the national bourgeoisie and the local oligarchy, it consists also of North Atlantic geopolitical power applied to shore up the hegemony of those who manage the neo-colonial structure on a daily basis in the interest of the North Atlantic. The national bourgeoisie is incapable of inclusion and the political education of the masses poses a direct threat to their hegemony, which means that under neo-colonialism the nation required to address the legacy of colonial domination is still born, in fact it was never conceived as the national bourgeoisie is sterile, barren. Fanon describes the product of this sterility and the price to be paid as follows: "The living expression of the nation is the moving consciousness of the whole of the people; it is the coherent, enlightened action of men and women. The collective building up of a destiny is the assumption of responsibility on the historical scale. Otherwise there is anarchy, repression, and the resurgence of tribal parties and federalism. The national government, if it wants to be national, ought to govern by the people and for the people, for the outcasts and by the outcasts. No leader, however valuable he may be, can substitute for the popular will; and the national government, ought first to give back their dignity to all citizens, fill their minds and feast their eyes with human things, and create a prospect that is human because conscious and sovereign men dwell therein." (Fanon 1963 pgs. 204-205). The salient question is the willingness and more importantly the capacity of the maximum leader and the nationalist party to do what is necessary to address the colonial legacy at the individual level vitally necessary to creating a new social order. The incapacity of the political elite to be the needed and necessary agent of change towards liberation is the result of more than the need to dominate the masses rendering them servile and subservient. The core reality is that the political elite is part of a national class that has failed and refused to regenerate themselves by committing discursive and worldview suicide. The national middle class, the national bourgeoisie and the oligarchs are all rooted in the subservient worldview of those who embrace North Atlantic hegemony. The political elite fears the masses as a result of this worldview and can only marginalise the masses through barbarism because of their continued adherence to this worldview. This political elite can only unleash the barbarism of neo-colonial domination as they remain human actors who are unapologetically the foot-soldiers of massa. What they have the capacity to do, have done and continue to do is to unleash the politics of racist hegemony which trumps the nation, replacing it with a multiplicity of racist nationalisms that divide the social order ensuring the overdetermination of the politics of race and the hegemony of the discourse of racist hegemony over the social order. Racist hegemony enables a penetration of neo-colonial domination of the society that outstrips that of the order of universal liberalism, masking grinding hierarchies of inequality as it infects the individuals of the social order with a racist hegemonist worldview that enables the fascist order that facilitates neo-colonial domination. The national middle class does not have the capacity to produce sustainably organic intellectuals and those that are produced by the entire social order are easily persuaded to migrate in the face of violence. In the 21st century we are still then searching for the intervention to breach the colonial/neo-colonial legacy that enables us to be finally conscious and sovereign humans in a social order where we are not brutalised, marginalised and burdened with inequality, having a stake in the daily affairs of the nation which gives us the realisation that we are the nation with a common destiny and history. The common neo-colonial reality is premised on our continued state of being nonhuman, deprived and marginalised which is the living expression of the potential of the national middle class, the national bourgeoisie and the oligarchy for that is all they are capable of.

This third section is the final section of the book written by Fanon in 1961 before his death the two sections that follow were added to these three sections from works he wrote previously. In these three sections Fanon raised the salient issue of the required intervention necessary to destroying the legacy of colonial domination towards liberation and becoming human to the best of all our abilities. The historical record of neo-colonial North Atlantic domination presents the incontrovertible proof that the dominant, hegemonic discourse of the postcolonial State has not only failed to address the salient legacy of colonial domination, it has heightened it and enabled its evolutionary path to an existential condition that eclipses that of colonial domination. For not only are the objective conditions of daily existence worse, they have worsened and continue to worsen in spite of all of us of the postcolonial world being free and sovereign individuals. This is the dominant reality which poses the question of how do we now effect the revolutionary change necessary to address this abysmal reality of daily existence? This question conjures up the strategic imperative then in the 21st century of having to deal with a hegemonic North Atlantic intent on protecting its right to hegemony as it made abundantly clear in the 1940s to the end of the twentieth century. The power relation has not changed and the blowback of this power relation is human deprivation and arrested development. The pressing need for revolutionary change is then only unobvious to those who benefit from or believe that one day they will benefit from the neo-colonial order and both these groups in the North Atlantic and in the neo-colonies are peddlers of delusion and denial.

The question of the how in the 21st century raises the damning conclusion of inevitability and futility of resistance if one believes that a revolution abolishes power relations, thereby creating this mythic revolutionary idyllic. A revolution simply impacts hegemonic power, replacing it with an alternate hegemonic power, the nature of which is determined by the individual power relations of the social order. In that transition before power hardens to become hegemonic power individuals and groups have the power to impact power relations, to condition such power relations in their own interests. The neo-colonial world is what it is in the 21st century because: 1. The masses surrendered to a methodology of decolonisation that was not in their favour by refusing to exert pressure on colonial power relations to effect a power breach and thereby write their interests upon the power relations in search of hegemony. The masses failed to exert the power they possessed which they soon lost. 2. In neo-colonial societies where the masses exerted their power and the breach of power was attained they either wrote their interests on the power relations in search of hegemony or they chose to surrender this power to the maximum leaders of the revolution. In the first instance, the masses in the revolution must continue writing their interests on power relations as they evolve or they will become passive recipients of power dominated by elite groups. In the second instance, the condition of the masses is no different from those of the neo-colonial condition in spite of the revolutionary propaganda. It is incumbent on those who bear the brunt of the assault of neo-colonial domination to act and create the necessary breach of power, failure to do so, well it's suffering as usual across generations. One reality we are all assured of is the sustainability of suffering under neo-colonial domination. The destiny of the masses is in the hands of the masses at the most micro levels of power exercised, that is the pressing reality of change which demands that this failed Marxist-Leninist discourse of revolution be thrown in the sprawling garbage dumps of the postcolonial world, where so many of us eke out a living, for it has failed us miserably with its blood lust born out of the white man's Enlightenment.

What is left to be understood is the nature of power relations in the neo-colonial world in the 21st century, especially in the realm of politics; the hegemony of the North Atlantic and the blowback from that is commonly accepted. This hegemony is far-reaching and cohesive as the neo-colonial world is fully integrated into the terminal expressions of the hegemonic power of the North Atlantic, whereby the neo-colonial world will cease to function if the USA and/or the EU shuts them out of these terminal expressions of white power. They will soon enter a period of existence that draws no parallel with colonial domination or its precolonial history. The neo-colonial world is then an addict totally dependent of the North Atlantic. The neo-colonial world has earnestly embraced the neo-liberal discourse of the North Atlantic and has earnestly worked at formulating and unleashing a neo-colonial discourse of neoliberalism, which has replicated the North Atlantic impact of this discourse with grotesque effects in the neo-colonial world. The core discursive concept of North Atlantic neoliberalism, Homo Economicus, is in the neo-colonial world redefined and reformulated through the matrices of the discourse of racist settler colonial exploitation and domination. In areas of the neo-colonial world where the demography allows, the minority races and the agents of the globalised transnational companies who dominate the local oligarchy, embrace this discourse of settler colonial neoliberalism as they are the main beneficiaries of the windfalls thereby ensuring their political action to dominate neo-colonial politics by any means necessary, especially neo-colonial fascism. The political elites of the neo-colonial world have embraced neoliberalism with fervour, some with a fanaticism for obvious reasons, especially those of the racist settler colonial exploitation discourse who now see the hegemony of neoliberalism in the North Atlantic as their opportunity to capture the state and turn the state and the social order into the living embodiment of a racist, settler colonial rabid exploitation state and social order, where the plunder of the assets of the state will flow into the hands of the local and transnational oligarchy who will always be externally grateful to their political hitmen for hire. The fixation of all of the political elite, especially the left and the ultra-right of the North Atlantic, with neo-liberalism does not infect the political elite of the neo-colonial world, what it does is enable the open, public drive for the racist, settler colonial state by signing on for the programme as it deepens the exploitation of the neo-colonial world to the ultimate benefit of the oligarchs of the North Atlantic. The resident dupes of this scenario are those of the masses who buy into this grand Ponzi scheme, which they are excluded from, but insist they are given the racial bond they enjoy with the public leader of this political line. Racism is the mobilising force in its most potent simplicity generated by the Manicheism of the neo-colonial world. Fanon describes this reality as follows: "African unity takes off the mask, and crumbles into regionalism inside the hollow shell of nationality itself. The national bourgeoisie, since it is strung up to defend its immediate interests, and sees no further than the end of its nose, reveals itself incapable of simply bringing national unity into being, or of building up the nation on a stable and productive basis." (Fanon 1963 pg. 159). The oligarchy in its quest for sustainable hegemony premised on the prosecution of self-interest as paramount, not that of the nation, dances with all political lines that ensure their hegemony – the left, the right and the center, as the issue is operational accords to ensure hegemony. This is then a rapacious oligarchy in the colonial mould who refashion themselves into world citizens who transition between the North Atlantic and the neo-colonial world simply as a survival strategy, which illustrates the circularity of the nature of North Atlantic exploitation of the colonial then the neo-colonial world. As world citizens are simply the present version of the colonial absentee planters/landowners/merchants of the white colonial empire who were intent on plunder for personal wealth accumulation. To have an oligarchy exhibit said behaviour in the 20th and 21st centuries potently explains why we remain the wretched of the earth!

The most potent impact of this servility of the elites of the neo-colonial world is the impact North Atlantic political discourse is having on political discourse in the neo-colonial world. All politicians in the neo-colonial world act upon their servility to the North Atlantic and the political discourse they now frame to effect political mobilisation is borrowed from the North Atlantic. Whether they be of the social democratic persuasion, the conservative pro aggressive capitalism persuasion or the openly racist conservative pro aggressive capitalist persuasion, they are all neoliberal, servile to the North Atlantic and their discourse sourced from the North Atlantic. And what they promise to the electorate does not coincide with the possible under their servile power relations with the North Atlantic, therefore upon accession to power they must now insist that the possible is limited because of the resistance posed by internal enemies. The rise of the openly racist conservative pro aggressive capitalist political line has dramatically changed the political discourse of the present neo-colonial world. The enemies of this openly racist political line are identified in the campaign, as with all other political lines, to ensure that the excuse has traction with accession to power but the nature of the enemies identified betrays the hidden agenda: a raw fascist/Nazi agenda, hence the identification of specific enemies within the social order namely minority races, the criminals and queers from minority races, political corruption spawned by the leftist agenda and economic collapse spawned by leftist corruption and the leftist socio-economic agenda. The intention is then to further weaken an already emaciated state to fully operationalise the plunder of its assets by the local oligarchy and the globalised transnational corporations. To cease all state policy interventions aimed at addressing the grave hierarchy of inequality that pervades the social order thereby compounding the inequality of the social order as the looting of the assets of the state escalates. To respond to the escalation in crime which is perceived as an insurgency of the poor by militarising the war on crime, where fascism drives social control and policing is placed in the hands of militias as state expenditure is cut in keeping with the discourse of austere, fascist, oligarchic, dependent capitalism. In this scenario crime is not an insurgency of the poor but the product of the growing hegemony exerted by transnational organised crime over the social order which this political line does not deal with as it is simply not an enemy, just another oligarchic enterprise. Social cleansing explodes whilst the hegemony of transnational organised crime expands and heightens. This fascist political line visualises only short term goals for the financial benefit of a rapacious oligarchy which transitions from the Third World to the North Atlantic and back, for as the state is plundered and the social order is militarised, anarchy becomes pervasive and at the tipping point the oligarchs will simply leave for the North Atlantic leaving their proxies in charge of their plantations. Been there done that!

This strategy, its use and its effectiveness reflects the reality that the neo-colonial social order in the 21st century is driven by the politics of racist hegemony where specific groups who identify themselves as separate, distinct races dominate the social order constituting the oligarchy bolstered by a hierarchy of inequality, that demands paranoia of the oligarchs expressed in the politics of racist hegemony. Where, as in the North Atlantic economic collapse, criminal insurgency and all forms of insecurity are the product of the assault of inferior races on the entitlement of the superior race. Tribe, ethnicity, race and class differences have now been reformulated for the political context of neo-colonial domination via a veneer of a threat matrix defined by Manicheism where difference in Manichean terms is weaponised in the politics of racist hegemony of the neo-colonial world. The Final

Solution of the North Atlantic has now been embraced, redefined and weaponised in a manner that is even more dangerous than North Atlantic fascism and National Socialism for this is servile, subservient racist hegemony free from the quest to conquer the world, for the aim is social control through social cleansing where the fit, able and the superior race has the right to plunder the State in its own interest. This has nothing to do with ending corruption and draining the swamp, this political movement is primarily concerned with privilege and impunity, let the plunder begin.

In the 21st century it is now publicly apparent that the inherent nature of neo-colonial domination is now in the political sphere mounting a concerted challenge to the discourse of universal liberalism and its masking of the true nature of neo-colonial domination. The new political strategy calls for the public embrace of the barbarity of neo-colonial domination, by insisting that this condition is normal and desirable and must be heightened as the prime political issue is the threats posed by the inferior races to those so chosen to rule. War is then normal to this social order and necessary to purge the human dross but servility and subservience to the North Atlantic is normal, acceptable and embraced by the political elites and the oligarchs. Racist hegemony and war is the essence of social control espoused by an oligarchy and a political elite in the 21st century trapped in a colonial slave idyllic which betrays their fitness for subservience, not even for postmodernity and progress of the North Atlantic variety. In the neo-colonial world mainstream politics have now embraced the colonial slave plantation idyllic of the politics of race based impunity, hence the need to experience Fanon's texts in the 21st century.

Chapter Four
War of Liberation, National Culture and National Consciousness

Power Relations, Legitimacy

In section four of the text the address Fanon gave to the second Congress of Black Writers and Artists, Rome, Italy, 1959 is presented where Fanon dealt with the strategic imperative of building a national culture in the decolonisation project. The methodology of building this national culture is then a major issue that Fanon engages with in this address. Fanon states: "We must rid ourselves of the habit, now that we are in the thick of the fight, of minimising the actions of our fathers or of feigning incomprehension when considering their silence and passivity." "we must realise that the reason for this silence lies less in their lack of heroism than in the fundamentally different international situation of our time." (Fanon 1963 pgs. 206-207). The international power relations impact the local power relations of the colonial and neo-colonial order, which constitutes the reality that any attempt at decolonisation and deneo-colonisation must be fully cognisant of the nature of the international power relations and its impact on local power relations. The issue is never the failure to resist and the passivity of the dominated, but the power relations that encapsulated the dominated and the opportunity that presented itself, or not at all, for organic change. The Haitian Revolution was the product of the action of the enslaved to exploit a conjuncture created by internecine warfare within the ranks of the North Atlantic colonial overlords in an attempt to erase the French Revolution. There was no such conjuncture to be exploited at the time of the Biafran secession from Nigeria and the subsequent war for the conquest of Biafra. The impact of North Atlantic hegemonic power on decolonisation and deneo-colonisation attests to the power wielded by the North Atlantic in the colonial to the neo-colonial world and their willingness to act to ensure their sustainable hegemony. Fanon then turns to the issue of the legitimacy of the nation following the decolonisation process. Fanon states:

"In this chapter we shall analyse the problem, which is felt to be fundamental, of the legitimacy of the claims of a nation. It must be recognised that the political party which mobilises the people hardly touches on the problem of legitimacy." (Fanon 1963 pg. 207). The fundamental issue is the legitimacy of the nation that supposedly emerges out of the decolonisation process which the nationalist party and the maximum leader that dominates the party are not concerned with. A nation cobbled together by dint of a constitution rooted in North Atlantic universal liberalism is not organic to the colonial terrain. A nation whose demographic composition and territorial boundaries are the product of North Atlantic colonial domination is not organic. A nation that is free and sovereign but continues to be dominated by North Atlantic overlords is not organic, but can this so-called nation be a nation and can it be sustainably legitimised? Not if it cannot be legitimised, but it can be operationalised, premised on neo-colonial fascism as the cementing agent of the matrix. The reality of colonial power relations is that there is resistance that is effective without revolution, for revolution is an imported Enlightenment construct of the North Atlantic. In the absence of revolution our resistance will be glossed over with the North Atlantic discursive construct of passivity, even servility. But resistance to the point of triggering brutality, in the absence of this idyllic termed revolution, is an effective response to the material, strategic conditions. The effectiveness of resistance erasing the impact of the colonial psychoexistential complex is then the salient issue. The answer to this must be framed by the reality that the psychoexistential complex is an instrument of North Atlantic power and it evolves as the strategy of North Atlantic power evolves over time/ space. The psychoexistential complex of the colonial era is not that of the neo-colonial era and the composition of this instrument of power in the 1950s is not what it is in the 21st century. Secondly, the assault of North Atlantic power on the rest of the world involves the formulation and unleashing of this instrument of power on countries, cultures and races who were never colonised by the North Atlantic as Russia, Japan and South Korea. There are then two terrains of engagement demanding two strategies of engagement: the decolonisation intervention to dismantle the colonial psychoexistential complex and the ongoing strategy of engagement to constantly disarm the evolving postcolonial assault of the postcolonial psychoexistential complex. When you fail to disarm the colonial psychoexistential complex the postcolonial psychoexistential complex is all pervasive and hegemonic, which impacts the quality and nature of resistance to power/force relations.

Colonial Assault on the Native

Fanon now insists that a process of reclaiming our history, our national culture from North Atlantic domination is necessary to the process of legitimising the nation as follows: "The passion with which native intellectuals defend the existence of their national culture may be a source of amazement; but those who condemn this exaggerated passion are strangely apt to forget that their own psyche and their own selves are conveniently sheltered behind a French or German culture which has given full proof of its existence and which is uncontested." (Fanon 1963 pg. 209). There is then a divide created between those who labour in the project to redefine the national culture assaulted by colonial domination and those who reject and assault the relevance of this project, who are immersed in hallucinatory whiteness, secure in their North Atlantic worldview of delusion. This is then one expression of the power relation where the North Atlantic intervenes to bring those of the reformulation and resistance project to their knees, their silence, their migration and their change of sides or selling out to the coloniser/neo-coloniser. It is a power relation loaded in favour of the local compradors, the Stevens and to the detriment of the forces of resistance. Fanon continues: "The claim to a national culture in the past does not only rehabilitate that nation and serve as a justification for the hope of a future national culture. In the sphere of psycho-affective equilibrium it is responsible for an important change in the native." (Fanon 1963 pg. 210). The discovery, formulation and claim of a past national culture in in fact therapeutic as it impacts the ravages of the psychoexistential complex on the native, thereby constituting hope for the future of the nation. To sell the legitimacy of the nation, the psycho-affective equilibrium of the colonised, of the colonial and postcolonial order must be addressed and one way to do this is via hope in the future of the nation and positive impact of this hope on the daily well-being of each citizen of the nation. Hope for the nation and in the nation is absolutely necessary for legitimacy, but the national bourgeoisie and the neo-colonial project can only dispense hopelessness, which erodes the very quality of daily human interaction in the social order. Where hopelessness drives nihilism and violence becomes the mediator of all human conflict in the social order. This neo-colonial reality points to the agenda of North Atlantic colonial domination which necessitated a well-crafted strategic instrument to drive decolonisation, which with the gift of independence was pre-empted. Fanon states: "When we consider the efforts made to carry out the cultural estrangement so characteristic of the colonial epoch, we realise that nothing has been left to chance and that the total result looked for by colonial domination was indeed to convince the natives that colonialism came to lighten their darkness. The effect consciously sought by colonialism was to drive into the natives' heads the idea that if the settlers were to leave, they would at once fall back into barbarism, degradation, and bestiality." (Fanon 1963 pgs. 210-211). The strategic aim of colonial assault via their instrument of power, the psychoexistential complex, was to convince the colonised that we are inferior races that are incapable of modernity/postmodernity and progress without the tutelage and oversight of the North Atlantic white man. We therefore needed to be dominated by the colonial overlord, represented by the colonial settler and the official, and under neo-colonialism these colonial representatives are replaced by a phalanx of North Atlantic officials from government, multilateral agencies as the IMF, the World Bank and UN agencies, NGOs', politicians, employees of globalised financial markets neoliberal capitalism and religious operatives. There is then a wave of North Atlantic white people that now assault the freedom and sovereignty of the minds of the postcolonial world by reinforcing the colonial dictum that we are inferior races intrinsically incapable of taking charge of our destiny. Kipling's white man's burden was never put to death by the postcolonial condition, simply embellished and heightened by our genetic incompetence. The basis of the North Atlantic colonial and postcolonial assault on us is the racialisation of thought and culture formulated in the discourse of white racist supremacy, constituting the most potent gift of the North Atlantic white man to the world. Fanon states: "And it is only too true that those who are most responsible for this racialisation of thought, or at least for the first movement toward that thought, are and remain those Europeans who have never ceased to set up white culture to fill the gap left by the absence of other cultures. Colonialism did not dream of wasting its time in denying the existence of one national culture over another." (Fanon 1963 pg. 212). Under colonial domination the modus operandi of domination was the dismantling of the native culture by attacking the native with the psychoexistential complex, then to fill the void created with a native who accepts their inferiority and acts upon it with subservience and servility. At the point of decolonisation, the failure to assault this racialized discourse with essentially the rebirth of native culture, driven by the discourse of native culture and the new individual constituted, enabled the rolling out of the neo-colonial project. The failure to attain this threshold meant the survival of the colonial project and its reformulation to fully exploit the postcolonial terrain towards realising the sustainable neo-colonial domination of the postcolonial world. This survival across space/time by the modus operandi of colonial domination is the grave failure of decolonisation that was vitally and strategically necessary to realising the neo-colonial project. One potent illustration of this failure to assault the white man's racialized thought at the point of decolonisation is the embrace of racialized thought as the necessary and effective instrument of decolonisation for colonised persons. Fanon states: "The historical necessity in which the men of African culture find themselves to racialize their claims and to speak more of African culture than of national culture will tend to lead them up a blind alley." (Fanon 1963 pg. 214). National culture can never be replaced in its potency for decolonisation by abstractions created by North Atlantic white supremacy, as 'African culture', where specificities of daily existence are all compressed together and normalised within categories invented by white colonial discourse to serve white colonial domination. Driven by hallucinatory whiteness, they refuse to see the diversity of the precolonial world and the colonial attempt to homogenise the colonial world by normalising it to fit within the white worldview. These postcolonial, supposedly liberationary concepts, follow passively the white man's model of normalisation masked in their claim to a racialized emphasis as they set out to destroy the diversity of the precolonial world, which must be rejuvenated and expanded towards the formation of national culture and the legitimate nation. Their agenda is then a fascist agenda expressed via a deeply hierarchized social order. On this strategy to racialize the response of the colonised to the challenge of decolonisation Fanon states: "Negro and African-Negro culture broke up into different entities because the men who wished to incarnate these cultures realised that every culture is first and foremost national, and that the problem which kept Richard Wright or Langston Hughes on the alert were fundamentally different from those which might confront Leopold Senghor or Jomo Kenyatta." (Fanon 1963 pg. 216). The concept of an 'African culture' is then the product of the white North Atlantic racist discourse in its attempt to reduce the diversity of Africa to a single expression, which denies national culture and identity. To adopt this racialized discourse as a liberationary tool is in fact an assault on African liberation for it denies the specificity of each existential experience and the mechanism employed to create a national culture that reflects this existential experience. The Africans and the African Diaspora must then by necessity reject this call to normalisation and return to the roots of their national culture from which all other political instruments should emerge. The return to the strength to resist spawned by cultural diversity, for with failure to accomplish this task, we remain normalised under the hegemony of white North Atlantic racist culture which encourages diversity that ensures our servility and subservience as we labour under the burden of black on black racism, which is the neo-colonial instrument of power exercised at the micro levels of human interaction. Fanon then insists that the embrace of racialized discourse by the colonised in the quest for decolonisation is a potent indicator of the user's subservience and servility to white North Atlantic hegemony. Fanon states: "Thus we see that the cultural problem as it sometimes exists in colonised countries runs the risk of giving rise to serious ambiguities. The lack of culture of the Negroes, as proclaimed by colonialism, and the inherent barbarity of the Arabs ought logically to lead to the exaltation of cultural manifestations which are not simply national but continental, and extremely racial." (Fanon 1963 pg. 217). The colonial assault on the Negro and the Arab constitutes a cultural terrain characterised by serious ambiguities, where non-white colonised persons in response to their embrace of the colonial assault signal their utilisation of the logical outcomes of this assault. These logical outcomes embrace extremely racist, national and continental expressions of the cultural forms they generate for decolonisation which indicate that they accept and act upon their inferiority and barbarity. With these actions the circle has been closed as the neo-colonial project is now on track.

Native Intellectual

In the text Fanon now deals with the native intellectual and the role of this specific individual in the process of decolonisation and nation building. Fanon states: "there remains nevertheless the fact that it contributes greatly to upholding and justifying the actions of politicians. It is true that the attitude of the native intellectual sometimes takes on the aspect of a cult or of a religion." "This stated belief in a national culture is in fact an ardent, despairing turning toward anything that will allow him secure anchorage." (Fanon 1963 pg. 217). The native intellectual is deeply alienated, even estranged from her/his non-white self and more so from his people. Having immersed herself/himself in white North Atlantic discourse, fully opening their psyche to its racist assault, constituting a non-white riven with grave contradictions, ambiguities and self-hate, yet this native intellectual purposely distances herself/himself from the masses. The native intellectual resides in a 'No Man's Land' of the soul; where she/he is too 'native' for the North Atlantic, yet perceives herself/himself as too 'evolved' for the masses. Self-hate, driving the air of inherent superiority that distinguishes them from their fellow non-whites, constitutes the cult of the native intellectual and the local university as a poor imitation of North Atlantic ivory towers. This deeply flawed and problematic native intellectual must then serve the native politicians and the North Atlantic agents of the neo-colonial order for that is their means to eat, to seek social prominence and some even believe it is an effective means to amass personal wealth. But there are those native intellectuals who are driven by the self-hate waged on them by North Atlantic racist discourse and intensified by their servility to seek to become whole in their ambivalence, self-hate and servility. The solution they devise can only be twisted and self-destructive, posing a most potent threat with its adoption by the masses. This search to devise a safe anchorage is rooted in the manufacture of a national culture, rooted in a discourse of the purity, sanctity and ultimate utility of a native precolonial culture, pinned in an era devoid of modern technology. This is a precolonial culture that is the idyllic, which is pre-capitalist and devoid of modern technology, thereby constituting a postcolonial Luddite utopia of non-white peoples. This discourse can only be the product of the mind of a native intellectual that sees only via the white supremacist discourse of the North Atlantic. Fanon states: "This is because the native intellectual has thrown himself greedily upon Western culture." "the native intellectual will try to make European culture his own." (Fanon 1963 pg. 218). The quest for whiteness then spawns the native intellectual alienated from the masses and more importantly, the agenda to drive decolonisation by a specific methodology which ensures the continued hegemony of the North Atlantic over the postcolonial world via the neo-colonial project. The native intellectual is not an organic intellectual and can never become one until the moment is encountered where the process of discursive and worldview suicide is unleashed and embraced sustainably. The native intellectual then poses a grave, potent threat to decolonisation as a liberationary process, for they can only affirm North Atlantic hegemony by their personal servility to whiteness and the desire for white affirmation.

Fanon insists that the native intellectual undergoes an evolutionary process that is easily discernible in his quest to rediscover his native idyllic as follows: "He sets a high value on the customs, traditions, and the appearances of his people; but his inevitable, painful experience only seems to be a banal search for exoticism." (Fanon 1963 pg. 221). The native intellectual is valorising all things native that will supposedly end his alienation from herself/himself and the masses, but in this valorisation all native cultural practices chosen reveal their exoticisation for the intent is fetishisation not liberation. The hallucinatory whiteness of the native intellectual prohibits the internalisation of all things native, but allows the embrace of the objects of the idyllic as fetishes and talismanic objects to act as the psychic oxycodone and oxycontin the native intellectuals' altered and servile worldview constantly craves in its addiction to whiteness. The native intellectual by extension must peddle to the masses an exoticised form of their culture, constituted by the native intellectuals, for the sake of the hegemony of the national politicians and the North Atlantic oligarchy over the masses. In this exoticised version of native culture the native intellectual must then exoticise the native as the repository of all truth and goodness, for the political end game of the native intellectual demands this device be formulated and unleashed. For the maximum leader of the people, of the masses, is the single individual premier repository created and affirmed by the exoticism of the native intellectual, which is in fact a political weapon to ensure the hegemony of the North Atlantic. Fanon states: "The native intellectual decides to make an inventory of the bad habits drawn from the colonial world, and hastens to remind everyone of the good old customs of the people, that people that which he has decided contains all truth and goodness." (Fanon 1963 pg. 221). The repository of truth and goodness that is the masses is then the answer to colonial bad habits, thereby placing this exotic instrument in the terrain of decolonisation with the maximum leader potently empowered by this discourse of exotic infallibility. Fanon states that in the writings of the native intellectual there are three evolutionary phases they journey through. The first phase encompasses the presentation of evidence by the native intellectual of the fruits of their pursuit of whiteness, they are now non-whites with white minds. Fanon states: "In the first phase, the native intellectual gives proof that he has assimilated the culture of the occupying power. The writings correspond point by point with those of his opposite numbers in the mother country." (Fanon 1963 pg. 222). The overwhelming number of native intellectuals never migrate from this first phase, in spite of decolonisation, and aid in the replication of this subservience in the neo-colonial condition. The native intellectual ensures the sustainability of North Atlantic hegemony, from colonial domination to the neo-colonial condition, by consciously and willingly acting on their worldview and the menu of choices it generates for action. In the second phase, the non-white intellectual finally decides to seek solutions for the deep void generated by hallucinatory whiteness where you invest all your endeavours to be a valorised human, white and imbued with whiteness, which genetically you can never be for you are condemned to be non-white. But the refusal to commit worldview and discursive suicide means that in your return to roots, to your non-white cultural foundation, you are in fact seeing and interpreting what you can see via your whiteness. You are then on a journey of roots to grasp specific cultural instances and remodel them in the image and likeness of your white worldview and discursive order, thereby creating a new revisionist non-white servile culture which will be unleashed to serve the neo-colonial project and the hegemony of the white North Atlantic, thereby framing the hegemonic neo-colonial condition. Fanon states: "In the second phase we find the native is disturbed; he decides to remember what he is." "But since the native is not a part of his people, since he only has exterior relations with his people, he is content to recall their life only." "old legends will be reinterpreted in the light of a borrowed estheticism and of a conception of the world which was discovered under other skies." (Fanon 1963 pg. 222). What is seen as native culture is selectively reinterpreted via a white worldview and estheticism, which is a project that can only actively support white North Atlantic hegemony over the masses who are the repository of this native culture, which the native intellectual insists will address their angst. The native intellectual cannot be a liberationary agent, not even a Frankenstein monster nor a Dr Jekyll and Mr Hyde, for they all carry the mark of Cain. The third phase in the evolutionary process is the proclamation of revolution in the name of the masses by the native intellectual which constitutes a most dangerous phase for the masses, decolonisation and the nation, for the essential question must deal with the discourse and source of this revolution, ultimately its nature. For a native intellectual yet to commit discursive and worldview suicide can only generate a revolution which is driven by the white esthetic and worldview, which results in a revolution to further damage native culture towards ensuring their servility in the neo-colonial project, by assaulting it with the native intellectual discourse of native culture formulated through white North Atlantic discourse. Fanon states: "Finally in the third phase, which is called the fighting phase, the native, after trying to lose himself in the people and with the people, will on the contrary shake the people." "he turns himself into an awakener of the people, hence comes a fighting literature, a revolutionary literature, and a national literature." "and to become the mouthpiece of a new reality in action." (Fanon 1963 pgs. 222-223). The native intellectual fails to become one with the masses, for which the masses are to blame, as they are trapped in a cultural lethargy which the native intellectual will dispel via revolutionary, real action. The native intellectual appoints himself awakener of the masses and undertakes real, revolutionary action to immerse the masses in their version of what native culture should and must be. They are emancipating the masses, from the lethargy driven by an inadequate culture and worldview to which it is attached, by formulating and unleashing a revolutionary discourse that constitutes the new world. They are then intent on writing on the minds of the masses this new discourse and its attendant worldview born out of the servility to whiteness by the native intellectual. This process is in fact revolutionary in the mind of the native intellectual, as finally under the aegis of neo-colonial domination, the masses will once and for all grasp the impact of modernity/postmodernity and progress making them the premier revolutionaries of the North Atlantic, having solved the problem that colonial domination failed miserably to overcome. For this most strategically and historically important accomplishment they will finally be accepted as white in their non-white skins or their chemically altered skin colour of their non-white skins. Fanon continues: "but the ideas that he expresses and the preoccupations he is taken up with have no common yardstick to measure the real situation which the men and the women of his country know. The culture that the intellectual leans toward is often no more than a stock of particularisms." (Fanon 1963 pg. 223). In her/his whiteness the native intellectual is incapable of resonating with the daily existential reality of the masses and their diverse survival strategies that operate in this existential reality. What the native intellectual presents as native reality and culture is the product of her/his whiteness and is unintelligible to the masses, for the product of the native intellectual is rooted and grounded in a worldview of particularisms that maintain the exclusions and hierarchies of the colonial order, but with potent differences. The native intellectual is constituting a discourse of the cult of the non-white intellectual as the repository of liberation, thereby enabling the laying on of the hands to all those who bear the hallmark of approval by this repository, hence the maximum leaders of the nationalist political movement, the national middle class, the local oligarchy and white North Atlantic domination. This particularist discourse of the native intellectual constitutes the neo-colonial social hierarchy which reformulates a colonial social hierarchy with potency the colonial order could never possess and exercise. It is formulated by non-whites for the domination of non-whites to the ultimate benefit of North Atlantic whites, thereby proving and indicating the importance of the native intellectual to the neo-colonial project, thereby solidifying their importance to the neo-colonial project which enables their quest to construct a structure of power in their favour under neo-colonial domination. Power, personal wealth and the exercise of power in the social order are only guaranteed by the sustainable operation of the intensely hierarchical order formulated by their discourse of the new, refurbished national culture. This discourse of particularism, expressed as a rigidly policed social hierarchy, is then the jaundiced view of native culture that the native intellectual is condemned to generate. Fanon states on this fatalistic condition as follows: "The man of culture, instead of setting out to find this substance, will let himself be hypnotised by these mummified fragments which because they are static are in fact symbols of negation and outworn contrivances. Culture has never the translucidity of custom; it abhors all simplification. In its essence it is opposed to custom, for custom is always the deterioration of culture." (Fanon 1963 pg. 224). The man of culture, this native intellectual can only generate a parody of native culture viewed through her/his white worldview, which generates the fixation with customs which is then proclaimed the basis of native culture, thereby denying the dynamism of native culture. Without this dynamism native culture constituted by the native intellectual is ossified, holding on to mummified expressions no longer relevant to daily existential reality, enabling the native intellectual and his white overlords to proclaim the urgent need for a huge injection of white modernity and progress to awaken native culture from its ossified slumber. Every project the native intellectual embarks upon can only benefit the white North Atlantic overlords and their domination of the neo-colonial world for the native intellectual is the white man's artifice, his instrument of power with a non-white face, even more powerful and vitally necessary than Steven was to enslavement. The native intellectual formulates the discourse of assault and clears the path for the intensive assault on native culture under neo-colonial domination that was not possible under colonial domination. The assault under neo-colonial domination is as under enslavement, but perfected by having non-white first line massas, the instrument of white power, under the domination of the external white overlord. Rape by proxy! Fanon continues: "But the native intellectual who wishes to create an authentic work of art must realise that the truths of a nation are in the first place its realities." (Fanon 1963 pg. 225). Again the native intellectual is alienated from the realities of the nation as her/his worldview and its driving discourse can only see as valid and real the realities of this nation generated by their white worldview. Their white perceptual grid constituted by her/his worldview dismisses the realities of the nation as being less than real, the babblings of primitive, backward people excluded from the veracity of science. The truths that spring from this reality can never be fit and proper truths in keeping with her/his whiteness, which then necessitates the native intellectual project to manufacture reality and constitute truth from this alien reality that is concordant with her/his whiteness. The neo-colonial social order is then driven by a vast divergence between: the reality and truth of the hegemonic oligarchy, the national middle class and the political elite and the reality and truth of the masses, hence the need for fascism and its explicit brutality as an instrument of power. There is no investment in the neo-colonial state in biopolitics towards seducing the masses to police themselves, for there is no core group of native intellectuals, oligarchs, national bourgeoisie/national middle class capable of visioning this process of the formulation of a neo-colonial discourse of biopolitics/biopower and the necessary mechanism of power and the instruments of power. The specificity of the worldview of members of these elite groups predisposes them to view power as massa did and exercised it on the plantation in the 18th century, in the 21st century, they are then and can only be hard core fascists plagued with black on black racism. In the neo-colonial world infusions of the discourse of biopolitics emanate from the North Atlantic in an attempt to replicate the North Atlantic reality in the neo-colonial world. What we have then are the masses, the underclass and the minority elite groups separated by a chasm of perception, a multiplicity of realities and truths that drive a hard, hierarchical social order noted for extreme inequality facing off each other, where violence is the preferred choice of resolving human conflict. The elite minority groups exhibit a paranoid fear of the masses and the underclass where the State is co-opted to police this chasm of divide in the interest of the elite groups. Fanon points out the strategic need for this chasm as follows: "Let there be no mistake about it; it is to this zone of occult instability where the people dwell that we must come; and it is there that our souls are crystallised and that our perceptions and our lives are transfused with light." (Fanon 1963 pg. 227). The search for wholeness in response to the alienation that is the result of the embrace of whiteness, must involve the entry to and immersion into the realm of the masses, a realm that is and must be unstable given its rejuvenating potency but its instability is masked, unseen by those who are outside viewing inwards. It is only those who share the discourse and worldview of this terrain will be able to see the instability and its rejuvenating power, to others it is an occult instability. The strategy of the native intellectual is then to render this region, realm and terrain stable and visible to her/his worldview and discourse thereby disarming the rejuvenating potency of the terrain of the masses. This then is the prime directive of the native intellectual, for this rejuvenating realm of the masses must be whitened, subjugated and rendered impotent. The neo-colonial condition is then premised on an ongoing power relation between the masses and the local and foreign progenitors of neo-colonial subservience which involves the control and conquest of the realm of the masses, for it is impossible to generate sustainable neo-colonial domination with this realm fully operationalised and maintaining its integrity. This is a battle primarily between discourses and worldviews where those of the masses must be silenced and relegated to the margins, becoming esoteric knowledges at best, buried and forgotten knowledges at worst. Hence the primary role of the native intellectual in the assault on the terrain of the masses which demands the constituting of organic intellectuals in the service of the masses as the counter to this agent of dominance and servility. This organic intellectual must be of the discourses and worldview of the masses and competent to deconstruct the worldview and discourse of the assault of neo-colonial domination towards contributing to the erection of instruments of power that mitigate the assaults of the adversary. The organic intellectual is a watcher, traverses a multiplicity of realms and is a translator of the discourse and worldview of the adversary for the masses in their discourses and worldviews. The organic intellectual has then to utilise the clarity of mass culture where the realities of action possible and probable of the masses are fully understood, accepted and strategy crafted to reflect this actional reality. Unlike the native intellectual, who can at best gaze upon the realm of the masses afflicted with translucidity where light, the image and reality can only be distorted to fit the reality that whiteness accepts and permits as real. In this war with the realm of the masses the organic intellectual is always marked for still birth and marginalisation, for the genesis project has to perish with miscarriages and still births. With a successful genesis these organic intellectuals must be marginalised, rendered impotent which illustrates the intensity of the engagements in this war. Fanon speaks to this reality as follows: "The colonised man who writes for his people ought to use the past with the intention of opening the future, as an invitation to action and a basis for hope. But to ensure that hope and to give it form, he must take part in action and throw himself body and soul into the national struggle." (Fanon 1963 pg. 232). The organic intellectual produces for the masses, which in itself is an action that encompasses personal sacrifices and actions that generate threats to life and an assurance of some semblance of normality and security. This act of production must be part of the national struggle, the defence of the realm of the masses which is absolutely basic, understood and compulsory for national liberation. The action of production of the organic intellectual is even more strategically necessary and problematic in a neo-colonial order given the fact that there was no decolonisation just a gift of independence. The problematic constituted by a decolonisation process, that was anti-colonial in name only, which ended in neo-colonial domination is illustrated by Fanon as follows: "To fight for national culture means in the first place to fight for the liberation of the nation, that material keystone which makes the building of a culture possible. There is no other fight for culture which can develop apart from the political struggle." (Fanon 1963 pg. 233). In a colonised setting the formulation of a national culture is only possible with national liberation for it is the foundation necessary to the building of a national culture. Any struggle for culture that is not rooted in political liberation is then aimless for it is impossible, for what is defined as culture being fought for is an aberration created by the assault of white North Atlantic domination via the neo-colonial order. In the decolonisation process rooted in the gift of independence there was no struggle for national liberation and no national liberation as decolonisation disappeared into neo-colonial domination, there is then no national culture only cultures constituting a realm of acute contestation. This acute contestation of cultures exposes the existence of realms of culture with their own discourses and worldviews, which simply cannot be welded into a national culture for it is held together by the quest for hegemony by minority groups of class, race and ethnicity utilising the State as the policeman of this terrain of acute and incessant contestation. The primary issue in this operational terrain is not then national liberation and the genesis of national culture, but the building up of capacity to resist the assault and then go on the offensive as an instrument of survival, for the neo-colonial condition in the 21st century does not afford much more space than for survival.

National Culture

Fanon at this point in the text defines national culture as follows: "A national culture is the whole body of efforts made by a people in the sphere of thought to describe, justify, and praise the action through which that people has created itself and keeps itself in existence. A national culture in underdeveloped countries should therefore take its place at the very heart of the struggle for freedom which these countries are carrying on." (Fanon 1963 pg. 233). There is no national culture in a social order under the domination of neo-colonialism as the masses never took the action to create themselves and keep themselves so created in existence sustainably. There is then no discourse and its worldview that speaks to and of the action taken by the masses to create themselves and ensure their sustainable existence. It is by undertaking the action to free ourselves that the action to create ourselves will be unleashed with the discourse and worldview that drives the process, which is the basis of the genesis of the culture of action. The gift of independence that enabled neo-colonial domination ensured that we are yet still to frame and launch the action to free ourselves, much less to sustainably exist thereafter. We are then emancipated slaves trapped in a netherworld, a wasteland of human misery termed underdevelopment, devoid of national culture, but burdened with cultures which are all attached to North Atlantic national culture which ensures our captivity. Skin bleaching cream anyone? What about some cosmetic surgery? Wigs, hair pieces, hair relaxer? Embrace the white esthetic which renders us permanently ugly, for we are not of the right and acceptable genetic code. Such is the result of the failure to produce a national culture rooted in national liberation. The salient issue is the failure to accept the pressing reality that underdevelopment is today sustainable because we remain discursively dependent on the North Atlantic, for this cultural dependence is constructed to ensure our sustainable servility, nothing else. Today's organic underdevelopment is then joined at the head with organic dependence, the Frankenstein monster that is the product of white North Atlantic hegemony over the neo-colonial world. Fanon comments on this organic subservience as follows: "There will be never such a thing as black culture because there is not a single politician who feels he has a vocation to bring black republics into being. The problem is to get to know the place that these men mean to give their people, the kind of social relations that they decide to set up, and the conception that they have of the future of humanity. It is this that counts, everything else is mystification, signifying nothing." (Fanon 1963 pgs.234-235). The national politicians were never intent on creating national culture, hence black republics and culture were never on the agenda. What was on the agenda, being now palpably apparent in the 21st century given the sustainability of the neo-colonial order, is neo-colonial subservience to white North Atlantic hegemony with its gift of sustainable underdevelopment. The interests of the oligarchy are then paramount to the detriment of the masses, and all other stated public intent is simply mystification that has repeatedly proven in the existential condition of the masses that they amount to nothing. A nihilist reality underpinned by fascist social relations. Fanon insists that the neo-colonial order in its power relations is a distinct and separate development from the power relations of colonial domination. The neo-colonial order is buttressed and driven by a fundamentally distinct discourse with its specific power relations which demands analysis that addresses this specificity. Fanon states: "There can be no two cultures which are completely identical. To believe that it is possible to create a black culture is to forget that niggers are disappearing, just as those people who brought them into being are seeing the breakup of their economic and cultural supremacy." (Fanon 1963 pg. 234). The social order of colonial domination and that of neo-colonial domination are entirely different and can't be reduced to each other using faulty argument, such as the domination and the dominator are the same, as the domination is not the same even though the dominator is the same. Black culture formulated under colonial domination is sterile as an instrument of power to assault the neo-colonial order. Those who constituted the nigger under colonial domination have been replaced by the new powered elites of the neo-colonial order, whilst there is no longer any need for the old, colonial slave plantation nigger in the neo-colonial order. The strategic imperative is for servile, subservient non-whites immersed in North Atlantic white culture where they view the world through white matrices of perception, see order in the world through the white worldview and unleashes action in the world that is the product of white discourse, cosmology, order and truth. Colonial domination never needed such non-whites as demanded by neo-colonial domination and those whites who insisted on niggers being all they needed under neo-colonialism simply were erased by the neo-colonial project. A new white discourse and worldview were demanded by the neo-colonial project and colonial whites averse to change were simply disposed of by the neo-colonial project, as there was no neo-colonial white solidarity with beached ex-colonial whites fighting to hold back the hegemony of the neo-colonial project, with few exceptions as apartheid South Africa and Mandela's neo-colonial black on black racist South Africa.

Fanon ends this portion of his presentation by reaffirming his position on the nexus between national liberation from North Atlantic domination and national culture as follows: "It is around the peoples' struggles that African-Negro culture takes on substance and not around songs, poems, or folklore." (Fanon 1963 pg. 235). National culture is the product of national liberation, without national liberation there are cultures no national culture, which is the terrain of neo-colonial domination. Fanon then insists that the fundamental tasks of all of us of the colonial world is as follows: "the liberation of the national territory; a continual struggle against colonialism in its new forms; and an obstinate refusal to enter the charmed circle of mutual admiration at the summit." (Fanon 1963 pg. 235). The prime task is national liberation which must be buttressed by the realisation, and relevant action, that colonialist domination is constantly evolving and even in a state of national liberation we can surrender to a newly evolved form of North

Atlantic domination. To avoid subservience to the North Atlantic we must then be wary of the institutional structures they dominate that are instruments of seduction and servility. The nature of our existential condition in light of our failure to effect national liberation is clearly apparent in the 21st century.

Nature of Colonial Domination

Fanon in the final section of his presentation presents an analysis of the nature and impact of colonial domination on the colonised which provides strategic insights into the terrain of neo-colonial domination, as there was a seamless transition in colonies via the instrument of the gift of independence to the neo-colonial project. Fanon states: "Colonial domination, because it is total and tends to oversimplify, very soon manages to disrupt in spectacular fashion the cultural life of a conquered people." (Fanon 1963 pg. 236). Colonial domination disrupts the cultural life of the dominated by being totalist and interventionist by oversimplifying the reality under assault. It is totalist because the white North Atlantic worldview and its cosmology is linear, binary, white humanist and ultimately white supremacist. This worldview invests in an order of binary, mutually irreconcilable opposites whose intense antagonism is registered in linearities for time and space, as there is still grave difficulty with the time/space construct, history and knowledge are never cyclical. Being totalist it must be interventionist, for it must change all realities into its own as mutual respect for difference is anathema to this worldview. The white North Atlantic worldview has then an inability to respect difference, which expresses its innate imperialist drive to oversimplify and to dominate. Simply ask Crazy Horse, Sitting Bull, Cochise, Geronimo and the victims at Wounded Knee about this inability to respect difference and the white will to imperialist domination by any means necessary. Fanon continues: "Every effort is made to bring the colonised person to admit the inferiority of his culture which has been transformed into instinctive patterns of behaviour, to recognise the unreality of his 'nation,' and, in the last extreme, the confused and imperfect character of his own biological structure." (Fanon 1963 pg. 236). The white imperialist, totalist, colonial assault is insisting that we accept and act upon the inferiority of our biological/genetic reality which can only generate an inferior culture and a sick, less than civilised at best nation. But this totalist assault is not complete at the point of our acceptance of our inferiority for we must now fill the void created by the assault for it to be totalist, a whole and complete with whiteness, which keeps us permanently in a state of incompleteness, disarmed and conquered which constitutes us the binary opposite of the white man. Fanon continues: "A national culture under colonial domination is a contested culture whose destruction is sought in systematic fashion." (Fanon 1963 pg. 237). The culture of the colonised is then under constant assault making it a contested culture, but since colonial domination is assaulting the human generators of native culture the cultural expression reflects this assault and its nature. The humans are contested humans making the culture they generate a contested culture which indicates the systemic assault of the colonial dominator. The fight to hold on to this contested culture by contested humans becomes an exercise in grasping inertia, mistaking it for dynamism and vibrancy, which means that there is no effective resistance at the cultural level as the culture atrophies mistaken for customs. Fanon insists that this results in as follows: "There is simply a concentration on a hard core of culture which is becoming more and more shrivelled up, inert, and empty." (Fanon 1963 pg. 238). The assault is in fact operationally successful as the native culture retreats, shrinks even becoming silenced, marginalised and esotericised, leaving a core of customs that is practised ritually as an expression of culture in response to the colonial assault. Operationally native culture cannot effectively resist and launch a counter offensive against colonial assault. Fanon states: 'The poverty of the people, national oppression, and the inhibition of culture are one and the same thing." (Fanon 1963 pg. 238). This inhibition of culture indicates the success of the assault on the native which enables colonial exploitation which expresses its outcomes as national oppression, underdevelopment and the poverty of the masses. This then is the nexus of white North Atlantic colonial domination: degenerated humans, degenerated culture, national oppression, underdevelopment and the poverty of the masses. To attain this condition, discourse, its mechanism of power and its instruments of power must be formulated and operationalised with the base driving discursive concept being white North Atlantic supremacy.

Reflexive Violence

The colonial assault on native culture results in the pushback from the colonised, which is manifested in growing aggressive behaviour of the reflexive type which does not pose a concerted threat to white colonial hegemony. Fanon states: "But these patterns of conduct are of the reflexive type; they are poorly differentiated, anarchic, and ineffective. Colonial exploitation, poverty, and endemic famine drives the native more and more to open, organised revolt." (Fanon 1963 pg. 238). The colonial assault on native culture cannot bring about the conditions for revolt against colonial domination as it results in a reflexive aggression which is focused internally on the native self and on native to native relations. This reflexive aggression is the product of the assault on the native self which insists that the non-white is inferior, primitive, backward and sub-human at best. Violence necessary to assault colonial domination has to emerge from a reservoir that is free from the clutches of reflexive aggression, as this self-hatred expressed via self-immolation is the major impediment to liberationary violence. Liberationary violence emerges from the existential condition of natives under colonial domination characterised by inequality, exploitation and chronic underdevelopment embracing instances of famine. The failure to effect liberationary violence as the premier instance of decolonisation coupled with the gift of independence means the continuity of the assault on the native's humanity under neo-colonial domination and the spiralling of native reflexive violence as we are all now free and sovereign. Fanon points out another indicator of this reflexive violence in the literature produced by natives under colonial assault as follows: "From being a reply on a minor scale to the dominating power, the literature produced by natives becomes differentiated and makes itself into a will to particularism." (Fanon 1963 pg. 239). The literature of colonised, native reflexive violence is transformed as it is driven by the will to structure colonial reality into hierarchical structures premised on difference defined and problematized by Manicheism. The colonised native is now illustrating the impact of the racist colonial assault upon discourse and worldview, which blossoms under neo-colonial domination, as the discourse of black on black racism with its mechanism of power being hierarchies of difference and its instrument of power being the policing of difference to the point of genocide. This will to particularism that blossoms under neo-colonial domination drives the native to deepen the reflexive violence, hence the cosmetic surgery, the chemical alterations of the body and the wearing of the good, beautiful symbols from the bodies of other races alien to yours. So whilst you speak of white racism and black victims, you have on your head a wig made from South Asian or Chinese hair or hair implants from the same source, you have chemically altered your skin colour and had a lip and nose job. Such is the nature of the blossoming of native reflexive violence under neo-colonial domination where there was no cleansing of the soul of the colonised with decolonisation where today we are all emancipated slaves. Fanon insists that it is futile to seek a new, rejuvenated native culture under colonial domination as they are mutually irreconcilable. This nature of the operational terrain, this act of futility it was launched in is also illustrated by the nature of nationalism that thrives and is effective in it. Fanon states: "This is why we arrive at the proposition which at first sight seems paradoxical: the fact that in a colonised country the most elementary, most savage, and most undifferentiated nationalism is the most fervent and efficient means of defending national culture." (Fanon 1963 pg. 244). The nature of the colonial assault on the humanity of the native and native culture constitutes a terrain of resistance where effective resistance utilising nationalism as an instrument of power is conditioned by the operational terrain. In this terrain only basic, rudimentary, elementary and violent nationalism plagued with reflexive violence is effective and efficient in its defence of native culture. This reflexive nationalism in defence of native culture, which flows into the gift of independence and the terrain of neo-colonial domination enables the construction of the neo-colonial social order rooted in fascism, black on black racism, underdevelopment and chronic inequality. The effective and efficient nationalism is then in the colonial terrain the product of the will to particularism, which spawns its demon under neo-colonialism that thrives on black on black racism and its magnification and fabrication of difference towards genocide.

Fanon is insisting that liberation from the assault of the coloniser and the impacts of this assault on the colonised, our culture and our social order was possible but the action was ours to do as the choice was ours to make.

Fanon in his presentation presents the outcomes of this liberationary action and points to the outcomes arising from the failure/refusal to embrace liberationary action. On the liberationary outcomes Fanon states as follows: "As soon as the Negro comes to an understanding of himself, and understands the rest of the world differently, when he gives birth to hope and forces back the racist universe," (Fanon 1963 pg. 243). The basis of liberation is then an awakening to the reality of our place in the white man's world premised upon: understanding of our non-white self, especially the impact of the racist assault on my psyche, understand the world and my place in it by focusing on power, power relations and hegemony and their impact on the hierarchical world order and my place in it. This process of embracing an alternate discourse and worldview that affirms my humanity stokes hope and with it a push back on the hegemonic racist universe. Being beached in a nation that willingly accepted neo-colonial domination the process is inherently stymied where one fights a battle for personal emancipation at great personal cost. Fanon continues: "After the conflict there is not only the disappearance of colonialism but also the disappearance of the colonised man. This new humanity cannot do otherwise than define a new humanism both for itself and for others." "A nation which is born of the people's concerted action and which embodies the real aspirations of the people while changing the state cannot exist save in the expression of exceptionally rich forms of culture." (Fanon 1963 pg. 246). A new humanity emerges from the defeat of colonial domination and its dismantling through a war of liberation waged by the masses. Colonialism and the colonised disappear, which constitutes a new humanity made up of non-whites who are now asserting their humanity in the formulation of a new humanism that is anathema to white humanism. This nation created by mass action must continue to be the vehicle for and the instrument by which the aspirations of the masses are expressed, made real, but it cannot accomplish this task without the formulation of, and unleashing of an enabling high culture in its diverse forms. The failure to wage the war of liberation results in the formulation of the neo-colonial condition where the colonial assault continues, evolves and blossoms under neo-colonial domination. The neo-colonial condition demands that the colonial assault on the humanity of non-white peoples be sustainable, reformulated and intensified with the impacts of this assault clearly apparent in the 21st century.

National Consciousness/International Consciousness

Fanon ends his presentation in 1959 by indicating that national consciousness is the highest form of national culture possible with national liberation. National consciousness outstrips narrow nationalism as it enables the formulation and unleashing of the universal dimension and positioning of the peoples of the nation and it enables the creation of universalising values that create the legitimacy of the new order. Fanon states: "it is the national consciousness which is the most elaborate form of culture." "National consciousness, which is not nationalism, is the only thing that will give us an international dimension." "the building of a nation is of necessity accompanied by the discovery and encouragement of universalising values." (Fanon 1963 pg. 247). The creation of a truly alternate reality to that of white North Atlantic colonial and neo-colonial domination is possible when the war of liberation is grasped and properly executed. This potent, inherent threat must then be defanged and any expression of this threat and its potential for development into an alternate reality destroyed, for the inherent superiority of white North Atlantic supremacy must always be affirmed with bloodletting. To affirm white North Atlantic supremacy with bloodletting is necessary to shore up the dominance of the non-white elites that continue to serve white hegemony and to unleash the spectacle when

necessary of the high price we will pay, even genocide in the 21st century, to challenge the dominance of the non-white servile oligarchs and the hegemony of their white overlords. Fanon ends his presentation as follows: "Far from keeping aloof from other nations, therefore, it is national liberation which leads the nation to play its part on the stage of history. It is at the heart of national consciousness that international consciousness lives and grows. And this two-fold emerging is ultimately only the source of all culture." (Fanon 1963 pgs. 247-248). The war of liberation that removes colonial domination enables the emergence of the two primary constituent elements of the alternate national culture of liberation: national consciousness and international consciousness. The neo-colonial nation is then devoid of, and cannot formulate this alternate national culture, for white North Atlantic hegemony working with compliant non-white oligarchs ensures that all there is, and can be, is servility in the international and national realms to the agenda of the massa.

Chapter Five
French Torture and Algerian Mental Disorders

Section five of the book forms part of the text Fanon created in 1961 before his death comprising sections 1 to 3 and 5 of the "Wretched of the Earth." In this section Fanon deals with the most telling impacts on the psyche of the Algerians by the instruments of war utilised by the French colonial overlords in the Algerian War of Liberation/Independence/Decolonisation. Fanon states: "But the war goes on; and we will have to bind up for years to come the many, sometimes ineffaceable wounds that the colonialist onslaught has inflicted on our people." "We shall deal here with the problem of mental disorders which arise from the war of national liberation which the Algerian people are carrying on." (Fanon 1963 pg. 249). Fanon in this section of his text is dealing with the mental disorders that have arisen from the specific nature of the instruments of war unleashed by the French colonial dominator on the Algerian people. Instruments of power powered by war which impact the Algerian individual to the extent of constituting mental disorders, even worse than those constituted by French colonial domination. Fanon states: "The truth is that colonialism in its essence was already taking on the aspect of a fertile purveyor of psychiatric hospitals." (Fanon 1963 pg. 249). Colonial domination was, by being the instrument of power utilised to assault the humanity of the native, already producing persons damaged and in need of psychiatric intervention. Colonial domination was then producing humans burdened with mental disorders, damaged humans. Fanon then states that the irony was the practice of psychiatric intervention in a colony where you are seeking to reintegrate the victim into the social order that is producing the damaged humans. The futility of this circular action then demands the end of colonial domination towards the liberation of the colonised from colonially induced mental disorders. Fanon states: "to the difficulties that arise when seeking to 'cure' a native properly, that is to say, when seeking to make him thoroughly a part of a social background of the colonial type." (Fanon 1963 pg. 250). The white North Atlantic scientific discourse of psychiatry is not then the solution to native mental disorders, but part of the colonial hegemonic power structure to constitute and maintain dominance over the native by any means necessary. The assault of the colonial instrument of power on the native concept of self and being human is then the thin edge of the wedge towards white colonial domination which constitutes the mental disorders. Fanon states: "Because it is a systematic negation of the other person and a furious determination to deny the other person all attributes of humanity, colonialism forces the people it dominates to ask themselves the question constantly: 'In reality, who am I?' The defensive attitude created by this violent bringing together of the colonised man and the colonial system form themselves into a structure which then reveals the colonised personality." (Fanon 1963 pg. 250). The constant assault on the humanity of the native problematizes self where you are forced to question your humanity, your identity, your history, your civilisation and your culture. This assault constitutes the defensive posture and attitude of the native which combines with the colonised man and the colonial system of domination to constitute the colonised personality. There is then a colonial personality that constitutes the ideal native desired by colonial domination. The failure to dismantle the colonial structure that constitutes the colonial personality in the run up to independence means that this structure survived, and is present and operational in postcolonial nations. This enabled the reformulation of the colonial personality through the formation of the neo-colonial structure of domination, where all and any form of discursive resistance to white colonial domination was disarmed by insisting that massa was gone replaced by non-whites. Massa day done! This position removed the white North Atlantic colonial dominator as the villain of the piece exonerating them for their sins perpetrated on non-white peoples the world over. The new enemies were now all non-white, both internal and external, where the masses were divided into race, ethnic, tribal and class differences for the sake of pursuing their servility. But the colonial personality was never addressed, never purged as it evolved and became even more potent under neo-colonial domination, exceeding the wildest expectations of white imperialist colonialists as Rhodes and Kipling. The basis of the potency of the neo-colonial assault is the changed power terrain where it is now desirable, fashionable and progressive to clothe your non-white self in whiteness, for it is no longer colonial domination but free will, all made possible by the non-whites who are dominant in the power relations of the neo-colonial world at the local level. What is now apparent is the strategy, that was unleashed by the political elites, the deep state and the discursive agents of the North Atlantic in the run up to formal independence, of a globalised assault on non-white peoples who were now approaching independence. This assault aimed to carry over the dependence of the colonised into the postcolonial era, reformulating it to enable the hegemony of the neo-colonial project on a global scale, which was driven by a consortium of assaults formulated for specific races and nations. In the 21st century the assault on China and the "middle class" of Africa and India is most visible. The colonial personality has now evolved into the neo-colonial/postcolonial personality which is strategically vital to white North Atlantic hegemony in the 21st century, driven by a globalised dynamic that pre-dated the hegemony of neo-liberal capitalism in the North Atlantic. White North Atlantic hegemony in the 21st century is premised on globalised white supremacist hegemony internalised, accepted and acted upon by servile, subservient non-white people. Put the skin lightening cream, the cosmetic surgery and the chemical and cosmetic alterations to the body in this context of power, this power relation. Fanon continues: "colonisation is a success when all this indocile nature has finally been tamed." (Fanon 1963 pg. 250). The terrain of colonial domination encompasses all of the targeted space of the colony under assault for colonial domination is driven by a totalist discourse and its attendant worldview. All humans, flora and fauna/biota and natural resources are and must be targeted thereby constituting totalist North Atlantic imperialism. Any action by the natives that limit this totalist assault is in fact assaulting the drive for totalist North Atlantic imperial, colonial domination. The basis of this totalist imperialism is docility of the targeted and with reference to natives this docility is indicated by mental disorders. Fanon states: "There is thus during this calm period of successful colonisation a regular and important mental pathology which is the direct product of oppression." (Fanon 1963 pg. 251). White North Atlantic domination constitutes a colonised native plagued with grave mental pathology. The continued existence and evolution of this structure under neo-colonial domination ensures that, whilst we insist that we are free and sovereign, we are plagued by mental pathology that is much more potent than that under colonial domination. We were sick in the head under colonial domination but today we are certifiable lunatics under neo-colonial domination.

Fanon now introduces the material he will present in this work dealing with the mental disorders arising from the Algerian war of liberation. Fanon states: "We shall mention here some Algerian cases which have been attended by us and who seem to us to be particularly eloquent. We need hardly say that we are not concerned with producing a scientific work." (Fanon 1963 pg. 251). Fanon is in fact presenting his work of antiscience, where he is deconstructing white North Atlantic scientific psychiatric discourse exposing its racist supremacist colonial agenda, as it is but another discursive agent of white North Atlantic racist, imperialist, colonial discourse. Fanon is then presenting cases that are strategically important to the Algerian war of liberation. Fanon states: "It seems to us that in the cases here chosen the events giving rise to the disorder are chiefly the bloodthirsty and pitiless atmosphere, the generalisation of inhuman practises, and the firm impression that people have of being caught up in a veritable Apocalypse." "we have already pointed out that a whole generation of Algerians, steeped in wanton, generalised homicide with all the psycho-affective consequences that this entails, will be the human legacy of France in Algeria." (Fanon 1963 pg. 251). The manner in which this war was fought, the strategies utilised by both protagonists, especially by France, and the use of widespread torture and murder framed the legacy left to the free Algeria that will impact the social order and the quality of life long after the end of the war. Fanon states: "The hitherto un-emphasised characteristics of certain psychiatric descriptions here given confirm, if confirmation were necessary, that this colonial war is singular even in the pathology that it gives rise to." (Fanon 1963 pg. 252). The colonial war to destroy the war of liberation is then unique amongst wars for the nature of the pathology it unleashes on the human psyche of the protagonists of the war both Algerian and French.

Fanon now presents Series A which comprises five cases.

Case No.1

Rape as a French instrument of war affirms revolutionary values.

The husband is an active member of the urban Algerian resistance but his wife is not a member of the resistance and takes no part in the guerrilla war. They both have a young daughter. In an engagement with the French the husband leaves a trail to the household, exposing the wife and child to the French, where the wife is arrested, transported to an interrogation centre and raped by two different French soldiers. Meanwhile the husband fled the urban operational area and joined with the guerrilla force in a rural setting where he receives the letter from the wife which instructs him to walk away from her as she has been dishonoured. The husband reacts to the rape by exhibiting symptoms of mental disorder and sexual impotence which land him in the mental hospital under Fanon's care. Fanon reports the conversation with the husband which illustrates the impact of the revolution on the place of women in the power relations of Algeria. The husband states as follows: "I came to realise that they'd raped her *because they were looking for me*. In fact, it was to punish her for keeping silence that she'd been violated." "it was the rape of an obstinate woman, who was ready to put up with everything rather than sell her husband. And the husband in question, *it was me*. This woman had saved my life and had protected the organisation." (Fanon 1963 pgs. 257-258). The wife preserved the integrity of the revolutionary organisation and the life of the husband by choosing rape and the dishonour of it over her own honour and life. The husband is insisting that the revolutionary values of the wife abrogates the potency of the weapon of French rape against the victims and Algerian males and he is bound by his gratitude to his wife to recognise the revolutionary values and act upon it. He must then continue to be her husband and return to the guerrilla war as a fit and able combatant, but he continues to illustrate the power the male centred Algerian culture with women in a subservient position has over his worldview. The husband states: "for it must be said I've seen peasants drying the tears of their wives after having seen them raped under their very eyes. This left me very much shaken." "I've seen civilians willingly proposing marriage to a girl who was violated by the French soldiers, and who was with child by them. All this led me to reconsider the problem with my wife." (Fanon 1963 pg. 258). The husband holds the position that the war of liberation from French colonial domination involved the maintenance and restoration of the hegemony of the discourse of purdah to its pristine precolonial glory. He therefore laboured under the delusion that war with the French coloniser left the discourse of purdah on the ground inviolate, but the French coloniser attacked the discourse of purdah using it as a weapon against the Algerian resistance. The efficacy of this assault upon the male was clearly illustrated by the mental disorder of the husband arising from the rape of the wife where he became a less than effective soldier which brought the intervention of the command structure. The discourse of purdah was then the basis of male dominance which was under assault by the French strategy of total war demanding a counter strategy. One counter strategy came from the women of Algeria who insisted that the revolutionary war and its success cannot abide by the discourse of purdah, one instance of this strategy is the action of the wife where she undergoes multiple rapes rather than give up the struggle, thereby destroying her status as a fit and proper wife/female. The wife chose the revolution over her position as dictated by the discourse of purdah, then indicated to the husband that she was now a soiled, dishonoured woman and wife. There is then a power relation between revolutionary values and the strategy to expel the French colonial dominator and the discourse of purdah and the gender power relations it drives. The French assault on purdah, utilising the instrument of industrial rape, is generating a crisis of gender power relations and the women must lead the way in resolving this power relation in their favour and that of the revolution. The husband states: "If they'd tortured her or knocked out all her teeth or broken an arm I wouldn't have minded. But that thing-how can you forget a thing like that? And why did she have to tell me about it all?" (Fanon 1963 pg. 258). To protect her honour, the husband expected that the wife will do anything except being dishonoured for that was her duty to his stature as dominant male, even to be an informer against the revolution. With this reaction of the husband one expects that rape in Algeria utilised by the French was on an industrial scale and the only effective counter measure was devised by Algerian women.

Case No. 2

The Will to Homicide

The patient took no part in the revolutionary struggle against the French, lived in an area where there was a steady stream of guerrilla activity with the villagers openly giving aid and support to the guerrilla bands. The French in its anti-guerrilla strategy decided to destroy the village where the patient lived and kill the males of the village, as a result twenty-nine men were killed. The patient was one such man lined up to be shot was wounded, feigned death and subsequently survived. With his recovery the patient presented with an intense drive to homicide. The patient states: "God is with me...but he certainly isn't with those who are dead...I've hellish good luck...In life you've got to kill so as not to be killed...When I think that I knew nothing about all that business...There are some Frenchmen in our midst. They disguise themselves as Arabs. They've all got to be killed. Give me a machine gun. All these so-called Algerians are really Frenchmen...and they won't leave me alone." (Fanon 1963 pg. 261). The patient who tried his endeavour best to evade the war is deeply impacted by the war simply because he is an Algerian male, hence fit for extermination. He then survives the mass murder event and responds to it by exhibiting a will to homicide which cannot discern between friend and enemy, for the Shaitan is the Frenchman and he is occupying the bodies of Arabs, he has therefore to kill all of them, making him a mass murderer on an industrial scale or genocidal. This patient was then the creation of the total war to maintain the colonial domination of France and action that was the product of the drive to exterminate a portion of an inferior race that refuses to be pliant, servile and subservient as the motivator to embrace servility on a sustainable basis.

Case No.3

Tit for Tat Murder

The patient is a nineteen-year-old soldier of the Algerian revolutionary movement who states his experiences as follows: "I left the town where I had been a student to join the Maquis. After some months, I had news of my people. I learnt that my mother had been killed point-blank by a French soldier and two of my sisters had been taken to the soldiers' quarters. Up to now, I have had no news of what happened to them. I was terribly shaken by the death of my mother." "I was the only man in the family, and my sole ambition had always been to manage to do something to make life easier for my mother and my sisters." (Fanon 1963 pg. 263). The French killed his non-combatant mother and disappeared his two sisters which begs the question which he did not address, if the action was as a result of his membership in the Maquis. He failed in his duty assigned to him and accepted by him under the discourse of purdah as the result of the death of his father. The assault on the women of his family by the French had the desired effect as it impacted his ability and discipline as a member of a disciplined fighting unit. The patient continues: "One day we went to an estate belonging to settlers, where the agent, who was an active colonialist, had already killed two Algerian civilians. We came to his house, at night, but he wasn't there. Only his wife was at home." "We decided to wait for her husband. But as far as I was concerned, when I looked at that woman I thought of my mother." "I wondered why we didn't kill her," "She flung herself upon me screaming 'Please, don't kill me...I have children.' A moment after she was dead; I killed her with my knife." "After that this woman started coming every night and asking for my blood. But my mother's blood-where's that?" (Fanon 1963 pg. 263). The French killed his non-combatant mother but the Maquis refused to kill the non-combatant wife of the colonialist who had killed two Algerian civilians. He was then duty bound to avenge his mother and he seized the opportunity when it arose and did so contrary to the rules of engagement of the Maquis, cognisant of the possible punishment for his action. The woman he killed now visits him at night as a succubus but such is the price he must pay for avenging his mother's blood as the Maquis refused to do so or aid his bid to do so. The mental disorder he presents with in the aftermath of his action, is it preferable to death by firing squad at the hands of the Maquis?

Case No.4

The French interrogator and the Weapon of Torture

The patient is a French policeman assigned to an anti FLN brigade where he was assigned to interrogations at the police headquarters. The patient states: "Sometimes we almost wanted to tell them that if they had a bit of consideration for us they'd speak without forcing us to spend hours tearing information word by word out of them. But you might as well talk to the wall. To all the questions we asked they'd only say 'I don't know.' So of course, we have to go through with it. But they scream too much." (Fanon 1963 pg. 265). The dominated inferior race has no consideration for the dominant, superior race for they dare resist, to mount a revolution and for that impertinence they must be made to pay. In this specific instance they are sent a potent message of the price they will pay for rejecting servility to the white, dominant race by the ruthless application of a methodology of torture designed to destroy the recipient, not to collect information supposedly vital to the French war effort. The application of this methodology of the generation of pain results in the death of the victim, which is the end accepted as normal. This is the methodology applied in Vietnam by both the French and the Americans and in post September 2001 to another case of non-whites engaged in insurgency against the white North Atlantic hegemony. The patient continues: "Nowadays as soon as I hear someone shouting I can tell you exactly at what stage of the questioning we've got to. The chap who's had two blows of the fist and a belt of the baton behind his ear has a certain way of speaking, of shouting, and of saying he is innocent." (Fanon 1963 pg. 265). The first stage of the methodology of torture as related by the interrogator is the use of the fist and the baton. The next stage is an escalation of the violence where the tortured is hung by the wrists for two hours as follows: "After he's been left for two hours strung up by his wrists he has another kind of voice." (Fanon 1963 pg. 265). Followed by the bath and other stages but the most potent stage approaching the end of life and the end of the process is the application of electricity as follows: "But above all it's after the electricity that it becomes really too much. You'd say that the chap was going to die any minute." (Fanon pg. 265). To die at the end of the process was perfectly acceptable, as the need for and the application of the methodology of torture brought joy to the patient as he had no questions as to the efficacy and humanity of the process as it was not applied to humans just sub-humans, as in the case of post

September 2001. The interrogator states: "Of course there are some that don't scream; those are the tough ones. But they think they're going to be killed right away. But we're not interested in killing them. What we want is information. When're we are dealing with these tough ones, the first thing we do is make them squeal; and sooner or later we manage it. That's already a victory. Afterward we go on. Mind you, we'd like to avoid that. But they don't make things easy for us." (Fanon pgs. 265-266). There is then greater elation, joy, pleasure and the assertion of white, male superiority and dominance over the sub-human by torturing and breaking the tough ones, regardless of the failure to extract information and the murder of the victim. The French torturer at that specific instance, in a special place of impunity, is an amoral, sociopath in the service of French colonial domination of Algeria. To break the tough ones, even if it results in their death, is the most desired accomplishment in this asocial space where you blame the victim for his death as all sociopaths do, for impunity allows this. The patient is now presenting with memory retention of the screams of his victims, especially when at home, as he is bringing his work in the space of impunity home as follows: "Now I've come so as I hear their screams even when I'm at home. Especially the screams of the ones who died at police headquarters. Doctor, I am fed up with this job. And if you manage to cure me, I'll ask to be transferred to France. If they refuse, I'll resign." (Fanon 1963 pg. 266). The patient wants then to be cured from his mental disorder by Fanon in order to carry on with his work of being a policeman. He can be cured and redeployed to other anti-FLN activities which all feed into search, seizure, torture and murder as what he was involved in before being transferred to the torture chamber. Fanon speaks of the event at the hospital where he worked, where the patient encountered an Algerian whom he 'interrogated' at the police headquarters who was also under treatment at the hospital because of this interrogation. The patient insisted that his anxiety attack was the result of seeing his victim at the hospital, whilst Fanon determined that the Algerian victim of torture at the hands of Fanon's patient, on seeing his torturer fled to a toilet where he was trying to commit suicide as he was convinced that his torturer was in the hospital to arrest him and return him to the torture chamber. The torturer had returned to finish the job. The impact of the methodology of torture on the victim, when compared to the impact on the torturer, illustrates the potency of this assault on destroying the lives of those who escape death at the hands of the torturer, as the staff of the hospital resorted to lies to convince the victim that the torturer was never in the hospital, this was an illusion of his. Whilst Fanon reports the marked improvement of his patient and his return to France on medical grounds, he describes the Algerian victim of his patient as an Algerian patriot. A patriot who paid a grave price for being a patriot.

Case No.5

A European Torturer who brought his Work Home

A police inspector married with three children voluntarily came to Fanon seeking his help. The patient was a torturer and was disposed to bring his work home by unleashing violence on his wife and three children including his twenty months old child. The patient states: "But there is a war going on in Algeria, and when they wake up to it it'll be too late. The thing that kills me the most is the torture. You don't know what that is, do you. Sometimes I torture people for ten hours at a stretch..." "You may not realise, but it's very tiring...It's true we take it in turns, but the question is to know when to let the next chap have a go. Each one thinks he's going to get the information at any minute and takes good care not to let the bird go to the next chap after he's softened him up nicely, when of course the other chap would get the honour and glory of it." (Fanon 1963 pg. 268). There is a war waging in Algeria between the Algerian liberation movement and France, with the patient on the frontline of this war as he is a torturer on an industrial scale seeking to break the back of the Algerian rebellion. But the action of torture is a personal pursuit of fame, glory and power through the extraction of strategic information from the victim by any means necessary. The torturers in the torture chambers are then caught up in a power relation towards power, dominance, fame and glory, to the detriment of the victim for they are subhuman meat holding strategic information, the extraction of which by any means necessary is the name of the game. Torture is then necessary but very tiring, for it's a competitive white male sport driven by self-interest and testosterone, simply barbarity on steroids. The patient continues: "Sometimes we even offer the chap money, out of our own pockets, to try to get him to talk. Our problem is as follows: are you able to make this fellow talk? You see you're competing with the others." "in fact, you have to be intelligent to make a success of that sort of work. You have to have a flair for it." "Above all, what you mustn't do is to give the chap the impression that he won't get away alive from you. He must go on hoping; hope's the thing that'll make him talk." (Fanon 1963 pgs. 268-269). The patient prides himself on being a proficient, scientific torturer as he administers enough pain to convince the victim that he is willing and able to continue the process for some considerable time, deliberately denying the relief death brings to the victim. The victim then clings to the hope of life purchased at the cost of informing where a choice has then to be made: life in exchange for information. Fanon comments that the patient expected Fanon to cure his current propensity to violence external of the torture chamber of impunity in order that the patient self-actualise his chosen calling to be a professional torturer of utmost lucidity and efficiency, capable of making the journey through zones of transition outside of the torture chamber, free from the behaviour pattern of the chamber of impunity. The patient needed Fanon to enable his quest to fully compartmentalise his daily reality by developing multiple consciousness and worldviews that will serve each compartment. The patient wanted Fanon to aid him in becoming a well-adjusted, cunning, flexible, multi-faceted predator as Ted Bundy. Fanon states: "This man knew perfectly well that his disorders were directly caused by the kind of activity that went on inside the rooms where interrogations were carried out, even though he tried to throw the responsibility totally upon 'present troubles.' As he could not see his way to stopping torturing people (that made nonsense to him for in that case he would have to resign) he asked me without beating about the bush to help him go on torturing Algerian patriots without any prickling of conscience, without any behaviour problems and with complete equanimity." (Fanon 1963 pgs. 269-270). The mental disorders of the patient are then a signal of his weakness, his less than perfect suitability, to his beloved vocation of scientifically applying torture to gather strategically vital information to wage war on the Algerian insurgency. Fanon was then sought out to privately and in secret work towards perfecting the scientific torturing machine, for that is the end prized and sought by the patient, simply remorseless barbarity without personal impact. The patient sought Fanon's help to evolve into the quintessential sociopath, asocial predator. What is clearly apparent in the case of the torturers is the worldview where the Algerians are to blame for whatever acts of barbarity unleashed by the French on them. The Algerians are expected to accept French domination with servility and subservience without a desire for freedom and self-determination. This position is the product of the white supremacist North Atlantic discourse of white entitlement, privilege and manifest destiny where they insist that they have the right to supremacy and are above the blowback, and will not accept responsibility for the blowback from their imperialist actions taken in the world. This position is especially articulated in the politics of the North Atlantic in the 21st century as it is at the core of the mainstream political discourse masked as "populist" of white supremacy mechanised and instrumentalised via fascist and national socialist structures of power relations. This 21st century manifestation makes it clear that the white race has the right to plunder and dominate the non-white races, but will not accept any form of blowback from this white supremacist imperialism from impacting the white fatherlands of the North Atlantic. This white racist fear of a black North Atlantic is now summed up with all its imagery in the non-white migrant hordes besieging and threatening to inundate and defile the white fatherland, and is now expressed via a mainstream political discourse of the white North Atlantic whose political intent is to intensify this fear to the point of motivating political action within the political mainstream. The threat implied is the inability of the political mainstream to control this dynamic once unleashed in the political mainstream.

Series B

Fanon now presents the cases of Series B which comprise mental disorders arising from the manner in which the total war in Algeria was pursued.

Case No. 1

Two young Algerians, thirteen and fourteen years old respectively murdered their European playmate.

The thirteen-year old boy in his conversation with Fanon states: "We weren't a bit cross with him. He was a good friend of ours. One day we decided to kill him, because the Europeans want to kill all the Arabs. We can't kill big people. But we can kill ones like him, because he was the same age as us." (Fanon 1963 pgs. 270-271). There was no personal animosity between the two Algerian boys and the European boy save and except the visualisation of a great existential battle being waged between two races, where the European is intent on exterminating the Arabs. The European boy had to die as he in himself represented the potent threat his race posed to the two Algerian boys. The two boys must make their contribution to saving their race from white genocide by murdering a boy they were capable of killing. The issue was their capacity to kill white people not their willingness to kill white people. The conversation continues: "We didn't know how to kill him. So we got the knife from home and we killed him." (Fanon 1963 pg. 271). They then settled on the use of a knife as the methodology of murder as they will be sure he was dead and the knife was available in their homes. In response to Fanon's question as to why they picked the victim the perpetrator stated: "Because he used to play with us. Another boy wouldn't have gone up the hill with us." (Fanon 1963 pg. 271). The will to kill the European boy arose and was facilitated by the willingness of the European boy to consider both Algerian boys as friends, unlike the other European boys in the area. Fanon indicates to the boy that he killed his friend who replies as follows: "Well then, why do they want to kill us? His father is in the militia and he said we ought to have our throats cut." Fanon replies: "But he didn't say anything to you? The boy replied: "Him? No." (Fanon 1963 pg. 271). The problem with the European boy was his race and what it represented to the Algerian boys, as the boy in himself presented no threat to the boys. Hence the reference to the boy's father and the threat he posed to both Algerian boys. The Algerian boy indicated to Fanon that he did kill the European boy, he had no regrets for his action and accepts his punishment. He has then made his contribution to the protection of the Algerian from the assault of the French. Fanon in his conversation with the fourteen-year old reported that when asked why did he kill, the fourteen year old failed to answer the question by asking Fanon the question if he had ever seen a European arrested and imprisoned after the murder of an Algerian. Fanon replied in the negative to which the boy stated: "And yet there are Algerians killed every day, aren't there?" (Fanon 1963 pg. 272). In response to Fanon's question of why he killed the European boy the fourteen-year old states: "I'll tell you why. You've heard tell of the Rivet business? Two of my family were killed then. At home, they said that the French had sworn to kill us all, one after the other. And did they arrest a single Frenchman for all those Algerians who were killed? Well, nobody at all was arrested. I wanted to take to the mountains, but I was too young. So X—-and I said we'd kill a European." (Fanon 1963 pg. 272). The fourteen-year old boy is seeking revenge for what was done to his family at Rivet but he was too young to be accepted in the resistance intensifying the literal drive to revenge, the shedding of European blood. The young European boy was then the sacrificial lamb that presented himself as the soft target which was gladly exploited by both boys. When asked by Fanon the following questions the fourteen years old replies as follows: "Boy: "in your opinion, what should we have done?" Fanon: "I don't know. But you are a child and what is happening concerns grown-up people." Boy: "But they kill children too..." Fanon: "That is no reason for killing your friend." Boy: "Well, kill him I did. Now you can do what you like." Fanon: "Had your fiend done anything to harm you?" Boy: "Not a thing." Fanon: "Well?" Boy: Well, there you are..." (Fanon 1963 pg. 272). Both boys, especially the elder, show the train of thought typical to a young teenage killer arising from a developing brain and personality, gravely impacted by the methodology of a totalist war being waged to preserve French colonial domination and the response from the Algerian liberation movement.

Case No. 2

Psychotic Break, Manhood and Personal Choice

The male individual completely devoted his life from age nineteen to perfect his skills as a multi-copying machine technician of the highest order. This was his sole concern and vocation as he severed his personal ties devoting himself to perfecting his craft. His immersion in his quest for excellence meant that with the outbreak of the struggle for liberation from French domination he showed no interest in the cause. Sometime in 1955 he framed the opinion that his parents considered him a traitor for evading the national cause for liberation. In response to this opinion he severed all ties with his parents retreating to the room in the house he shared with them. One day in the streets the psychotic break enveloped him as he heard a voice calling him a coward but there was no one in the street. In response he locked himself up in his room and abandoned his prized job and his quest. The psychotic break repeated in the room much worse than in the street and in response he stopped eating. The accusatory voice stated: "Traitor, traitor, coward…all your brothers who are dying…traitor, traitor." (Fanon 1963 pg. 274). On the fourth day of his psychotic break he left home and walked straight to European town seeking to be arrested by the French and face the full brunt of their war machinery. But he entered and walked the streets of European town undisturbed, as he apparently was seen as European by the French security structure, and this worsened his condition as he now saw contempt for him in the eyes of the Algerians under scrutiny of the French security, whilst he walked freely in European town. He then encountered some soldiers armed with machine guns outside of the French Staff headquarters and attacked one soldier attempting to seize his machine gun whilst shouting "I am Algerian." (Fanon 1963 pg. 275). He was subdued and subjected to days of torture until he was deemed mentally unfit by the French interrogators and sent for expert analysis. The patient states; "All I wanted to do," he said, "was to die. Even at the police barracks I thought and hoped that after they'd tortured me they would kill me. I was glad to be struck, for that showed me that they considered that I too was their enemy. I could no longer go on hearing the accusing voice, without doing something. I am not a coward. I am not a woman. I am not a traitor." (Fanon 1963 pg. 275). The quest for perfection is measured by the yardstick of commitment expected from the Algerian male to national liberation. To choose the quest for perfection over commitment to national liberation questions your manliness, your fitness to be male, to be dominant over females therefore all that signals manhood, cojones as big as a bull. To choose the quest for perfection illustrates cowardice, traitor and less than man, a woman, a bitch. The patient had then to affirm his manhood, manliness and revoke his bitchhood by seeking and inviting death at the hands of the French. A totalist war in defence of colonial domination opposed by a war of liberation that tore apart the fabric of the colonial social order, from which the change or the maelstrom could have emerged, or a mixture of both.

Case No. 3

Torture, Alienation and Anxiety

A twenty-one year old French woman came to Fanon seeking help presented with symptoms of anxiety complex which impacted her studies and her social relationships. In her statement to Fanon she reveals the situation she found herself in which contributed to her anxiety complex. The patient states: "My father was highly placed in the civil service. As soon as the troubles started, he threw himself into the Algerian manhunt with frenzied rage. I saw without being able to do anything about it the slow metamorphosis of my father. The fact was that every time I went home I spent entire nights awake, for screams used to rise up to my room from down below; in the cellar and in the unused rooms of the house Algerians were being tortured so as to obtain information." (Fanon 1963 pg. 276). The patient has witnessed the impact of the French war against the Algerian liberation movement on her father as he became transformed from a civil servant to a torturer, utilising his home as the torture chamber. The patient is impacted further by the actual torture sessions carried out at her home and the sounds of the victims she heard from the cellar and unused rooms of the house. The patient was then sharing a home with her father the torturer, other torturers, the victims and the torture chambers all under the management of her father. The patient continues: "You have no idea how terrible it is to hear screaming all night like that. Sometimes I used to wonder how it was that a human being was able to bear hearing those screams of pain-quite apart from the actual torture. And so it went on. Finally, I didn't ever go home." (Fanon 1963 pg. 276). The acts of torture impacted the patient and her relationship with her father, in response she stayed away from the home she shared with her father and the torture chambers where in fact she became estranged from her father. The patient states: "The rare times my father came to see me in town I wasn't able to look him in the face without being terribly frightened and embarrassed. I found it increasingly difficult to force myself to kiss him." (Fanon 1963 pgs. 276-277). In fact, the patient was alienated from her father and from the people of the village she grew up with as a result of her father waging war on these villagers. Her father had then alienated her from himself and the villagers she grew up with and considered part of her comfort zone. The patient states: "For you must understand that I had lived a long time in the village. I knew almost all the families that lived there. Every time I went home my father told me that fresh people had been arrested. In the end I didn't dare walk in the street any more, I was so sure of meeting hatred everywhere. In my heart I knew that those Algerians were right. If I were an Algerian girl, I'd be in the Maquis." (Fanon 1963 pg. 277). The patient now expected to be a victim in the streets of the village given the assault on the villagers by the structure under her father's command. Alienated from her father and comfort zones of her childhood the patient comes to the position that the only resort of the Algerian is resistance. The patient received word that her father, along with the military detachment he attached himself to, was injured in an ambush by the Algerian resistance and subsequently died. The patient now speaks of her father's funeral as follows: "There wasn't a single person who didn't know that my father had the whip hand of all the interrogation centres in the whole region. Everyone knew that the number of deaths under torture reached ten a day, and there they came to tell their lies about my father's devotion, his self-sacrifice, his love for his country, and so on. I ought to say that now such words have no meaning for me, or at any rate hardly any." (Fanon 1963 pg. 277). The patient insists that the officials who spoke at her father's funeral all uttered lies of praise for her father such as his devotion, his self-sacrifice and patriotism for her father's true legacy was the number of persons who died per day at the hands of the torturers of some ten per day. But for the officials her father's record was pristine, one to be emulated which potently exhibited his devotion to duty to France. To the cause of preserving French colonial domination of Algeria her father's "high moral qualities conquered the native population." (Fanon 1963 pg. 277). It is then morally necessary to do all that is possible to conquer the Algerian people, making torture then morally necessary in the colonies, even though illegal in the North Atlantic, hence the offshore US torture sites in response to the attacks of September 2001.

Case No. 4

War, Children of Algeria and PTSD

In Case No. 4 Fanon is presenting an analysis of the disorders of children of Algeria who were refugees, the children of fighting men or orphans of civilians killed by the French sent to live at various centres in Tunisia and Morocco. These children were displaced as a result of the war and bore the marks of the war on their bodies and their psyche. Fanon lists the following characteristics of these children's behaviour as follows: "a) In each of these different children there exists a very marked love for parental images." "b) These children are very much affected when they are scolded. They have a great thirst for peace and for affection." "c) Many of them suffer from sleeplessness and also from sleepwalking." "d) periodical enuresis/ bedwetting." "e) Sadistic tendencies. They quarrel frequently among themselves despite a deep fundamental affection." (Fanon 1963 pg. 278). Fanon is describing what is termed today Post Traumatic Stress Disorder (PTSD) which is the product of deep, impactful trauma which results in deeply troubled humans with a propensity for self-harm and /or acts of violence against others. This PTSD is the product of the war of colonial domination of the liberation movement, which scars the victims of the methodology of warfare adopted. PTSD is today part of the daily life of those of us who live in the Third World, which is the result of the collapse of the independence postcolonial project.

Case No. 5

This is the final case Fanon presents for Series B which deals with mental disorders of Algerian refugee women before or after childbirth. Fanon states: "This name puerperal psychoses is the name given to mental disorders which occur in women around childbirth." (Fanon 1963 pg. 278). Fanon indicates that some 300,000 refugees have fled to the Morocco-Tunisia borders constituting a humanitarian catastrophe as they are living in subhuman conditions plagued with malnutrition, illnesses, improper shelter and water supplies. This flow of internally displaced Algerians is the direct result of the terror unleashed by the French on the civilian population to force them out of areas where the resistance is active through a scorched earth methodology of counter insurgency. A strategy used by the white North Atlantic throughout the colonial and neo-colonial worlds as Vietnam, Malaysia, Kenya, Aden, Angola, Mozambique and others, with Yemen today being the prime example of genocide as the counter insurgency instrument to settle a sectarian war. Added to the inhumane subhuman living conditions of the refugee camps Fanon speaks to the insecurity of the camps as follows: "The atmosphere of permanent insecurity in which the refuges exist is kept up by frequent invasions of French troops, applying 'the right of following and pursuit,' bombardment from the air, machine-gunnings "To tell the truth there are very few Algerian women who give birth in such conditions who do not suffer from mental disorders." (Fanon 1963 pg. 279). Algerian women are giving birth in conditions of intense peril to themselves, their infants and the survival of both mother and child. This environment is the product of war on civilians/non-combatants, combined with famine, which amounted to war induced genocide as a methodology of war common to white North Atlantic imperialist action in the colonial and then the neo-colonial world to this day in the 21st century, as in Yemen. This existential reality is indicated by the nature of the delusions afflicting these refugee mothers. Fanon states: "In the same way the form which the delusions take are many and diverse. We may find a delusion of persecution against the French who want to kill the new-born infant or the child not yet born; or else the mother may have the impression of imminent death, in which the mothers implore invisible executioners to spare their child." (Fanon 1963 pg. 279). It is obvious that these delusions are plausible expectations of actions on the part of the French that are highly probable and possible given the existential reality the child was born into. Fanon ends this case with the position that he was, amongst other practitioners, called upon to intervene into the life of pregnant women and mothers of new-born infants in an existential reality that assaulted the life chances of both mother and child. Fanon states: "The circumstances of the cured patients maintain and feeds these pathological kinks." (Fanon 1963 pg. 279). How can you effect cures when the existential conditions drive the pathology, which points to the need for drastic change to the existential conditions, which necessitates victory over the French colonial overlord for there is no guarantee that surrender to the French will end the assault?

Series C.

In Series C Fanon presents the impact of torture on the victims. Fanon states: "In this series we will group together patients to a fairly serious condition whose disorders appeared immediately after or during the tortures." "we realise that the characteristic morbidity groups correspond to different methods of torture employed, quite independently of its evil effects, whether hidden or glaring upon the personality." (Fanon 1963 pg. 280). Disorders arise from torture but the morbidity produced as a result of torture varies with methods of torture employed, which means that there are methods of torture that wreak havoc on the human body and psyche which make recovery very problematic presenting a grave burden for the victim to bear through the rest of her/his life.

Category No. 1

Specific Methods of Torture

Fanon states: "We here refer to brutal methods which are directed towards getting prisoners to speak, rather than to actual torture. The principle that over and above a certain threshold pain becomes intolerable here takes on singular importance. The aim is to arrive at quickly as possible that threshold." (Fanon 1963 pg. 280). This category consists of brutal methods of torture that maximises the exertion of pain to the recipient in order to break their resolve quickly, for white North Atlantic torture is defined and driven by a discourse of the ontology of man, which insists that human resolve can be broken with the application of the necessary volume of pain at a given time. The North Atlantic Enlightenment has then spawned a discursive science of torture with its methodology of application perfected under colonial domination, with the original laboratory being the enterprise of First Peoples and African enslavement. This discourse of torture of non-white sub humans was reconstructed and re-released/ reissued post 9/ 11. Fanon continues: "Certain methods of torture used in Algeria seemed to us to be particularly atrocious; the confidence of those who had been tortured are our reference." (Fanon 1963 pg. 280). The French colonial apparatus then unleashed in Algeria in defence of its colonial hegemony a regime of torture that was premised on seeking the greatest output with the highest application of pain in the shortest possible time frame. French colonial torture in Algeria eclipsed that of the Gestapo of Nazi Germany illustrating the inherently fascist basis of colonial domination. The methods of torture listed by Fanon are as follows: "a) Injection of water by the mouth accompanied by an enema of soapy water given at high pressure." "b) Introduction of a bottle into the anus." Both forms/styles of torture that follow Fanon terms "motionless torture" where the victim is mercilessly beaten for moving whilst being forced into a physical position the mechanics of which forces movement. The intent of this is the battle between the victim and gravity, physical fatigue and weakness driven by the ever present expectation of blows and the pain derived from for moving. This is physical, mental and emotional torture all rolled up into an episode of great and grave stress. Fanon states: "c) The prisoner is placed on his knees, with his arms parallel to the ground, the palms of his hand turned upward, his torso and head straight. No movement is allowed. Behind the prisoner a policeman sitting on a chair keeps him motionless by blows of his truncheon." "d) The prisoner is placed standing with his face to the wall, his arms lifted and against the wall." (Fanon 1963 pgs. 280-281). As in the case of c) with d) any movement is punished with blows raining down on the victim with his face to the wall which means he cannot see when the blows will commence or are on their way which potently illustrates your powerlessness. Sensory deprivation in the face of an imminent threat is the boost to the effectiveness of the blows which unhinges the psyche of the victim. It is simply a snuff movie that you are starring in. Fanon indicates that in his experience in Algeria you must distinguish amongst torture victims between those who knew something of value and those who knew nothing. Fanon states that those who knew something and survived the torture session/s very rarely become patients of the hospitals. The significant number of persons presenting themselves for consults at the hospitals belong to those who knew nothing and were not members of any organisation. The non-combatants who were of little intelligence value, picked up in sweeps by the French colonial security structure and tortured, were the dominant group of persons seeking consultations at the hospitals. This reality illustrates the manner in which especially the Algerian resistance prosecuted the war against French colonial domination and the manner of response by the French colonial overlord where the strategy insisted that all Algerians will be punished for embracing revolt.

Symptoms arising from these methods

Fanon now presents the symptoms presented by psychiatric cases arising from the methods of torture of category 1. Fanon states: "a) Agitated nervous depression: four cases." "They are depressed and spend most of their time in bed; they shun contact, and are liable to suddenly show signs of very violent agitation the significance is always difficult to grasp." "b) Loss of appetite arising from mental causes: five cases. These patients present serious problems, for every mental anorexia is accompanied by a phobia against all physical contact with another." "c) Motor instability: eleven cases. Here we have to deal with patients who will not keep still. They insist on being alone" (Fanon 1963 pg. 282). The symptoms of the damage done to victims of French methods of torture in Algeria indicate the potency of these methods of torture to deconstruct the psyche of the victim, literally leaving it shattered in the aftermath where surviving the event creates a new crisis of daily life and quality of life. Fanon points out that two positions are common to victim of torture in category 1. These are: "First that of suffering *injustice*. Being tortured night and day for nothing seemed to have broken something in these men." (Fanon 1963 pg. 282). This is the response of men tortured, even in spite of having nothing of use to the French, they then feel powerless and understand their powerlessness which drives the position of injustice. What these victims fail to accept is their powerlessness demanded their torture, for the instrument of war must not and cannot be selective in its application, for the target is all Arabs. Fanon continues: "Secondly, there was *indifference to all moral arguments*. For these patients, there is no just cause." (Fanon 1963 pg. 283). The victims of the torture are insisting that they want no words of a moral argument on the justness of their cause what they want is revenge, the application of force to the perpetrators that traumatised them, a barbarous force that purges their soul of the pain of powerlessness, even though vicarious.

Category No. 2

Torture by Electricity

In this category Fanon placed Algerian patriots tortured by electricity who survived the event. In the cases Fanon encountered he discovered two common outcomes of these cases. Fanon states: "a) Localised or generalised coenesthopathies" three cases. These patients felt 'pins and needles' throughout their bodies; their hands seemed to be torn off, their heads seemed to be bursting, and their tongues felt as if they were being swallowed." "b) Apathy, aboulia, and lack of interest: seven cases. There are patients who are inert, who cannot make plans, who have no resources, who lives from day to day." "c) Electricity phobia. Fear of touching a switch, of turning on the radio, fear of the telephone." (Fanon 1963 pg. 283). A method of torture that targeted those who were considered to be likely operatives of the Algerian liberation movement clearly shows its potency in deconstructing the human psyche with telling after effects which highlights the reason for its unleashing.

Category No. 3

The Impact of Truth Serum

In this category Fanon presents the issues that arise with the application of pentothal to persons who are under arrest for the purpose of extracting information vital to the French war effort against the Algerian war of liberation. These are persons in receipt of pentothal who are not presenting with mental disorders under medical guidance, but persons who under arrest are being administered pentothal under medical guidance for the express purpose of extraction of information. On the medical efficacy of pentothal administered under medical supervision Fanon states: "It has been generally observed that it is difficult to control the progressive disintegration of physical processes when using this method. Very often a spectacular worsening of the illness was observed, or new and quite inexplicable symptoms appeared. Thus, generally speaking, this technique has been more or less abandoned." (Fanon 1963 pg. 284). Pentothal administered essentially deconstructs the psyche of the patient, essentially expressed via the physical processes of the patient's body which both worsened the original symptoms and even stimulates the development of new symptoms. To utilise pentothal to extract information from an individual is then an exercise in which the only certain outcome is the destruction of the interrogated, which questions the accuracy of any information collected. On the culpability of French medical operatives in this Algerian scenario, Fanon states: "In Algeria, military doctors and psychiatrists have found a wide field for experiment in police quarters." "it ought equally in the case of Algerian patriots to serve to break down the political barrier and make confession easier for the prisoner without having recourse to electricity; medical tradition lays down that suffering should be avoided. This is the medical form that 'subversive war' takes." (Fanon 1963 pg. 284). The French medical structure justifies the application of pentothal, in spite of its deleterious effects on the recipient, for the express purpose of experimentation to perfect the necessary and efficacious chemical means by which to extract vital information from the enemy. The quest for effective non-physical torture is then simply a discursive construct, utilised in the quest for the hegemony of medical science and its structure over information extraction in the subversive war against the Algerian war of liberation.

The Pentothal Effect

Fanon now lists the symptoms exhibited by the recipients of pentothal under interrogation as follows: "a) Verbal stereotypy: The patient continually repeats sentences of the type of 'I didn't tell them anything. You must believe me; I didn't talk.' Such stereotypes are accompanied by a permanent anxiety state." (Fanon 1963 pg. 285). The recipient has a grave fear of what she/he disclosed under intoxication and the assault on the movement that will result from her/his disclosure which generates the repeated statement of tenacity under assault and a state of permanent anxiety. Fanon states: "The sense of culpability toward the cause he was fighting for and his brothers in arms whose names and addresses he may have given here weighs so heavily as to be dramatic. No assurance can bring peace to these broken consciences.") (Fanon 1963 pg. 285). The guilt arising from the vent where the intoxicated is convinced that she/he did inform the French of vital information that should not have been disclosed. The victim becomes guilt expressed via a state of permanent anxiety in spite of the reality of her/his interrogation, which destroys their functionality as a human in a social order which can end in suicide or self-hurt. Fanon continues: "b) Intellectual or sensory perception clouded. The patient cannot affirm the existence of a given visible object. There is a fundamental inability to distinguish between true and false. Everything is true and everything is false at the same time." (Fanon 1963 pg. 285). The ability to perceive and affirm the existence of a given object is non-functional which is driven by the inability to distinguish between true and false which stems from the ravages of the drug administered and the post administration power relations. Again the recipient is rendered non-functional in a social order. Fanon continues: "c) Fear, amounting to phobia, of all private conversations. This fear is derived from the acute impression that at any moment a fresh interrogation may take place." (Fanon 1963 pg. 285). A phobia results after pentothal ingestion, driven by a fear of private conversations, for these are the basis for being grabbed again and another ingestion of pentothal. There is then a crippling fear of a second ingestion and the only means to evade this is by shutting your mouth, silence and withdrawal from personal contact with the perfect solution being suicide. Fanon continues: "d) Inhibition. From this comes the impression of a quasi-inhibition, with physical slowing down, interrupted sentences, repetition, and faltering, etc." (Fanon 1963 pg. 285). The survivor of interrogation via pentothal is very deliberate in what they speak and in how they interpret what others say to them where the entire process is slowed down, repetitious, faltering and inhibited arising from the course of the interrogation where your words uttered haunt you as a legacy does. The effects noted by Fanon of pentothal on the individual interrogated all add up to an individual whose ability to function normally in a social order is severely impaired, if not destroyed. This is a legacy of the colonial domination of Algeria that survived the French defeat, just as the legacy of the US invasion of Iraq survives in the expression of the Islamic State and the torture unleashed on some of its key leaders under US hegemony of Iraq. Torture does breed sociopaths which are unleashed on the neo-colonial world in the 21st century with the repeat of colonial methodology of the subversive war.

Category No. 4

The strategy of Brainwashing

Fanon indicates that there are two centres of torture by brainwashing in Algeria and he is simply interested in presenting the psychiatric effects of both centres. These two centres are: for intellectuals and for non-intellectuals.

Alienating the Intellectuals through Brainwashing

The prisoner is pressured to play a part, in fact a role defined by the French script, of a game to undermine the will of the intellectual and those of his audience utilising a school of psycho-sociology applied to the power relations of factories in the US. The prisoner is then called upon to dispense a specific discourse which is an assault on the discourse of the Algerian revolution. The discursive constructs are as follows: "a) Playing the game of collaboration. The intellectual is invited to collaborate and at the same time reasons for collaboration are brought forward. He is thus obliged to lead a double life: he is man well known for his patriotism who is imprisoned for preventative reasons." (Fanon 1963 pg. 286). The intellectual is a prisoner in preventive imprisonment the reason for being obvious, his support of the Algerian revolution. He is then faced with a choice between the preservation of himself or destruction by torture, but the only path to salvation is by becoming an active double agent for the French. Which is in fact no effective choice for he is the loser under all possible and probable outcomes arising from his actions. "b) Making public statements on the value of the French heritage and on the merits of colonisation." "c) Taking the arguments for the Algerian revolution and overthrowing them one by one." "d) Leading a totally pathological communal life." (Fanon 1963 pg. 287). Fanon cites one case where a person with a university education was interned and subjected to brainwashing for months on end. Eventually he was released by the French and he was convinced that he had successfully played the game with the French and sought to reconstruct his life especially his activity in the war of liberation. At the point where he re-established contact with the leaders of the war he previously dealt with his certainty collapsed replaced with guilt. Fanon states: "Where would the game end? Here once again we had to reassure the patient, and to free him from the burden of guilt." (Fanon 1963 pg. 288).

Symptoms of Brainwashing

"a) Phobia of all collective discussion." (Fanon 1963 pg. 288). The victim has a phobia of speaking in the company of three or more people premised on mistrust and reticence. "b) The impossibility of explaining and defending any given position." (Fanon 1963 pg. 288). Everything affirmed can and will be denied at the same instant with the same conviction applied to each instance. Fanon states: "This is certainly the most painful sequel that we encountered in this war. An obsessional personality is the fruit of the 'psychological action' used in the service of colonialism in France." (Fanon 1963 pg. 288). This then was the use of North Atlantic psychological action to destroy the credibility of chosen intellectuals with the war of liberation and the masses and to marginalise these intellectuals from the war of liberation and themselves, in other words to apply psychological action, North Atlantic scientific medical discourse, for the express purpose of destroying these individuals burdened with guilt and fear expressed via the obsessional personality, phobia and other indications of the fact that these individuals are now alienated from their selves. This methodology of incapacitation was utilised in stark contrast to that of torture, with the very same intent, but an entirely different methodology thereby expanding the reservoir of knowledge of the white North Atlantic in disarming the Arab threat posed to the hegemony of the white North Atlantic. In the aftermath of 9/11 the Arab threat became an Islamic/Arab threat, thereby bringing this reservoir of scientific, Western medical knowledge into play once again.

Torture as Brainwashing the non-intellectuals

Those classified by the French colonial overlords as non-intellectuals but in need of brainwashing as they are active in the war of liberation are seized and a torrent of torture unleashed on their bodies in the attempt to break their resistance. To discontinue torture and to eat you must comply, which then becomes a game of power between the French and the Algerians seized and tortured. Fanon states: "On the contrary, the body is dealt with: it is broken in the hope that national consciousness will thus be demolished. It is a thorough breaking in." (Fanon 1963 pg. 289). On the mental disorders of this group Fanon states: "Here, the disorders met with are not serious. It is the painful, suffering body that calls for rest and peace." (Fanon 1963 pg. 289). The body needs to be healed, but what of hate and the quest for revenge arising from this brutal experience, seen in its use in offshore torture sites where those identified as Islamic extremists are held and subjected to this brutal regime of torture as the means to brainwashing and then released or escape. The North Atlantic playbook in the 21st century remains the same as it was under the colonial era, what they boast of now is their advances in the scientific application of pain, for that is all they can boast of.

Series D

Psychosomatic Disorders of Algeria

In Series D Fanon presents the most potent ideas of this section of "Wretched of the Earth" where he is in fact discrediting North Atlantic medical scientific discourse at the very level of the idea, illustrating the need for an alternate non-Western discourse of medicine which is specifically efficacious to our reality. Fanon states: "A marked increase in mental disorders and the creation of conditions favourable to the development of specific morbid phenomena are not the only consequences of the colonial war in Algeria." (Fanon 1963 pg. 289). Mental disorders and specific morbid phenomena are not the only products of the war in Algeria. Fanon insists that there is a pathology of atmosphere which is giving rise to a specific morbidity that he has included in Series D. Fanon states: "Quite apart from the pathology of torture there flourishes in Algeria a pathology of atmosphere," "We propose to group together in this fourth series the illnesses met with among Algerians, some of whom were interned in concentration camps. the main characteristics of these illnesses is that they are of the psychosomatic type." (Fanon 1963 pgs. 289-290). This pathology of atmosphere is the threat perceived by Algerians that arise from the war in Algeria where the Algerian moves to devise a survival strategy, a coping mechanism which embraces a psychosomatic disorder. Fanon continues: "This pathology is considered as a means whereby the organism responds to, in other words, adapts itself to, the conflict it is faced with, the disorder being at the same time a symptom and a cure. The organism in fact chooses the lesser evil in order to avoid catastrophe." (Fanon 1963 pg. 290). Faced with the perceived, potent threat to life the Algerian chooses a solution that supposedly assures survival but the solution is a pathology, and this pathology is the only viable coping mechanism available in the terrain of the war against Algerian liberation because Algeria is under French colonial domination. French colonial domination of Algeria and the totalist war it is waging to ensure its hegemony over Algeria posits only a pathology as a survival solution to Algerians. But the solution offered incapacitates those who accept and apply it as a solution. You then develop symptoms of illnesses which are manifested in the brain, in psychic processes, not in the organic basis of the functioning human body. These psychosomatic disorders are of especial importance to the task of presenting the impact of colonial domination on the native and the impact of the methodology of the war against Algerian liberation now impacts the colonised Algerian even further.

Algerian Psychosomatic Pathology Arising from French Colonial Domination

Fanon now insists that there is a specific group of pathologies presented which arise solely in the context of Algeria under French colonial domination and must therefore be explained within the specificity of colonial domination of Algeria. Fanon states: "Like all other wars, the Algerian war has created its contingent of cortico-visceral illnesses. With the exception of Group G described below, all the disorders met with in Algeria have already been described during the course of 'traditional wars.' Group G seems to be specific to the colonial war in Algeria." (Fanon 1963 pgs. 290-291). Fanon insists that all of the psychosomatic pathologies are common to traditional wars save and except the home grown pathology constituted by colonial domination in Algeria. This uniquely colonial Algerian pathology has then to be studied via an alternate discourse as there are grave falsities with the version produced by French colonial medical discourse. Fanon states: "This particular form of pathology (a generalised muscular contraction) had already called forth attention before the revolution began. But the doctors described it by portraying it as a congenital stigma of the native, an 'original' part of his nervous system where," (Fanon 1963 pg. 291). This Group G pathology which manifested itself in colonial Algeria before the war of liberation presents as generalised muscular contraction which is a psychosomatic disorder. Fanon states: "Generalised contraction with muscular stiffness. These symptoms are found in patients of the masculine sex who find it increasingly difficult to execute certain movements: going upstairs, walking quickly, or running. The cause of this difficulty lies in a characteristic rigidity which inevitably reminds us of the impairing of certain regions of the brain (central gray nuclei)." (Fanon 1963 pg. 292). This generalised contraction of the muscles of males immobilises them, ensuring that they are no use to the colonial enterprise contributing to the discourse of the lazy, shiftless, shirking dodgy Arab. The French colonial medical discourse insisted that this pathology is the product of the underdeveloped nature of the Algerian, Arab nervous system. The Arab nervous system has then through its underdevelopment, even its subhuman condition, the proclivity to generate this pathology. This then has nothing to do with French colonial domination and its impact on the Algerian psyche, for under French colonial domination the Algerian, the Arab can attain heights of development denied to them by their genetic nature. Clearly a white supremacist, scientific racist medical discourse. Fanon's position on this pathology arises from an alternate discourse which is rooted in a liberationary axis as follows: "This contracture is in fact simply the postural accompaniment to the native's reticence, the expression in muscular forms of his rigidity and his refusal with regard to colonial authority." (Fanon 1963 pg. 291). The native is reticent in the face of French colonial domination as her/his feelings, emotions and position must not be expressed easily for personal survival demands that. This reticence is expressed via muscular contractions for the inner thoughts must be expressed somehow and these inner thoughts amount to a rejection of colonial domination. Group G pathology is then the collective expression of the psychosomatic expression of the rejection of colonial domination. Pathology framed to express rejection of colonial domination is also very useful in rendering the Algerian, the Arab of very little to no use to the colonial machinery. Which is very similar to the number of the African enslaved reporting ill to the slave hospital every day of the sugar crop raising grave anxiety in the owner, given the ability of this resistance to damage the earning power of the plantation during its peak earning season. Then there was the grave paranoia over the use of poison by the enslaved.

Fanon lists the psychosomatic symptoms of the groups other than G as follows: "a) Stomach ulcers. Very numerous. The pains are felt predominantly at night, with considerable vomiting, loss of weight, sadness and moroseness, and instability in exceptional cases." "b) Nephritic colic. Here again we find pains which came on intensely at night." "c) Menstruation trouble in women. Either the women affected remain three or four months without menstruation, or else considerable pain accompanies it," "d) Intense sleeplessness caused by idiopathic tremors. The patients are young adults, to whom all rest is denied because of a generalised slight shaking reminiscent of a total case of Parkinson's disease." "d) Hair turning white early. Among the survivors of the interrogation centres, the hair often turns white suddenly, either in patches, in certain areas, or totally. Very often this is accompanied by serious debility and sexual impotence." "f) Paroxysmal tachycardias. The cardiac rhythm accelerates abruptly:" "These tachycardias are accompanied by anxiety, and by an impression of imminent death:" "The patient does not seem able to 'release his nervous tension." "He is constantly tense, waiting between life and death." (Fanon 1963 pgs. 291-292)

In the list of psychosomatic disorders Fanon presents, inclusive of Group G, potent evidence emerges to confirm that a colonised race, people and culture is one deeply plagued with mental disorders which impair our ability to resist domination and thereby remake and refurbish ourselves in a liberationary continuum. What is painfully obvious is the existential reality that with the gift of independence the colonial mental disorders passed unhindered into the operational terrain of independence, thereby making a necessary and potent contribution to the neo-colonial project. The question then is the nature of this neo-colonial operational terrain, the impact on the psyche of the individual and the manner they present but this is not the task nor interest of those of the neo-colonial world who serve white North Atlantic scientific, medical discourse and hegemony. This reality they must suppress by expressing white scientific medical discourse of our mental disorders which cannot expose the continued impact of white North Atlantic domination on our psyches in the 21st century. The conclusion is inescapable as colonials we were constituted sick in the head but as neo-colonials the operational terrain is simply lunacy constituting normal as an expression of lunacy, with all of us sick in the head insisting that we are normal. Under white North Atlantic neo-colonial domination lunacy is the normal, where we are normalising lunacy to create normal/lunacy the perfect binary duality joined at the hips operationally, which explains our state of functional schizophrenia.

Algerian Criminality and the War of Liberation

The Depersonalised Colonial/Neo-Colonial

Fanon now presents the final portion of the final Section of the "Wretched of the Earth" which drips the potency of Fanon's alternate scientific medical discourse when he deals with criminality and the impact of the national war of liberation. Fanon states: "It is not only necessary to fight for the liberty of your people. You must also teach that people once again, and first learn once again yourself, what is the full stature of a man; and this you must do for as long as the fight lasts." (Fanon 1963 pg. 293). There is no liberation without violent engagement, but there can be no success without a process that creates, defines and unleashes an ontology and epistemology that serves us, that is libationary, that is our creation and our instruments of power. You can never hope to defeat the hegemonic white North Atlantic by using its ideas created to generate its hegemony against it. Liberation begins and ends only at the level of the idea. Fanon continues: "A people's victorious fight not only consecrates the triumph of its rights; it also gives to that people consistence, coherence, and homogeneity. For colonialism has not simply depersonalised the individual it has colonised; this depersonalisation is equally felt in the collective sphere, on the level of social structures. The colonised people find that they are reduced to a body of individuals who only find cohesion when in the presence of the colonising nation." (Fanon 1963 pgs. 294-294). A colonised individual is depersonalised, alienated from self, culture, past and the precolonial identity, existing daily in a depersonalised social order where only the domination of the colonial overlord can restore some semblance of functional order. We are broken down to be constituted dependent personalities who insist that only the white man can do it right, for all things modern and progressive only proceed from the white man. This depersonalised individual situated/located in a colonial social order is plagued with deep, potent inferiority complexes and is always seen mistaking action for overcompensation. In the neo-colonial condition the depersonalised individual does not disappear and the power relations of the colonial social order never collapsed, it simply evolved into the depersonalised neo-colonial plagued with deeper inferiority complexes, which are actionized in a social order that is ever more fractured and individualised to the point where black on black racism becomes the standard action expression of our inferiority complexes and the overcompensation thereof. This fails to hide and solve the morbid failure and incapacity of thought process to address the daily existential realities of neo-colonial life. Those charged with the task of creating discourse all show a morbid failure and fear to challenge the status quo always seeking to shore up a failed discursive hegemony to the point of being braindead. The reason for this is their failure to create discourse as the daily reality demands, for this is a task way out of their pay grade as white North Atlantic hegemony through the depersonalised, inferior neo-colonial can only demand that the overlord supplies these ideas which they will faithfully apply, even when they are drastic failures. The reality is that the ruling neo-colonial elites have lost control of the ground in this neo-colonial social order, and that portion of the ground involved in the criminal life is presently posing the most potent threat to their position of dominance. In specific instances the criminal life is now an insurgency against the neo-colonial project where the colonial power relation has evolved and worsened their lot in life. Fanon continues: "The fight carried out by a people for its liberation leads it, according to circumstances, either to refuse or else to explode the so-called truths which have been established in its consciousness by the colonial civil administration, by the military occupation, and by economic exploitation."

(Fanon 1963 pg. 294). The war of liberation generates the ability to destroy the truths colonial domination has assaulted and depersonalised us with, thereby affecting liberation. Those who made the transition to neo-colonial domination via the gift of independence failed to generate that choice and remain depersonalised, which evolves to neo-colonial depersonalisation buttressed by the continued potency of colonial truths. Fanon continues: "Armed conflict alone can really drive out these falsehoods created in man which force into inferiority the most lively minds among us and which, literally, mutilate us." (Fanon 1963 pg. 294). The depersonalised, colonised human, is a human plagued and burdened with inferiority which renders them subservient and servile to the white North Atlantic in the strictest sense of the term, which is the inability to create discourse free from the limitations imposed by colonial falsehoods of the nature and potential of the non-white races which continue to constitute individuals in the neo-colonial project. This discursive inability is manifested in a variety of forms, one being the constant quest to migrate to the North Atlantic from the neo-colonial world which excludes and silences any quest to build the neo-colonial nation. The depersonalised neo-colonial is drawn to the North Atlantic for the prime reality that it is only in the belly of the North Atlantic in the 21st century the neo-colonial individual can seek some measure of wholeness, with the expectation that it does in fact exist and is attainable, unlike the neo-colonial terrain. The non-white races of the neo-colonial terrain are seeking wholeness in the spaces afforded them by the hegemonic discourse of biopolitics/biopower with individuation as the outcome of its mechanism of power. North Atlantic individuation is the holy grail of the depersonalised, inferiorised neo-colonial individual and will continue to be so as long as the neo-colonial condition exists such is the depravity of this condition.

The Laziness of the Native and the Designed Inferiority Effect

Fanon now deals with one of the colonial truths which is the laziness of the native. Fanon states: "How many times have we not heard men from the colonised countries violently protesting against the pretended laziness of the black man, of the Algerian, and of the Vietnamese." (Fanon 1963 pg. 294). The colonial discourse of the laziness of the non-white races evokes protest from non-whites that deny their laziness, which indicates the impact of the colonial discourse expressed in the driving need to deny non-white laziness rather that assaulting colonial domination. Why must we aid and abet colonial domination with our complicity is not then the issue. Fanon states: "The native's laziness is the conscious sabotage of the colonial machine; on the biological plane it is a remarkable system of auto-protection; and in any case it is a sure brake upon the seizure of the whole country by the occupying power." (Fanon 1963 pg. 294). To loudly protest against the white supremacist discourse of non-white laziness means in fact that you have internalised the designed inferiority effect and you are now protesting the lies told about you because you are not a shiftless, lazy nigger, you are a good nigger exemplified, by your assault on resistance to colonial domination. Fanon states: "it is time to stop remonstrating and declaring that the nigger is a great worker and that the Arab is first-rate at clearing ground." (Fanon 1983 pg. 294). The handwringing and remonstrating is simply the mannerism of a servile being who accepts and acts upon his inferiority which he believes and accepts. This is not then an anti-colonial domination protest but a lament for inclusion, for acceptance, which drives the quest for migration to the North Atlantic on the pilgrimage devoted to wholeness. In the neo-colonial world these lamentations and remonstrations pass themselves off as "blackness", "black nationalism" and various forms of nationalism and self-determination of non-white peoples which all emanate from a white worldview and the refusal to construct an alternate liberationary discourse, for what is desired is a place at the table of the white North Atlantic, no longer consigned to being under the table and the scraps thereof. There is then no concern for the manner that the table is stocked with all that is desired and the cost thereof to specific sections of the social order. Much worse, there is a refusal to accept the reality that access to the table is always selective and has progressively become so over the course of the 21st century, and being white gives one no assurance of a place at the table.

The Nature of Colonial/Neo-Colonial Power Relations

Fanon now comments on yet another instance of native compliance with colonial domination which is the compliance with colonial laws, such as the willing payment of rates and taxes levied by the colonial overlord. Native compliance then illustrates a complex, fluid power relation with macro and micro instances that encompass the entire social order which generates a social order which is not mores, norms and values driven and defined, but transactionally defined by power relations, which require no masking for it's colonial power in your face unlike the North Atlantic. In this specific colonial order, Fanon insists that there are no discursive linkages between power and mores, norms and values for power blatantly subverts the bid for power of these discursive constructs that are of use to power in the North Atlantic. In the colonial order power lays itself bare, naked for all to behold and fear the majesty of power in its all-embracing impunity. In the neo-colonial condition nothing changes as the local oligarchs, the legacy of colonial domination, entrench their power together with the local political elite and the operatives of North Atlantic hegemony where power is expressed publicly as fascism. Fanon states: "Under the colonial regime, gratitude, sincerity, and honour are empty words." (Fanon 1963 pg. 295). The colonial order is then the discourse of the law of the jungle, of the survival of the fittest made flesh. A human approximation of the world of nature that is a deliberate distortion of nature, especially that of mammals that live in a social order as apes, monkeys, wolves, hyenas, lions, elephants etc.; where in these social orders norms define behaviour and the exercise of power and dominance. The colonial/neo-colonial continuum can only then be a fascist expression of hegemonic power devoid of any root in nature and the precolonial history of human civilisation. Fanon continues: "During these last years I have had occasion to see that Algerian honour, self-sacrifice, love of life, and scorn of death have taken on no ordinary forms." (Fanon 1963 pg. 295). The Algerian war of liberation has then transformed the Algerian individual by constituting the hegemony of long suppressed and silenced Algerian honour, self-sacrifice, love of life and scorn of death which is dismantling the power structure of colonial hegemony and deconstructing the depersonalised colonised Algerian. Without this war of liberation there can be no cleansing of the soullessness of the colonised. With the transition to neo-colonial domination, the soullessness persists and evolves to the point where neo-colonial fascism rooted in graphic social inequality and underdevelopment breeds nihilism on an industrial scale. Nihilism is then the product of neo-colonial domination and the solution devised to grapple with bare, naked, fascist neo-colonial power.

Non-whites are Criminogenic

Fanon now engages with the colonial discourse of the criminality of the North African for white North Atlantic colonial domination, in its depersonalisation of the colonised, insisted that we are all criminogenic, having the disposition to criminality is in our inferior DNA, our culture, our worldview and our religion. This wild beast must then be tamed by the white North Atlantic master race for we all pose grave, lucid threats to white hegemony and civilisation which demand we cannot be left up to our own devices, for the security of white premier, apex civilisation is paramount which demands that we must then be dominated. Fanon states: "Before 1954 magistrates, policemen, barristers, journalists, and legal doctors agreed unanimously that criminality in Algeria was a problem. It was affirmed that the Algerian was a born criminal. A theory was elaborated and scientific proofs were found to support it. This theory was taught in the universities for over twenty years." (Fanon 1963 pg. 296). Before the commencement of the war for liberation in 1954, the discourse of the criminality of the Algerian was hegemonic in the colonial social order as it was unchallenged by a mass anticolonial movement. This discourse of the criminality of the Arab of Algeria was fully supported by an instrument of power in the scientific theory of the criminal Arab buttressed by scientific evidence. This French colonial discourse of the Arab, buttressed by its scientific instrument of power, informed the actions of the colonial state whilst it assaulted the self of the Arab towards her/his depersonalisation and enabled its use of the criminal justice system as an instrument of social control. Fanon reveals the inherent stigma of the Arab in this discourse of criminality as follows: "the inherent stigma of the Algerian people: they were born slackers, born liars, born robbers, and born criminals." (Fanon 1963 pg. 296). Every Arab carried this stigma in colonial Algeria and was summed up via this stigma when dealing with the white colonial state and its agencies. But the potency of the stigma and its strategic intent is revealed with its use in and impact on Arab interrelations, for this is the operational terrain on which divide and conquer is sustainably written. Fanon's approach to his study of this colonial discourse is as follows: "We propose here to repeat the official theory, and to recall to mind the concrete bases and the scientific arguments used to create it. Later on we shall go over the facts and try to reinterpret them" (Fanon 1963 pg. 296). Fanon is now presenting a critique of the white colonial discourse of Arab criminality with emphasis on its scientific, academic form inclusive of all its scientific evidence cited in support. A critique which reveals the nature of Fanon's worldview at this stage of his life. Fanon now begins the critique by restating the core discursive concepts of the discourse and the theory derived from it. The core discursive concepts are as follows: "*The Algerian frequently kills other men*. There are no minor delinquencies. When the Algerians, and this applies equally to all North Africans, puts himself outside the law, it is always outside to the maximum." "*The Algerian kills savagely*. The Algerian, you are told, needs to feel warm blood, and to bathe in the blood of his victim. These magistrates, policemen, and doctors hold serious dissertations on the relationship between the Moslem and blood. The savagery of the Algerian shows itself especially in the number of wounds he inflicts, some of these being unnecessary once the victim has been killed." "*The Algerian kills for no reason*. Very frequently magistrates and policemen are nonplussed by the motives of a murder; it may arise out of a gesture, an allusion, an ambiguous statement, a quarrel over an olive tree which is possessed in common, or an animal which has strayed by an eighth of an acre. From thence springs the frequent impression that the social group is hiding the real motives." "Finally, robbery as practiced by an Algerian is always coupled with housebreaking whether or not accompanied by manslaughter, and in any case with aggression against the owner." (Fanon 1963 pgs. 296-297). The Arab is designated by this white colonial discourse a savage, brute with a blood lust who poses a salient threat to white security in the colonies and the expected impact of this Arab when you allow him unfettered entry into the heartland of white civilisation, i.e. Europe, the grave need arises to protect the white race from this savage brute by any means necessary, including genocide unleashed within an operational terrain of internal colonialism or the order of the banlieues. The discourse of the criminality of the North African is then an instrument to constitute the Arab savage, brute driven by bloodlust especially a white bloodlust. Illustrated by the application of the very same discourse to Tunisia and Morocco necessary to creating a North African criminality expressed as the discourse of the Arab. Fanon states: "Similar though less weighty observations were made in Tunisia and Morocco, and thus the question shifted more and more onto the ground of North African criminality." (Fanon 1963 pgs. 297-298). The strategic intent is to create a colonial discourse of the Arab which is the basis of the assault on the Arabs of Algeria, Tunisia and Morocco to depersonalise them in order to dominate them, to colonise them. The operational basis of this assault demands that the colonial Arab now internalise, accept and condition her/his worldview, behaviour and menu of possible action upon the colonial discourse of the Arab. There are then functional instances of every single colonised, non-white defined and operationalised by white racist colonial North Atlantic discourse. Yes, Ahmed, Steven, Chicken George, Gunga Din and Hop Sing are REAL, not simply white racist invective. Under neo-colonial domination there is a frenzied attempt by the supplicants of white domination, in politics and academia, to mystify and mask the existence of these non-white supplicants of white hegemony constituted by white racist discourse to serve white hegemony. These supplicants, even replicants, relentlessly insist that nigger, Oreo and Uncle Tom are racist white invective which must be banished from use, which is frantically seeking to mask the reality that the prime directive of white hegemonic discourse is to constitute all non-whites into various types of supplicants, replicants, niggers. There is then a typology of niggerhood, for we are all systematised, and one potent way to achieve this is to devise a typology of criminality that systematises all of us. Fanon states: "All these elements which cluster around Algerian criminality have appeared to specify its nature sufficiently clearly to enable a tentative systematisation to be built up." (Fanon 1963 pg. 297). The aim of this systematisation is the generation of the science of these inferior races, expressed ultimately as the universal typology with its universal laws that drive the typology. There is then in the colonial/neo-colonial continuum the ongoing engagement to constitute specific forms of the inferior races in the image and likeness of white North Atlantic hegemonic discourse. Pliant, servile, submissive and totally consumed with the quest for a condition that is unattainable: whiteness. When we fail to discern and perceive these persons for what they are and can only be, and place our trust in them, that signals to massa that we are also pursuing the unattainable: whiteness.

Academic Scientific Medical Discourse of the Criminality of the Arab

Fanon presents the work of the psychiatric school of the university of Algiers where several teams worked to collect the scientific date to prove the theory of the criminality of the Arab by focusing on as follows: "several teams worked with the aim of specifying the forms of expression of this criminality and of establishing a sociological, functional, and anatomical interpretation for them." (Fanon 1963 pg. 298). The academics of the school of psychiatry of the university of Algiers were then working strenuously to create a scientific discourse of Arab criminality by developing a knowledge of Arab criminality, that will inform colonial power in its domination of the Arab. This is the very same role allocated to neo-colonial universities today. Fanon indicates that the doctors produced by the medical school of the university of Algiers were immersed in this scientific discourse of Arab criminality produced by the school of psychiatry and the doctors accepted the criminality of the Arab as scientific fact and acted upon this fact. Fanon states: "Moreover, I remember certain among us who in all sincerity upheld and developed these theories we had learned. We even add 'It's a hard pill to swallow, but it's been scientifically established.'" (Fanon 1963 pg. 298). The science then justifies the inherent racism of the discourse and its attendant scientific medical instrument of power, potently illustrating that white North Atlantic science is then a cult in the service of power. This scientific, medical instrument of power then insists that the Arab is as follows: "The North African is a criminal; his predatory instinct is well known; his intense aggressivity is visible to the naked eye. The North African likes extremes, so we can never entirely trust him." "He is insensible to shades of meaning, and Cartesianism is fundamentally foreign to him;" "The North African is a violent person, of a hereditary violence. We find him incapable of self-discipline or of canalising his impulses. Yes, the Algerian is a congenital impulsive." (Fanon 1963 pg. 298). The Arab is all body, instinct, drives and impulses as he has no mind save and except that determined by his body, physicality and base drives which means he is essentially uncivilised. This is the essence of the Arab which ensures he can only be a criminal, a violent predatory criminal with diminished capacity when compared to the white race, which means that the Arab is sub-human. Fanon continues: "But we must be precise. This impulsiveness is largely aggressive and generally homicidal." (Fanon 1963 pg. 298). This congenital impulsive Arab has then a predilection to murder, a propensity to murder. The Arab is then a race immersed in a drive to murder. Fanon raises the issue of the melancholia that Arabs present with and the tendency to suicide that arises from the melancholia, which contradicts the scientific, medical discourse of the homicidal tendencies of the Arab. This mainstream discourse recognises the melancholia, the tendency to suicide but not the contradiction posed to the position of Arab homicidal tendency. The Arab afflicted with melancholia does not commit suicide she/he commits murder, thereby creating a uniquely Arab typology of melancholia. Fanon states: "The melancholic Algerian does not commit suicide. He kills. This is the homicidal melancholia which has been thoroughly studied by Professor Porot in the thesis of his pupil Monserrat." (Fanon 1963 pg. 298). A scientific, medical discourse of the Arab that is constructed to serve power, i.e.- French colonial domination of Algeria, which creates its own reality in its quest to constitute servile Arabs to affirm that this constructed reality is in fact real, hence the schizophrenia of those in the neo-colonial condition who continue to drink and feed the white man's Kool Aid to their children. Fanon points out that the nature of the causality constructed and utilised in the scientific, medical discourse allows the scientific hit job done on the Arab. Fanon states: "First we must notice intellectual aptitudes. The Algerian is strongly marked by mental debility. The native, it is stated by them, presents the following characteristics: Complete of almost complete lack of emotivity. Credulous and susceptible to the extreme. Persistent obstinacy. Mental puerility, without the spirit of curiosity found in the Western child. Tendency to accidents and pithiatic reactions." "His congenital aggressivity finds ways of expressing of expressing itself on the slightest pretext. It is a state of aggressivity in its purest form." (Fanon 1963 pgs. 299-300). This relentless assault, this semiology of the scientific, medical discourse of the

Arab is compelled to come to a conclusion that enables the colonial strategy of domination and constituting servile, pliable Arabs that resonates with the scientific, medical discourse. It then needs a scientific, medical rationale to justify its fitness to exist, to operate.

Fanon now presents the scientific, medical rationale as follows: "For Professor Porot, the life of the native of North Africa is dominated by diencephalic urges. It is as much as to say that in a way a native North African is deprived of a cortex." (Fanon 1963 pg. 301). The Arab is then sub-human. Fanon quotes from an actual statement on this as follows: "The Algerian has no cortex: or, more precisely, he is dominated, like the inferior vertebrates, by the diencephalon. The cortical functions, if they exist at all, are very feeble and are practically unintegrated into the dynamic of existence." (Fanon 1963 pg. 301). The rationale is then an expression of base, crude, scientific racist discourse created to justify white colonial domination and the assault on the Arab to depersonalise them towards reconstituting them as servile Arabs. This is white North Atlantic racism wrapped up in a scientific veneer, powerfully illustrating the potency of the delusion of the cult of science, and the ends to which the white North Atlantic power elite will go to ensure its hegemony across the colonial/neo-colonial continuum.

The strategic intent of this constructed scientific racist medical discourse is then for Fanon apparent as he states as follows: "There is thus neither mystery nor paradox. The hesitation of the colonist in giving responsibility to the native is not racism nor paternalism, but quite simply a scientific appreciation of the biologically limited possibilities of the native." (Fanon 1963 pg. 301). The French colonialist in North Africa has then added to the arsenal of domination a scientific racist discourse justifying domination, which with the transition to neo-colonial domination, the discourse is modified to fit the new strategic conditions. The justification for neo-colonial domination initially relegated the scientific racist discourse to the margins, whilst a discourse of the cultural impediments of the neo-colonial that arrest the path to development became hegemonic. Then this discourse evolved to emphasise the weaknesses of the institutions of the neo-colonial order and the fragility of civil society, which served the assault of the multilateral lending institutions as the World bank and the IMF on the neo-colonial order. With the hegemony of neoliberal discourse in the North Atlantic, the emphasis switched to the miracle of unfettered capitalism in the neo-colonial order and the spectacular rise of the middle class. Today in the second decade of the 21st century, the scientific, racist discourse is back and once again utilised as a weapon by the political elite, agencies of the State and academia. But with two discourses driving two separate instruments of power, where in one the characteristics of this scientific, medical Arab are utilised, purged of the fascist, national socialist and eugenic explanations for these characteristics, are unleashed within a globalised assault to depersonalise and reconstitute replicants. In the other the characteristics of a servile race are once again married to a white supremacist scientific medical theory and unleashed in the globalised operational terrain, driven by a political agenda to exert openly and brazenly in the white North Atlantic the hegemony of a new power relations where the masks to the operational nature of political power are removed, i.e. operational power is unmasked in a bid to further defang the limits to power that still do exist in a bid to grant further impunity to the oligarchies of the North Atlantic. In the second decade of the 21st century, the white North Atlantic has now embraced the brutal, oligarchic power driven impunity of neo-colonial fascism and inequality as its desired model.

The Colonial/Neo-Colonial Continuum

This is simply indicative of the colonial/neo-colonial continuum which falsifies the delusion that what obtained under colonial domination is now past and of no impact and relevance to the 21st century.

Scientific racist medical discourse

In the final part of this section of the book Fanon presents an analysis of the discourse of A. Carothers an international expert on Africa. Fanon quotes Carothers on the nature of the African as follows: "The African makes very little use of his frontal lobes. All the particularities of African psychiatry can be put down to frontal laziness." (Fanon 1963 pg. 302). Carothers has then formulated and unleashed a discourse which is justifying for all times the need for the white man to dominate the African. This Carothers' discourse becomes part of the superstructure of the colonial/neo-colonial complex, rest assured when you imagine it is silenced, it exists in the superstructure impacting the formation of new discursive constructs for the 21st century. Fanon states: "According to Dr. Carothers, the likeness existing between the normal African native and the lobotomized European is striking." (Fanon 1963 pg. 302). To enable a comparison between equals, the European has to be lobotomized in order to enable an effective comparison with a native African, such is the extent of the inherent inferiority of the African compared to the white master race. Note the issue here is not to rail at the racism, leave that for those plagued with hallucinatory whiteness forever pleading for a space at the table, but to focus on the strategic intent of this discourse and how it is impacting the policing of non-white peoples in the North Atlantic today, right now! We don't need the cry of Steven we need the cold, crisp, precise analysis of Steve Biko. What must be noted is the fact that Carothers' book Fanon is referring to was published in 1954. In the decade of the move to independence or wars of liberation, Carothers is utilising scientific racism in a post-world war two context to insist that the African was incapable of utilising freedom as the white North Atlantic does. This is potently illustrated by Carothers' position on the Mau Mau insurgency of colonial Kenya as follows: "We should point out before concluding that Dr. Carothers defined the Mau-Mau revolt as an expression of the unconscious frustration complex whose reoccurrence could be scientifically avoided by spectacular psychological adaptation." (Fanon 1963 pg. 303). The Mau Mau insurgency is not the result of British colonial domination where the best land of the Kenyan plateau was placed under white settler control, displacing and marginalising the vast majority of the Kikuyu, expressed as an acute land hunger. There was then no colonial racist domination, what there was in fact, scientifically, was simply a Kikuyu frustration complex and an unconscious one at that. If the Kikuyu were to spectacularly psychologically adapt to this unconscious frustration complex, then there will be no need for the insurgency. Which when applied to reality on the ground it translates to being made by force to accept white racist colonial domination by any means necessary. Carothers' role is to add a discourse that justifies the colonial action by denying the reality, through creating an alternate reality that serves the colonial agenda.

Fanon now deals with the conclusions of this scientific racist discourse of the African and the North African. Fanon states: "the layout of the cerebral structures of the North African are responsible both for the native's laziness, for his intellectual and social inaptitude and for his almost animal impulsivity. The criminal impulses of the North African are the transcription into the nature of his behaviour of a given arrangement of the nervous system." (Fanon 1963 pg. 303). Everything that the African and the North African is stems from the specific structure and arrangement of their nervous system. The North African and the African is a product of a nervous system that is vastly different from and inferior to that of the white race. The white race can do no more than dominate the African and the North African when both races interact, for the nervous system of the African renders them uncompetitive. This discourse then creates space for colonial political discourse as follows: "Discipline, training, mastering and today pacifying are the words most frequently used by the colonialists in occupied territories." (Fanon 1963 pg. 303). Already the discourse for the neo-colonial condition has appeared under colonial domination as discipline, mastering and training, still in use in the 21st century having been constantly redefined to suit the discursive context. The favourite term now is pacifying in the context of the neo-colonial crime spree where it has been further militarised to match the militarisation of policing, where pacification is now crime suppression. This scientific racist discourse remains in circulation in the discursive terrain of the white North Atlantic having established the causal link to African and North African criminality with their underdeveloped nervous system. This marginalised circulation ends at the point in time in the realm of political discourse and power relations a grave threat is perceived as emanating from Africans and North Africans and the discourse kicks into retrofitting for frontline use. This is clearly seen in the case of North African and African migration to Europe in the 21st century and in the specific case of the US, where the threat is ever present since 1865, but became acute with two terms of office of a black president in the 21st century.

The Quality of Life in the Colonial/Neo-Colonial Continuum

Fanon ends this section with his position on the nature of colonial domination, its impact on the psyche of the colonised and the manner this reality influences the war of liberation. Fanon states that under colonial domination life has a specific reality and impact as follows: "For a colonised man, in a context of oppression like that of Algeria, living does not mean embodying moral values or taking his place in the coherent and fruitful development of the world. To live means to keep on existing. Every date is a victory: not the result of work, but a victory felt as a triumph for life." (Fanon 1963 pg. 308). Substitute "neo-colonised man" for "colonised man" and you have an accurate description of daily life and reality under the neo-colonial regime of the 21st century, which attests to the fact that there is a continuum that encompasses the colonial and the neo-colonial conditions. In the colonial/neo-colonial continuum there is no qualitative distinction between life under colonial domination and that under the freedom of independence, in fact life has significantly worsened under the neo-colonial where living continues to be driven by the quest to exist. The colonial social order inherited at independence has continued evolving structurally unchanged and entrenching its inequality under the neo-colonial order. Fanon then insists that the very nature of this colonial order forces the colonised to face the reality of their self-hate. Fanon states: "Up above there is Heaven with the promise of a world beyond the grave, down there below there are the French with their very concrete promises of prisons, beatings-up, and executions. You are forced to come up against yourself. Here we discover the kernel of that hatred of self which is characteristic of racial conflicts in segregated societies." (Fanon 1963 pg. 309). In a colonised condition as Algeria the quest to stay alive, for daily existence demands that you do battle with yourself as a survival strategy for the burden of self-hatred is the gravest impediment to any survival strategy of the colonised. Heaven is the realm where entry is premised on death after the grave, not daily life, as Algeria is a living Hell for life before death in Algeria is the realm, the territory of French colonial hegemony. To choose life over death means you have chosen Hell over Heaven which exposes your self-hate and how it is debilitating to your interests, the question then is your response or none at all to this discovery. This self-hate is expressed via a number of actions and behavioural patterns of the colonised, one of which is the use of violence as the means to resolve interpersonal conflict in the colonial social order. Fanon states: "The Algerian's criminality, his impulsivity, and the violence of his murders are therefore not the consequence of the organisation of his nervous system or of characterial originality, but the direct product of the colonial situation." (Fanon 1963 pg. 309). The colonial assault to depersonalise the dominated constitutes a colonial personality where self-hate is expressed via graphic acts of violence against fellow colonised persons, not against the coloniser/dominator. Which illustrates the effectiveness of the colonial assault where the effects of this assault is turned inwards to self and fellow members of the colonised, not the massa. A condition of self-hate that blossoms under neo-colonial domination into the genocidal wars of black on black racism, where you take into your own non-white hands the task of eliminating your non-white race enemy, thereby exonerating the white race from the task of the Final Solution that it so desires.

Fanon ends this section by stating: "Once again, the objective of the native who fights against himself is to bring about the end of domination. But he ought equally to pay attention to the liquidation of all untruths implanted in his being by oppression. Under a colonial regime such as existed in Algeria, the ideas put forward by colonialism not only influenced the European minority, but also the Algerians. Total liberation is that which concerns all sections of the personality." (Fanon 1963 pgs. 309-310). The basis of liberation is the colonised engaged in a fight against herself/himself for the self is flawed, damaged under the control of the coloniser. Liberation is only possible and achievable where the entire personality is fully purged of the implants of the coloniser that depersonalised us and rendered us problematized at the level of the psyche. Under the regime of the gift of independence there was no such fight against oneself, hence there was no liberation which enabled the colonised personality to thrive and evolve into the neo-colonial personality, noted for its self-hate plaguing free and sovereign citizens of a free and sovereign state. Fanon ends by defining what is the state of independence as follows: "Independence is not a word which can be used as an exorcism, but an indispensable condition for the existence of men and women who are truly liberated, in other words who are truly masters of all the material means which make possible the radical transformation of society." (Fanon 1963 pg. 310). Are we in the neo-colonial world masters of the means by which the colonial social order is radically transformed to the point where it's is no longer recognisable as it is a brave new world? To radically transform the colonial world into a postcolonial world the inherent characteristics, structure and outcomes of the colonial order have to be transformed into a state of existence that is 180 degrees apart from the colonial condition. Neo-colonial domination in the 21st century is premised on the colonial/neo-colonial continuum, where the colonial social order and its local and international relations of power have survived and evolved across time, preserving the dominance of the developed, white North Atlantic and the subservient, underdeveloped, non-white ex-colonial world. This reality emphasises the fact that we do not control the material means to radically transform our colonial social order, which includes the neo-colonial political elite and the oligarchs of the neo-colonial social orders. The political, economic and social elites of the neo-colonial world refuse to recognise and grasp power to lead the process of radical transformation for various reasons: personal commitment to and acceptance of white North Atlantic domination, fear of the price to be paid for resisting the power of the North Atlantic state expressed as an unacceptable personal cost and simply being not interested as the quest is for personal benefit and power by any means necessary. Whilst the masses recognise the back breaking burden placed on them by the elites, expressed as their daily struggle for survival, simply immerse themselves with survival or marching in lockstep with the agendas of the elites or both. The independence project in the 21st century has then failed, palpably written in the blood, sweat, pain, hunger, suffering and arrested development of the masses of the huge urban sprawl of the ghettoes/shanty towns/massive holding pens of the neo-colonial Frankenstein monster. There is no independence for the vast majority of the masses of the neo-colonial world for we have all failed the

Fanon litmus test. We have formed then social orders comprising collectives of servile non-whites, subservient to white North Atlantic states and their ruling elites and in this travesty we insist we are free and sovereign citizens of free and sovereign states with a serious face. Independence is today just a word used as an instrument of exorcism in an attempt to nullify the potently apparent failure of the independence project by defanging its potential political impact.

White North Atlantic Psychology and Psychiatry and Fanon

In the ever pressing search for self-medication amongst the neo-colonials there is now the quest for the "healing" and the "answers" that are provided by white North Atlantic psychology and psychiatry. An academic degree in psychology instantly turns a neo-colonial replicant into an expert, a person endowed with expertise that the social order is in dire need of, an inherently superior person differentiated from the herd of replicants of the neo-colonial condition. But you are an expert of a white North Atlantic discourse that vehemently denies your humanity, as it deconstructs your non-white persona and seduces you to erect on the ruins your persona as replicant of massa. You are then no expert, but a willing accomplice to the agenda to render all of us replicants in the service of massa. Your psychology is incapable of healing us, non-whites, for it is constituted to only destroy our being, essence and psyche thereby problematizing all of us, including yourself. When we visit you in search of healing you can only deepen the wounds, for what you define yourself by is what has all of us sick in the head, including yourself. It is simply ludicrous to hear you speak of black consciousness and the deprivations of the white man, whilst you serve the massa by viewing yourself and the world through the discourse that assaults us to the point of servility.

What is now apparent from the discourse of Fanon is that mental disorders are segregated by race between whites and non-whites and differentiated into typologies that encompass the various non-whites and the manner in which they present. In the United States of America, a white male and an African male raised in very similar living conditions present mental disorders arising from lived traumatic experiences entirely different. There are then white mental disorders and African mental disorders arising from very similar lived traumatic experiences simply because one is the dominating race and the other is the dominated race, where the dominating race has unleashed a discourse with its mechanism of power and instruments of power to police the non-white races into a sustainable existential condition of servility. The same applies to the white female and the African female, but there is a vast difference in the nature of the mental disorders between the African female and the African male. This segregated structure of mental disorders is even more apparent in the case of whites and the First Peoples of America, and in the manner First Peoples present compared with Africans and Hispanics. There are then specific discourses that sustainably assault specific non-white races with its mechanism and instruments of power which coalesce in an operational form of the colonial/neo-colonial continuum for that race in America. There are distinct colonial/neo-colonial continuums operating in America that are attached to the bodies, that envelops it as a "soul" of the non-whites under assault producing distinct lived experiences of white oppression, thereby creating a diversity of oppressions held within the operational ambits of distinct colonial/neo-colonial continuums. There are then distinct orders of power that enmesh the non-white races affixing the "souls" to their bodies for the assigned purpose of surveillance and punishment of these non-white races. There is no similar order of power for white folks as they are of the mainstream social order, which means that the white mainstream social order assigns non-white races its membership, its distinct order of power and defines the nature of surveillance and punishment. America is then a segregated society on the basis of race and its structure of power where internal colonialism defines and determines the nature of race relations and the order of race power. Internal colonialism demands race power and an order of power. The American colonial/ neo-colonial continuum is then operationally founded upon American internal colonialism, which pumps out a range of depersonalised non-white persons in search of the path to being functioning replicants. The liberal, democratic discourse that constitutes "America" is simply a mask for the operational "AmeriKKKa", the racially segregated white colonial metropole with its non-white Bantustans all wrapped up into a single package of internal colonial domination in the 21st century.

The conclusion is then evident that there is no healing possible for non-white races under treatment from white North Atlantic hegemonic psychology and psychiatry, only further deconstruction of our already problematized and dysfunctional psyche. White North Atlantic psychology and psychiatry has then to maintain this "soul" draped over the bodies of non-whites, thereby propagating the oppression and the depersonalisation towards constituting replicants.

Colonial/Neo-Colonial Continuum

In the final section of and in fact the entire work "The Wretched of the Earth" it is apparent that Fanon's discourse is alluding to a discursive concept, that I have termed the colonial/neo-colonial continuum, where the power relations of the colonial order flow unchanged into the neo-colonial order thereby framing the power relations that develop into the neo-colonial condition. The first continuum that developed under white North Atlantic domination was the enslavement/colonial continuum where the former slaves were told that they were now free subjects of the colonial dominator, but soon learned that they were now subject to an assault on their free personage that even exceeded the protocols of enslavement. The slave order became the basis of the colonial order and the assault on the non-white subject races heightened, expanded and intensified as it evolved under the colonial order. This first continuum impacted the second continuum as independence must be emasculated by ensuring that it was not decolonisation and to ensure emasculation independence must be defanged by the non-whites that were being freed, hence the need for willing, servile actors to hand independence to. Without the existence of servile non-whites to hand independence to there could have only been wars of liberation and decolonisation. The enslavement/colonial continuum's primary task was to constitute this body of replicants throughout the white North Atlantic colonial empires and gradually give them space in the colonial social order to take root and thrive awaiting the day of their call to duty to massa. When the call came in the decades of the 1940s, 1950s and 1960s they answered their call to massa's service dutifully and fulfilled their task by creating the operational conditions for the formation and expansion of the colonial/

neo-colonial continuum to this day in the 21st century, thereby obviating the need for a world war of wars of liberation following the second world war and the resultant hegemony of decolonisation, rather than the hegemony of the colonial/neo-colonial continuum. We, the colonised, then created the colonial/neo-colonial continuum with our own effort to effectively enslave ourselves, our children and the generations that follow. We sowed the wind and we always have and will continue to reap the whirlwind.

In this continuum there are core discursive concepts that drive the production of discourse with their attendant mechanism of power and instruments of power that police the power relations of this continuum to ensure its hegemony. The absolute right of the white North Atlantic to exercise hegemony over the world must never be challenged by a non-white power, as China today. The right to defend this hegemony abrogates all law, morality, ethics and principles, but the same does not apply to the actions of the enemy. All races under the hegemony of the white North Atlantic have no right to self-determination, much less to make choices the white North Atlantic considers detrimental to white North Atlantic hegemony. The salient issue then is to sustainably impact power relations to ensure that they are always favourable to white North Atlantic hegemony. The preferred means to sustainably attain this is to depersonalise the non-white races hegemony is exercised over and build on this ruin, a replicant, whose worldview is rooted in servility by being operationally problematized, in other words we are sick in the head. This core discursive construct entered a stage of crises having to deal with the possibility of decolonisation engulfing the colonial empires which hastened the demise of the political voice of the settlers and the formulation and unleashing of the instrument of power of

the gift of independence, the rest is now the history of suffering. In the 21st century the assault on the non-white races continues and is now heightened as a result of the digital revolution, for hegemony has evolved and is under contestation from various points of engagement. The discourse has responded, as it always will do, but will the spaces created now enable the former colonial empires, now the neo-colonial world, to grasp finally decolonisation after the rabid failure of the independence project? I simply don't know!

Fanon's Goodbye

In the Conclusion to "Wretched of the Earth" Fanon wrote his final words, his goodbyes. Fanon states: "Let us waste no time in sterile litanies and nauseating mimicry. Leave this Europe where they are never done talking of Man, yet murder men everywhere they find them," Fanon 1963 pg. 311). The legal strictures and the moral standards that the North Atlantic applies to their enemies are never applied to their actions and those of their allies and servile lapdogs. The North Atlantic is driven by a quest for hegemony which is expressed via the methodology of imperial penetration and domination, where all actions to attain and maintain dominance emanating from this methodology are permissible and acceptable even when they flout the rule of law of the North Atlantic, the neo-colonial targets and international law. North Atlantic imperial power is then amoral and illicit in its daily operational mode as it abhors all forms of self-determination, especially in the neo-colonial states it dominates, for in these weak, underdeveloped states the will of the masses expressed that is not compliant with the will of the North Atlantic massa will be overthrown and destroyed. This is a North Atlantic desire for power that infects the oligarchies that dominates their social orders to the point where they are presently consorting with their grave enemies in the war on terror to remove the Assad government of Syria. An oligarchy where the desire for power has overwhelmed their basic understanding of limits to power, as they insist that there are none to their power. The North Atlantic oligarchy in the 21st century has now been infected with the desire for unlimited power that drove the elites and petty dictators of the neo-colonial world to epic social disasters and wars of genocide. What the North Atlantic spawned in the neo-colonial world is now coming home to roost. Fanon continues: "That same Europe where they were never done talking of Man, and where they never stopped proclaiming that they were only anxious for the welfare of Man: today we know with what sufferings humanity has paid for every one of their triumphs of the mind." "as long as we do not imitate Europe, so long as we are not obsessed by the desire to catch up with Europe." "When I search for Man in the technique and style of Europe, I see only a succession of negations of man, and an avalanche of murders." (Fanon 1963 pg. 312). The only Man the North Atlantic refers to is the white race and the rest of us non-whites are less than this white race, hence we are there to be murdered, dominated and rendered servile in the interest of the White Man, the only human on Earth. The white North Atlantic willingly and deliberately lies to us as they murder us, as they negate our humanity and constitute us "things," sub-humans which have been "thingified" in their image and likeness for their benefit, simply because we desire their acceptance, we desire their affirmation and we lust after continuously a place at their table and we pay any and all prices possible to quench these desires. We are to blame, we are the ones who create the monsters, we are the ones who raise the white children who then continue their white destiny to the next generation and we are the ones who complain about massa, whilst we kill each in an orgy of aimless gun violence driven by black on black racism. We see no other quest worthy of life but to imitate the white North Atlantic and that is our recurring surrender to domination and arrested development.

Fanon now describes the condition of our servility and the impact of being dominated by the white North Atlantic as follows: "A permanent dialogue with oneself and an increasingly obscene narcissism never ceased to prepare the way for a half delirious state, where intellectual work becomes suffering and the reality was not at all that of a living man, working and creating himself, but rather words, different combination of words, and the tensions springing from the meanings contained in words." (Fanon 1963 pg. 312). We are in a half delirious state despite our attempts to self-medicate where the self-medication is in itself problematic as they involve an intoxication with self, expressed as a constant dialogue with self and an obscene narcissism which complement each other. This narcissism and the constant conversation with self, is the product of the depersonalisation of colonial domination, then prepares the way for the development of the half delirious state where intellectual work is in fact suffering for it is simply words, combinations of words with meanings nothing else, as we are not living people, humans involved in the act of creation by ourselves for ourselves.

We are all the servile products of white North Atlantic domination, serving this hegemony not ourselves, a servile act that denies our humanity and constantly alienates us from our specific human selves. In the neo-colonial condition the alienation is heightened for we insist that we are free sovereign humans, citizens of free, sovereign nations we then are not half delirious but fully delirious for we vehemently deny our servility whilst labouring over words and meanings that will never amount to intellectual output that is for ourselves by ourselves. The most potent indication of our chronic servility in the 21st century. Fanon continues: "The pretext of catching up must not be used to push man around, to tear him away from himself or from his privacy, to break and kill him. No, we do not want to catch up with anyone." (Fanon 1963 pg. 314). In the neo-colonial condition the need and drive to catch up is used to justify the continuation of colonial barbarity in a social order supposedly comprising free and sovereign citizens. Barbarity is excused in order to catch up with those who unleashed barbarity in order to colonise us, thereby following the North Atlantic model. Fanon continues: "If we want to turn Africa into a new Europe, and America into a new Europe, then let us leave the destiny of our countries to Europe. They will know how to do it better than the most gifted amongst us." (Fanon 1963 pg. 315). We do want to turn the ex-colonial world into another North Atlantic, hence our willing embrace of the neo-colonial condition, but we are yet to see this evolutionary change made manifest in the Third World. But in our fully delirious state of existence we can never see and much less act upon the reality that the independence/neo-colonial experiment has collapsed, failed.

Fanon's final words in this his last book pose a challenge to all of us, especially those of us in the neo-colonial world, which we have failed to shoulder from the commencement of the independence experiment to the 21st century. Fanon states: "For Europe, for ourselves, and for humanity, comrades we must turn over a new leaf, we must work over new concepts, and try to set afoot a new man." (Fanon 1963 pg. 316). There is no alternate body of knowledge, no contending discourses challenging white North Atlantic hegemony in the neo-colonial world. This is why we are in the neo-colonial condition and it escalates its strangulation of our population, for in this existential environment there can be no genesis of a new man, only generations of humans seeking to leave, migrate from the neo-colonial world to the North Atlantic for this is the only paradise sought in light of our paradise never attained, now lost forever. And in these human flows of the 21st century and the impact they are unleashing on the politics of the North Atlantic, the organic crisis of the binary duality of neo-colonial exploitation/domination and white North Atlantic dominance/wealth extraction is now made manifest.

Chapter Six

Selections from "Toward the African Revolution"

Selections from the collection of Fanon's unpublished writings published after his death in English in 1967 as "Toward the African Revolution" will now be presented in this chapter chosen on the basis of the continuity of the discourse of these selections with the discourse of "Wretched of the Earth."

The Strategic Terrain of Decolonisation in the late 1950s

This article written by Fanon was published in *El Moudjahid*, No. 27, July 22, 1958 deals with the strategic terrain of the decolonisation process in the late 1950s in which Fanon identifies the signal strategic realities of this terrain and how they impact the process of decolonisation in the colonial world. Fanon states: "The second upheaval of this period, unquestionably, is the conquest by the peoples of the lands that belong to them." (Fanon 1967 pg. 120). The second upheaval of this period of the twentieth century is the decolonisation process where those who own the conquered lands are retaking what is theirs from the conquerors. For Fanon there are other realities that will impact this second upheaval as the cold war, the threat of human annihilation by an atomic war and the retreat of colonialism itself. Fanon states: "this phenomenon of liberation, of triumph of national independence, of retreat of colonialism, does not manifest itself in a unique manner. Every new sovereign state finds itself practically under the obligation of maintaining definite and preferential relations with the former oppressor." "The parties that lead the struggle against colonialist oppression, at a certain phase of the combat, decide for practical reasons to accept a fragment of independence" (Fanon 1967 pg. 120). There is no unique manner the decolonisation process exhibits when enacted, as there is a potent strategy the North Atlantic colonisers utilise to retain hegemony over the colony then switch to the neo-colonial strategy where the intent is to create a sustainable dominant relation with the former colony termed neo-colonialism. Fanon then recognises that at a specific juncture in the anti-colonial struggle, the anti-colonial movement will accept a servile condition termed independence rationalised with the position that they can restart the process of anti-colonial agitation and struggle to complete the process at a later date, which never happened. The servile condition quickly concretised to a sustainable form of domination termed neo-colonialism. Fanon termed this the "rights" of the former coloniser as follows: "The actual rights of the occupant were then perfectly identified. The important thing was obviously the real rights that the occupier meant to wrench from the people, as the price for a piece of independence. The acceptance of a nominal sovereignty and the absolute refusal of real independence-such is the typical reaction of colonialist nations with respect to their former colonies." (Fanon 1967 pg. 121). The unleashing of the neo-colonial strategy is premised on having the rights of the coloniser affirmed by the newly independent. These rights of the former coloniser abrogate sovereignty and independence to create a new domination/dominated and dependent relationship between free and sovereign actors. For Fanon the neo-colonial strategy and its condition is as follows: "Neo-colonialism is impregnated with a few ideas which both constitute its force and at the same time prepare its necessary decline. In the course of the struggle for liberation, things are not clear in the consciousness of the fighting people. Since it is a refusal, at one and the same time, of political non-existence, of wretchedness, of illiteracy, of the inferiority complex so subtly instilled by oppression, its battle for a long time is undifferentiated." (Fanon 1967 pg. 121). There is then a battle of unequal forces taking place between the coloniser and the anticolonial movement, where the anticolonial movement has to battle against the assault of the coloniser and the debilitating legacy of colonial domination simultaneously, but we do it in an undifferentiated manner which makes up prone to accept the proposals of independence premised on the "rights" of the coloniser in the era of independence. What is then necessary under the colonialism/ neo-colonialism continuum is differentiated assaults on this continuum towards liberation where the legacies of domination, especially the inferiority complex, must be addressed separate and apart from the assault on the "rights" of the colonial/neo-colonial dominator. The role of this undifferentiated anticolonial assault in the surrender to neo-colonial domination for Fanon is as follows: "Neo-colonialism takes advantage of this indetermination. Armed with a revolutionary and spectacular good will, it grants the former colony everything. But in so doing, it wrings from it an economic dependence which becomes an aid and assistance program." (Fanon 1967 pg.121). The neo-colonial agenda driven by the discourse of neo-colonial domination in its power relations with the anticolonial movement exploits the indetermination of the movement as it fails to deal with the double assault launched by the neo-colonial agenda against it. With the guile of the seducer the colonial dominator now adopts the role of the policeman of democratic ideals and North Atlantic ethical practices, preaching democratic capitalist revolutionary ideals where it once dominated, brutalised and unleashed arrested development through the barrel of a gun and racist depersonalisation, towards encapsulating the newly independent in a soul of dependence yet being free where exploitation and the transfer of wealth and resources outstrips that of the colonial era. Which is potently symbolised by aid addiction tied to dependence and sustainable underdevelopment across space and time, which is neo-colonial domination potently expressed in the 21st century. Fanon continues: "Neo-colonialism, because it proposes to do justice to human dignity in general, addresses itself essentially to the middle class and to the intellectuals of the colonial country. Today, the peoples no longer feel their bellies at peace when the colonial country has the value of its elites. The people want things really to change and right away. Thus it is that the struggle resumes with resumed violence. In this second phase, the occupant bristles and unleashes all his forces. What was wrested by bombardment is reconverted into results of free negotiations. The former occupant intervenes in the name of duty, and once again establishes his war in an independent country." (Fanon 1967 pg. 122). In phase one of the neo-colonial project the middle class and the intellectuals of the colony and newly independent state are seduced by the North Atlantic, to the exclusion of the masses who experience no change in their existential condition with independence. Under the independent neo-colonial regime, the masses then go into revolt against the neo-colonial elites and instability even civil war, a war of secession and ethnic war erupt, which launches phase two where the former colonial massa and the North Atlantic intervene militarily to restore order, peace and democracy which amounts to a re-conquest of the ex-colony. Phase two adopts a variety of action modes where the deep state and the political elites trigger a crisis to justify an intervention by removing a native leader they simply don't want, as he does not fit the mould of a compliant neo-colonial servile leader. Such as the case of the removal of Patrice Lumumba of the Congo and Kwame Nkrumah of Ghana or the intervention is facilitated by the internal politics between the masses and the ruling neo-colonial elites. Whatever the reason for the intervention, the deep state of the North Atlantic is always at the tip of the spear of North Atlantic action and in the aftermath they never leave as they maintain their operational presence well into the 21st century protecting the interests of the North Atlantic. Phase two of the neo-colonial process hardens the domination of the North Atlantic over the independent country, a throttling hold that is yet to be broken. The reality is that excuses were found, and will always be found, to justify aggression to protect the interests of the North Atlantic by ensuring and heightening the subservience of the neo-colonial world, clearly illustrated by the USA today in the 21st century. Fanon states: "All the former colonies, from Indonesia to Egypt, without forgetting Panama, which have tried to denounce the agreements wrung from them by force, have found themselves obliged to undergo a new war and sometimes to see their sovereignty again violated and amputated." (Fanon 1967 pg. 122). The language of seduction makes for the military and covert force of dominant power unleashed on subservient states who dared challenge the right to domination by the North Atlantic, such are the wages of the neo-colonial condition. Fanon states: "The notorious "rights" of the occupant, the false appeal to a common past, the persistence of a rejuvenated colonial pact, are the permanent bases of an attack directed against national sovereignty." (Fanon 1963 pg. 122). There is then a permanent assault on the national sovereignty of the newly independent states premised on as follows: the recognised "rights" of the coloniser recognised by the independent regime, the unchallenged and rejuvenated discourse of the pact between coloniser and newly independent nation that was founded upon white colonial domination, hence an acceptance of white domination and a forgiveness of all the sins of the white coloniser, seen in the call for aid not reparations and compensation for white brutality and arrested development, with the continued operational existence of our depersonalisation and its concomitant inferiority complex. White power! With this operational matrix evolving and growing in power since the 1940s, 1950s and 1960s behold our poverty and powerlessness in the second decade of the 21st century on a comparative basis with the North Atlantic, in spite of our independence, as it is devoid of national sovereignty even self-determination.

Fanon now insists that we must view the drive to enmesh us in neo-colonial domination is heightened by the creation of zones of influence which intensify our dependence on the former colonial massa. Fanon states: "The concern to maintain the former colony in the yoke of economic oppression is obviously not sadism. The reconversion of the colonial economy, the industries engaged in processing raw materials from the underdeveloped territories, the disappearance of the colonial pact, competition with foreign capital, constitute a mortal danger for imperialism. For countries as Great Britain and France, there arises the important question of zones of influence." (Fanon 1967 pgs. 122-123). Old colonial imperialism in its quest for neo-colonial dominance faces the grave threat from US penetration of these ex-colonies, of especially Britain and France, which will upset the bid to constitute these former colonies as the exclusive preserve of the former massa. These zones of influence are then an attempt to replicate the mercantilist basis of colonies and control of colonial markets under the neo-colonial order. Neo-colonial dominance, premised on a zone of influence dominated by the former colonial massa, constitutes an acute form of neo-colonial domination and underdevelopment compared to that premised on competition amongst North Atlantic predators for dominance. Fanon's words of warning are as follows: "Every struggle for national liberation must take zones of influence into account." (Fanon 1967 pg. 124). Fanon is instructing us to be wary of the geo-political power relations that will impact any attempt by us to challenge the hegemony of the North Atlantic as follows: "This is because any difficulty that is put in the way of the supremacy of the West in any given section of the world is a concrete threat to its economic power, to the range of its military strategic bases, and representing a limiting of its potential." (Fanon 1967 pg. 124). All challenges to the hegemony of neo-colonial domination will be dealt with as a challenge to North Atlantic interests and will be suppressed by any means necessary, including deep state incursions, with no respect for the will of the majority of the supposedly free and sovereign people of a free and sovereign nation. Our right to self-determination as free and sovereign citizens are simply powerless words we have embraced from the North Atlantic of no effect when we pose threats to the hegemony of the North Atlantic over us. For power must always subvert law, ethics and morality, simply a case of white power expressed in your face! For Fanon this treachery of the West, some say hypocrisy others say moral relativism, is the expression of a psychological problem as follows: "And here we touch upon a psychological problem which is perhaps not fundamental but which enters into the framework of the dialectics that is now developing. The West, whose economic system is the standard (and by virtue of that fact oppressive), also prides itself on its humanist superiority. The Western "model" is being attacked in its essence and in its finality." (Fanon 1967 pg. 125). The North Atlantic insists that its predatory capitalism is the only relevant and effective economic system to engender humanism, but the manner in which it suppresses challenges to its interests in the neo-colonial world does not and cannot engender humanism. This then is the expression of a psychological problem the white North Atlantic is presenting, which impacts the power relations between the neo-colonial world and the white North Atlantic. A white massa/messiah complex enmeshed in a white supremacist discourse which justifies the right to dominate the world and to brutally suppress all resistance, for it is for our own good as it is only through the hegemony of the white massa/messiah we can reach the white promised land and never forget the white massa/messiah never lies, as the First Peoples of North America and Australia learnt the hard way. Fanon's solution for the neo-colonial world is as follows: "The negation of political *beni-oui-ouism* is linked to the refusal of economic *beni-oui-ouism* and of cultural *beni-oui-ouism*. It is no longer true that the promotion of values passes through the screen of the West." (Fanon 1967 pg. 125). To destroy political subservience or being a yes man, we of the neo-colonial world have to destroy being economically and culturally subservient/yes men, Steven, Chicken George, Gunga Din and Hop Sing. Our core problem then is our subservience to the West, where we run all our values, our worldviews through the screen mesh of the white North Atlantic thereby adopting the psychology of beni-oui-ouism, a yes man, a white ass kisser, simply shameless. Fanon then issues a warning on the nature of neo-colonial subservience as follows: "All the colonial countries that are waging the struggles today must know that the political independence that they will wring from the enemy in exchange for the maintenance of an economic dependence is only a snare and a delusion, that the second phase of total liberation is necessary because required by the popular masses, that this second phase, because it is a capital one, is bound to be hard and waged with iron determination." (Fanon 1967 pgs. 125-126). The gift of independence is granted on the grounds that the ex-colony is now under the domination of the former massa where economic, political and cultural domination masks the fundamental domination at the level of the idea, of the worldview. In this operational terrain of dependence and servility, the crisis of legitimacy soon arises as the masses move in search of the second phase of their liberation, this time from the political elites of a free nation. This drive for the second phase by the masses is beaten back brutally by the political and military elites in conjunction with the state apparatus of the neo-colonial dominator. The failure to resolve this power relation of the demand for the second phase effectively destroys the social order as extremism in all its forms becomes the norm of daily life. Fanon ends this article as follows: "The wolves must no longer find isolated lambs to prey upon. Imperialism must be blocked in all its attempts to strengthen itself. The peoples demand this; the historic process requires it." (Fanon 1967 pg. 126). In the 21st century the results of our dismal failure to heed the warning of Fanon is manifest with an overwhelming number of lambs isolated and slaughtered by white North Atlantic imperialism such as Yemen, the Democratic Republic of the Congo, the Central African Republic, Haiti and Libya and so on and on!

The Significance of the Algerian War of Liberation

In *El Moudjahid* No. 31, November 1, 1958 Fanon published an article on the significance of the Algerian War of Liberation to the power relations of the decolonisation process and the neo-colonial condition. Fanon states: "it was not rare to note a suggestion of hostility, indeed of hate, in the attitude of the colonialist worker toward the colonised. This can be explained by the fact that the retreat of imperialism and the reconversion of the underdeveloped structures specific to the colonised state are immediately accompanied by economic crises that the workers in the colonialist countries are the first to feel." "At the critical point at which the colonised peoples fling themselves into the struggle and demand their independence a critical period elapses in the course of which, paradoxically, the interest of the 'metropolitan' workers and peasants seems to go counter to that of the colonised peoples." (Fanon 1967 pgs. 144-145). The point at which the struggle for liberation from colonial domination impacts the earning power of the workers and peasants of the colonial metropole negatively, results in the workers and peasants being opposed to the war of liberation and in support of continued colonial domination. Workers and peasants support colonial domination not only as a result of their loss of earnings and job insecurity arising from anticolonial struggle, but in keeping with nationalist and race solidarity where they affirm white supremacy and the manifest destiny of the race. The revolutionary class consciousness of the working class in the North Atlantic is a myth propagated by Marx's idyllic. During the American civil war, the English workers displaced by the lack of slave grown cotton from the slave plantations of the US South openly supported African enslavement, the Confederacy and white supremacy as the solution to their hardships, not an anti-capitalist alternative in a country which first abolished African enslavement and the African slave trade and sought to pressure other European colonial countries to follow suit by force by various means. To embrace Marx's idyllic is then to open oneself to make grave mistakes in the strategic measures utilised in a war of liberation from colonial domination. Fanon now deals with the fundamental nature of colonial power relations premised on the hegemony of the white North Atlantic coloniser as follows: "The colonised have this in common, that their right to constitute a people is challenged. To diversify and legitimise this general attitude of the colonialist we find racism, hatred, contempt on the part of the oppressor, and correlatively stultification, illiteracy, moral asphyxiation, and endemic undernourishment in the oppressed." (Fanon 1967 pg. 145). The colonised have no right and will not be allowed to constitute a people through the formulation and application of our discourse of being and national culture.

We, by dint of being dominated by the white North Atlantic coloniser, must be constituted by colonial discourse to be servile, subservient servants of the colonial overlord. This constituted product of colonial domination is then the product of racism, hatred and contempt which ensures we are stultified, illiterate, amoral and perpetually undernourished both physically, emotionally and intellectually. We are then the product of colonial domination immersed in self-immolation driven by self-hate, inferiority complexes and arrested development which continues under neo-colonial domination, but significantly much more potent than under colonial domination, for we are free, sovereign citizens of free, sovereign nations.

Fanon now presents his position on the nature of French colonial domination of Algeria as follows: "The Algerian war occupies a choice place in the process of the demolition of imperialism." "French colonialism in Algeria has considerably enriched the history of barbarous methods used by international colonialism." (Fanon 1967 pg. 146). The Algerian war of liberation and the counter war to preserve colonial domination are noteworthy historical events for the lessons they provide on the power relations involved when you engage with white North Atlantic domination in the quest to be free self-determining humans. The barbarity the French unleashed on the Algerian population was singular in its use of violence to break the back of Algerian resistance, but this barbarity remains absolved in the official history of white North Atlantic domination. Whilst the eventual Algerian, Arab victory over white France can never be placed in its historical context for it is an instance of defeat at the hands of an inferior race, as the British army at Isandlwana at the hands of the Zulu. But the white colonial supremacists of France were plagued with recognising the impact of the Algerian war on their quest to maintain their colonial empire intact in spite of the loss of Vietnam. They were then in denial, having drunk the Kool Aid they brewed for consumption by the colonised, and in this condition refused to accept the loss of empire, hence their hatred for de Gaulle and his intervention to save the empire using a triage methodology. Fanon states: "the French colonialists tend to consider de Gaulle as a traitor or as a peddler. As a matter of fact, the general is once again saving the colonialists interests by laying out a community which, being unequal, organised for the sole profit of a metropolis, maintains important colonial structures intact. But had it not been for General de Gaulle's intervention, the collapse of the empire shortly would have ensued. An apparent traitor to his trust, general de Gaulle is in reality the momentary saviour of a certain colonial reality." (Fanon 1967 pg. 149). Fanon posits the case of de Gaulle and his strategy to save the French colonial zone of influence rather than lose the French colonial venture to wars of liberation, which France was incapable of prolonged engagement with. General de Gaulle chose the neo-colonial option, expressed through various political forms, in an effort to save and redesign a French zone of influence for the postcolonial world. The French white supremacist colonialists branded de Gaulle a traitor, but the lesson is the fact that the empire collapsed and what is left is the neo-colonial condition. The lesson in this to all of us, is the reality that there will be always a white supremacist hard line in white North Atlantic politics that demands the intensification of the neo-colonial condition, especially the public indicators of our servility and subservience to the white North Atlantic, especially to the USA. In the white North Atlantic today this line is presently challenging the hold on political power of the post-World War 2 liberal line of neo-colonial domination with a liberal, smiling face and blood on their hands. This liberal smiles and blood line is anathema to the white supremacist North Atlantic political discourse and pursuit of this white racist line is now threatening to dismantle the neo-colonial order of servility erected after the second World War, whilst replacing it with a neo-colonial order broken up into blocks and alliances facing off with each other, very much similar to the condition of Europe in the run up to the first world war. As the white supremacist colonialists arrayed against de Gaulle, they are formulating actions and strategies for a neo-colonial world that has changed and evolved in such a manner that makes the application of these actions and strategies a destabilising factor, rather than the means to recreate a hegemony that was the product of an era long since disappeared, a by-gone era. There is then a major misfit between reality and discourse and reality and actions wished for and sought, such is the formula for the collapse of empire, for the position of strength that informs the strategy is a figment of the white supremacist imagination. Simply, the result of drinking the Kool

Aid mixed and dispensed for servile neo-colonials or being seduced by your lies formulated to seduce the enemy.

African Liberation

In *El Moudjahid*, No. 58, January 5, 1960 Fanon published an article on the nature, conditions and requirements for African liberation or the liberation of the colonised areas of the African continent. Fanon states: "It is rigorously true that decolonisation is proceeding, but it is rigorously false to pretend and believe that this decolonisation is the fruit of an objective dialectic which more or less assumes the appearance of an absolutely inevitable mechanism." (Fanon 1967 pg. 170). There are no historical forces that will inevitably result in the decolonisation of Africa that are the product of and driven by class conflict. There are no objective conditions that exist external of the actions of man that drive decolonisation in Africa, for the decolonisation of Africa is only accomplished and made possible with the actions of Africans. Fanon is then debunking the crude, mechanistic dialectic of Marx and Engels in "The Communist Manifesto." Fanon states: "Optimism in Africa is the direct product of the revolutionary action of the African masses, whether political or armed-often both at one and the same time." (Fanon 1967 pg. 171). The optimism that liberation from colonial domination engenders is the product of mass revolutionary action whether political or armed. The hegemony of the neo-colonial condition over the postcolonial world is the product of the failure of the masses to undertake revolutionary political or armed action and the reasons for this failure are complex, which involve the very nature of colonial domination and its impact on the colonised. Fanon continues: "Well! The African peoples must likewise remember that they have had to face a form of Nazism, a form of exploitation of man, of physical and spiritual liquidation clearly imposed, that the French, the English, and South African manifestations of that evil need to engage their attention, but they must be prepared to face this evil as an evil extending over the whole of the African territory." (Fanon 1967 pg. 171). Colonial domination is inherently evil, as it is a multifaceted assault on the humanity and the wellbeing of the colonised, as it is the source of the fascist and national socialist forms of North Atlantic white supremacy, which were hatched in the laboratories of colonial domination from slavery onwards with the non-white colonised as the lab animals experimented on. Colonial domination was also exploitation of the resources and labour power of the colonised, with the wealth generated exported to the North Atlantic which deepened our exploitation, our arrested development and our dependence. Colonial fascism and chronic exploitation together imposed on us physical and spiritual liquidation, which constituted servile, subservient colonised non-whites in the service of white North Atlantic hegemony. The great tragedy which we brought upon ourselves is the neo-colonial condition where nothing has changed, the fascism continues but now its black on black fascism driving black on black racism, the chronic exploitation, the export of our wealth to the North Atlantic has intensified, whilst our underdevelopment has spawned misery for the masses in the face of obscene ostentatious lifestyles of the oligarchs of the neo-colonial world and the race to enter the billionaire club in the North Atlantic. In the 21st century the key reality of the neo-colonial world is the graphic inequality of neo-colonial social orders and the inequality between the neo-colonial world and the North Atlantic. Inequality is the potent expression of the colonial/neo-colonial continuum in the 21st century. Fanon states towards the end of the article as follows: "We Africans say that for more than 100 years the life of 200 million Africans has been life at a discount, contested, a life perpetually haunted by death." (Fanon 1967 pg. 173). Under neo-colonial domination life for the postcolonial Africans has not qualitatively changed as life for the significant majority of the masses in Africa is still discounted, contested with their death ever in pursuit of them. The single difference under neo-colonial domination is the fact that the perpetrators of the continued assault on the humanity and development of Africans are the fellow Africans who exercise their servility to the white North Atlantic and act upon their personal lust for power and wealth by exercising the colonial methodology of exploitation and domination in the 21st century. In the 21st century the postcolonial African is still in need of liberation and this liberationary action is in her/his hands. Fanon states: "Africa will not be free through the mechanical development of material forces, but it is in the hands of the African and his brain that will set into motion and will implement the dialectics of the liberation of the continent." (Fanon 1967 pg. 173). Fanon in his final work had then to explain the false starts to decolonisation manifested in Africa, for in order to ensure victory in the second phase we must understand the reasons for the failures in first phase, hence Fanon ensured that he left his analysis published in English as "The Wretched of the Earth" towards the realisation of success in the second phase.

In Part Five, the final part, of "Toward the African Revolution" two undated articles comprise this part which Fanon left unpublished. One article came from his notebooks detailing his revolutionary activity to create a pipeline of supply to the Algerian revolution, through Mali via the Sahel and the Sahara to the revolutionary forces, as the French were disrupting the supply lines from Tunisia and Morocco. In March 1960 Fanon was appointed the delegate of the Algerian revolutionary forces to Accra, Ghana, then under the rule of Kwame Nkrumah and a beacon of Pan African revolutionary action. Fanon and the Algerian delegation to Mali set off from Ghana during which Fanon recorded his thoughts in his notebooks from which the selection was published.

The Pitfalls of Decolonisation in Africa

Absence of Ideology

Fanon states: "Colonialism and its derivatives do not, as a matter of fact constitute the present enemies of Africa. In a short time, this continent will be liberated. For my part, the deeper I enter into the cultures and the political circles the surer I am that the great danger that threatens Africa is the absence of ideology." (Fanon 1967 pg. 186). Colonialism and neo-colonialism are not the primary enemies of Africa for the grave threat to the postcolonial Africa comes from the condition of the African where there is action in a colonial and postcolonial context devoid of ideology which are the actions of a servile, subservient actors. Decolonisation demands an anticolonial worldview which defines the alternative to colonial and neo-colonial domination and the mechanisms necessary to attain this desired outcome. This then is the defining role of ideology, which in its absence illustrates the intellectual poverty of the postcolonial actors wielding power over the African process of change. This intellectual poverty betrays the servility of the ruling elites to the white North Atlantic. Fanon links this absence of ideology to the instability of the newly independent nations and their ruling elites of Africa as follows: "In Africa, on the other hand, the countries that come to independence are as unstable as their new middle classes or their renovated princes. After a few hesitant steps in the international arena the national middle classes, not feeling the threat of the traditionally colonial power, suddenly develop great appetites. And as they do not yet have any political experience they think they can conduct political affairs like their business. Perquisites, threats, even despoiling of the victims. All of which is regrettable, for the small states have no other choice but to beg the former metropolis to remain just a little longer in these pseudo-imperialist states, an extremist militarist policy leads to a reduction of public investments in countries which in certain respects are still medieval. The discontented workers undergo a repression as pitiless as that of the colonial period. Trade unions and opposition political parties are confined to a quasi-clandestine state. The people, the people who had given everything in the difficult moments of the struggle for national liberation wonder, with their empty hands and their bellies, as to the reality of their victory." (Fanon 1967 pgs. 186-187). The servile, subservient inexperienced middle class of Africa first surrenders to the former colonial massa, willingly embracing neo-colonial domination and dependence for the politics of the nation is conducted in the interest of the middle class as there is no concept of national destiny. The middle class under the tutelage and protection of the white North Atlantic then sets about the task of looting the assets of the nation and suppressing all real and perceived sources of dissent. Under the hegemony of the middle class colonial suppression is unleashed, but this phase is controlled by non-white faces, with the inexorable result of deepening the underdevelopment legacy left by the colonial massa to the independent nation as political oppression and authoritarianism heightens underdevelopment. The masses in their grinding poverty in spite of the anticolonial mass movement and their subsequent independence are forced to question the efficacy of resistance, for resistance resulting in success brought only intense suffering. This is deliberate to dissuade a resurgence of mass action in the second phase of the resistance for the middle class, the military elite and the oligarchs are now practising devotees of colonial fascism protected by their white North Atlantic overlords. These states must then be chronically unstable, subject to inertia, chronic decay and violence, even genocide. This is then the genesis of the neo-colonial condition in crisis in the 21st century where your young population is voting on their living conditions and life chances with their feet the world over. Fanon insists that these states are chronically unstable as a result of the nature and characteristics of the middle class who inherit these independent states from the colonial massa, especially seen in their propensity to engage in aggression, both internally and externally, they are then holders of a colonial fascist worldview which they without hesitation apply by their actions taken. Fanon states: "In reality the colonised states that have reached independence by the political path seem to have no other concern than to find themselves a real battlefield with wounds and destruction. It is clear, however, that this psychological explanation, which appeals to a hypothetical need for release of pent-up aggressiveness, does not satisfy us. The triumphant middle class are the most impetuous, the most enterprising, the most annexationist in the world," (Fanon 1967 pg. 187). Those nations in receipt of the gift of independence under the political leadership of the middle class indicate a penchant for war and violence, both internally and externally, as there are always enemies at the door to be neutralised. There is no adequate psychological explanation for this neo-colonial middle class propensity, for the explanation lies in the power relations between the middle class and the masses and the power relations between the middle class and the white North Atlantic hegemon. The middle class is a relatively small insecure class as it has few, if any, points of groundings with the masses, their hallucinatory whiteness alienates them from the masses for they consider the masses inferior and a fetter on progress white North Atlantic style. Very soon after independence when faced with the backlash from the masses the middle class resorts to fascist colonial repression in order to retain their hold on political power. The threat of the masses is not the only potent threat, as there is the threat of the military arising from the fact that both the white North Atlantic and the middle class political elite pour resources into the military after independence, resources denied to the masses to address their chronic poverty and deprivation. The middle class then undertakes external wars as distractions, events to engage the military other than in seizing political power and to satisfy the agenda of white North Atlantic interests. This insecure and lumpen class then destroys the newly independent country in order to save it for themselves, an action which potently illustrates the mental deficiencies of colonised/neo-colonialized non-whites the world over. This lumpen political elite in control of the neo-colonial state, fully propped up by the white North Atlantic, could not have ever embraced the vision Fanon shared with others as Nkrumah for postcolonial Africa. Fanon states his vison as follows: "African Unity is a principle on the basis of which it is proposed to achieve the United States of Africa without passing through the middle-class chauvinistic national phase with its procession of wars and death-tolls." (Fanon 1967 pg. 187). The gift of independence places the hegemony of the national middle class on the political terrain of the newly decolonised state but this hegemony unleashes the chauvinistic, servile, subservient middle class' propensity for aggression, wars arising from their embrace of colonialist fascism. Fanon's alternate political path to defeat this inevitable self-destructive middle class politics is African Unity, premised on the creation of the United states of Africa which destroys the artificial boundaries and nation states created by white North Atlantic colonial domination. This alternate political path was stillborn, as any challenge to national middle class hegemony was defeated by the alliance of the neo-colonial political elites and the political elites and the deep state of the North Atlantic, with the continuing bloodbath that has characterised the postcolonial history of Africa to the 21st century. This lumpen middle class has turned postcolonial Africa into a blood stained land noted for human suffering, oppression and underdevelopment characterised by grinding, stifling inequality.

The Murder of Patrice Lumumba of the Democratic Republic of the Congo (DRC)

DRC was granted independence from brutal Belgian colonial domination and exploitation in June 1960 with Patrice Lumumba as its Prime Minister, on the 17th January 1961 Lumumba was murdered by the Belgian deep state working through Congolese secessionist paramilitaries. The political elites and the deep state of Belgium and the USA never wanted an independent DRC under the political rule of Lumumba, but were forced by the will of the DRC masses to place Lumumba in political power over the independent DRC. Immediately thereafter the deep state launched their covert/overt operations to destroy Lumumba's political dominance by any means necessary. In this final article Fanon is writing his analysis of Lumumba's murder during Fanon's final year of life, for Fanon died in December 1961. Fanon states: "the one discovered that something very serious was being plotted against Congo's independence and against Africa." "it became clear that a whole very precise procedure was about to be put into motion." "But this fact does not explain the deterioration that has progressively spread through the Congo; this fact does not explain the coldly planned, coldly executed murder of Lumumba. This colonialist collaboration is insufficient to explain why in, February 1961, Africa is about to experience its first great crisis over the Congo." (Fanon 1967 pgs. 191-192). Those seeking to explain the failings of the neo-colonial order insist on the covert operations of the deep state of the North Atlantic and the pressure wielded by the political elites of the North Atlantic, thereby exonerating the complicity of, and the vital input made by the Congolese neo-colonial political elites, oligarchs and military in the murder of Lumumba. Even before the murder of Lumumba, independent Congo was paralysed by ethnic wars, political intrigue and the propensity of state officials to utilise their state jobs to plunder the Congo rather than to develop the Congo. Congo's independence was then a still birth and it officially died when Lumumba was murdered. Fanon continues: "Lumumba believed in his mission. He had an exaggerated confidence in the people." "He only forgot that he could not be everywhere at once and that the miracle of the explanation was less the truth of what he set forth than the truth of his person." (Fanon 1967 pg. 193). Lumumba found himself in a power relation with the masses of the Congo which ultimately allowed his demise, as he was not the President of the DRC but its Prime Minister, and Lumumba was the only politician in the Congo that exercised the ability to influence the action of the masses, but he never used this link to develop a national consciousness which gave him the power to deal with his political enemies. The truth of his person cannot develop a national consciousness which impacts politics and the order of the state, for all there was on the ground was a cult of Lumumba the miracle worker, for there was no truth/ discourse of Lumumba at the ground level that was a political weapon. Lumumba, the miracle worker, was then naked in the face of the covert plots to kill him. Lumumba, the miracle worker of the masses must be joined to Lumumba, the devotee of the Congo, which meant Lumumba must die! Fanon states: "Why? Because the enemies of Africa had understood. They had realised quite clearly that Lumumba was sold-sold, to Africa of course. In other words, he was no longer to be bought." (Fanon 1967 pg. 193). In the run up to independence political and economic forces in the DRC quickly formed the opinion that Lumumba must be eliminated, this opposition rallied with the support of the Belgian and the US deep state. The die was now cast. These same DRC political and economic forces, including the military high command, were not in search of being convinced that Lumumba posed a grave threat to their interests, therefore when Lumumba earned the mistrust of the USA they were there to facilitate, to act not to be convinced. The deep, potent threat Lumumba posed to the white North Atlantic and the elites of the DRC was his willingness to dance with the "other" side and he paid for it with his life and the destruction of the DRC, his beloved. Fanon states: "And there were other Africans, not altogether puppets, but who are frightened the moment the question of disengaging Africa from the West comes up." (Fanon 1967 pg. 194). There was then a crude consensus amongst the elite, for even those who did not pride themselves on the servility and subservience to the white North Atlantic agreed, Lumumba now posed a potent threat to the future of the DRC as there was no DRC divorced from the West, in spite of brutal and brutalising Belgian colonial domination.

Fanon then insists that Lumumba's deadly mistake was to embrace the UN and expect a timely, expeditious and effective intervention into the ethnic wars triggered by the secessionists of Katanga province, funded and armed by the Belgians. Fanon states: "First of all by Lumumba himself when he asked for the intervention of the UN. It was wrong to appeal to the UN. The UN has never been capable of validly settling a single one of the problems raised before the conscience of man by colonialism, and every time it has intervened, it was to come concretely to the rescue of the colonialist power of the oppressing power." (Fanon 1967 pg. 194). Lumumba, faced with a joint, concerted covert operation to remove him from the politics of the DRC by any means necessary, facilitated this move by appealing to the UN for their intervention into the Katanga secessionist affair which was the creation of the Belgian deep state. This UN intervention, rather than giving Lumumba operational space/time, simply hastened his demise for the UN is the tool of the white North Atlantic neo-colonial agenda, clearly attested to in the case of Rwanda and its genocide. The lack of mass action, at this critical juncture in the period encompassing the run up to independence and his murder, was the root and branch of Lumumba's operational weakness. Simply visualise the mass action that broke the back of the coup d'état and restored Hugo Chavez to power in Venezuela in 2002 to grasp the extent of Lumumba's weakness. Fanon continues as follows: "In reality the UN is the legal card used by the imperialist interests when the card of brute force has failed." "Lumumba's mistake was then, in a first period to believe in the UN's friendly impartiality. He forgot that the UN in its present state is only a reserve assembly, set up by the Great, to continue between two armed conflicts the 'peaceful struggle' for the division of the world." (Fanon 1967 pg. 195). The UN in the 21st century continues to illustrate the reality that it was never meant to be impartial, as it was constructed to seduce and encapsulate the efforts of the newly independent world following World War Two by concentrating resources and time to a multilateral organisation funded and dominated by the white North Atlantic, which keeps you as the proverbial hamster on the mill of futility whilst your masses suffer. Fanon states: "Africans must remember this lesson. If we need outside aid, let us call our friends. They alone can really and totally help us achieve our objectives because precisely, the friendship that links us is a friendship of combat." (Fanon 1967 pg. 196). Rather than the UN Lumumba needed an intervention force of Africans, but in the failure to form the United States of Africa what is the mechanism in existence to marshal such a force, ah yes, the UN. As we all dance the dance of circular futility, from generation to generation with the same outcome: the deepening suffering of the masses.

Denial, delusion or simply madness derived from the colonial/neo-colonial continuum, no all of the above.

Fanon now states that Africans, as all neo-colonial peoples, have made a mistake as follows: "Our mistake, the mistake we Africans made, was to have forgotten that the enemy never withdraws sincerely. He never understands. He capitulates, but does not become converted. Our mistake is to have believed that the enemy has lost his combativeness and his harmfulness. If Lumumba is in the way, Lumumba disappears. Hesitation in murder has never characterised imperialism." (Fanon 1967 pg. 196). We have all been seduced by the white discourse of freedom and sovereignty because of the incessant drive of our inferiority complex for a seat at the white man's table, rather than in his kitchen. This unrelenting desire to be accepted demanded that we accept and act on the belief that we were now free and sovereign and will be treated as such, which in its historical operation is a grand delusion. They murder, they remove from and place in power without care nor concern for the price paid by the masses for these imperialist actions of impunity amongst a community of free nations. The current best examples being Iraq and Libya.

Fanon ends this article as follows: "For no one knows the name of the next Lumumba. There is in Africa a certain tendency represented by certain men. It is this tendency, dangerous to imperialism, which is at issue. Let us be sure never to forget it: that fate of all of us is at stake in the Congo." (Fanon 1967 pg. 197). Some of the names of the next Lumumba were: Eduardo Mondlane, Amilcar Cabral, Steve Biko and Walter Rodney, all murdered as Lumumba was. Sadly, there are much more, too many to list, for imperialism lives through its neo-colonial device which potently indicates that we have failed to learn the grave lesson and act strategically in response to which Fanon cited for all of us. That is the crux of the issue of white North Atlantic domination, for we alone are to blame and we refuse to accept blame by relentlessly speaking of the given of the white man's racism, without doing anything strategic about. Which shows that we are simply begging for a place at massa's table, we simply do not want to challenge massa, nor change the power relations. I have scant time for complainers, for they are soul suckers who sell you out to massa for scraps from his table.

Closing Words

I have written this deconstruction of the discourse of Frantz Fanon of decolonisation, violence and the power relations of the neo-colonial condition in a state of liberation, having exited the racist worldview of the white North Atlantic in times past in my life. I live in a neo-colonial world but I am not of this world, for my soul inhabits a space that effectively locks out the ravages of the neo-colonial condition on my worldview, my concept of self and my psyche. In this free soul-space I have no anger, hate and self-hate issues, all I have is the anxiety generated by being fixed within a small geographic space for way too long in my life. When liberated you are called upon to migrate ceaselessly, to roam, which is the necessary counterbalance to your soul rootedness, for you must constantly perfect your ability to constantly be unattached, to be not of the existing world for the grave pitfall arises with desire. For desire is the plaything of power in its perpetual quest for domination, and since no human can ever escape power, except to become the only human on earth, then power, its driving quest and its power relations are a given of human existence. Fanon's discourse is then about power, power relations and desire; and liberation is then about extricating oneself from a specific discourse of power, power relations and its desire at the level of the idea, but it continues to impact you at every moment of your existence. What in effect you become with liberation is a multi-dimensional human capable of discerning, interpreting, perceiving and acting in the terrain of at minimum two discourses and two mechanisms of power. You see all the minefields of the neo-colonial condition and the white North Atlantic supremacist discourse, but like Neo, you are yet to enter into the operational terrain where Zion is now hegemonic no longer hiding deep beneath the earth. But the salient issue is not seeing the discourse of Zion exercising hegemony, but to have seen these discourses, their mechanism of power, their instruments of power and their order of desire, that is the expression of Liberation. The path demands that we Exit the Racist Worldview.

Epilogue
The Neo-Colonial Condition of the 21st Century Illustrated

The power relation between the North Atlantic and the Third World especially its former colonies, which arises from North Atlantic hegemony, is illustrated and enforced by the levels of poverty that plague the Third World. Inequality, poverty and deprivation are then an instrument of power of North Atlantic hegemony operationalised within the neo-colonial condition. It is a product of North Atlantic hegemony and an instrument of exerting North Atlantic hegemony, inseparable, joined at the hips. North Atlantic hegemony produces poverty, inequality and deprivation because of the nature of its hegemonic power relation whilst it utilizes poverty, inequality and deprivation as instruments vitally necessary to exerting power. This hegemonic power is conceptualized, operationalised and exerted as the product of a discourse of white supremacy and its worldview which demands hegemony at the level of the idea over the inferior races, expressed at the level of material existence, where their inferiority is made palpable by their poverty. Whilst illustrating that our inferiority makes us poor, not neo-colonial domination. This discursive instrument has multiplied its potency, in the North Atlantic since the 1980's with the drive to hegemony over the political discourse of the North Atlantic by the discourse of neo-liberalism. The present hegemony of financial market neo-liberal capitalism, especially in the USA has now realized the application of poverty as an instrument of hegemony in the North Atlantic. This has resulted in the creation of a neo-feudal social order under the hegemony of financial market neo-liberal capitalism.

The 2018 Global Multidimensional Poverty Index (MPI) of the UNDP presents an estimate of 1,334 million people living in poverty distributed globally as follows: Sub-Saharan Africa 560 million persons, South Asia 546 million people, East Asia and the Pacific 118 million people, Arab States 66 million people, Latin America and the Caribbean 40 million people and

Europe and Central Asia 4 million people. The two areas of the planet that experienced a complex and lengthy period of colonial imperialist contact and conquest are the homelands of poverty in the world in 2018. This indicates that colonial domination left these regions chronically underdeveloped, prone and susceptible to embracing the neo-colonial condition, which maintains the colonial propensity to poverty, deprivation and inequality. This neo-colonial condition is then an evolved power relation derived from colonial domination and colonial domination was driven and defined by the discourse of white supremacy, operationalised by its white supremacist worldview. The neo-colonial condition is then the product of a power relation involving non-white races who have embraced and act upon, the image of themselves handed them by the discourse of white supremacy and the whites of the North Atlantic social order. This is not simply being compliant with the demands of white politicians, bureaucrats and capitalists, this is a condition of worldview and discursive subservience, of being a servile driver on massa's plantation, whilst massa's drivers insist that we are a free and sovereign nation and people, who cherish dearly our democracy. There can be no neo-colonial condition without a phalanx of non-white groups intent on action in the interests of massa, whose interests they insist are theirs. This phalanx, ever dutiful to its role as the fifth column, must relentlessly formulate and launch operations utilizing instruments of power that assault all attempts to challenge the hegemony of this phalanx. This relentless battle for their supremacy, which in fact is for the enduring hegemony of North Atlantic white supremacy, is then what constitutes the neo-colonial condition and the grinding futility of our life on a daily basis, where we are taught that as a non-white race we deserve our lot in life. This is the piercing daily lesson, that relentlessly invites us to nihilism, for this is the existential condition hegemonic white supremacy, through its compliant phalanx, desires for all of us. For nihilism justifies the slow, methodical, organised genocide made manifest in the 21st century, unleashed on us since first contact.

References

Fanon, Frantz (1963): "The Wretched of the Earth" Grove Press USA

Fanon, Frantz (1967): "Toward the African Revolution (Political Essays)" Grove Press USA

Readers can access my website at https://www.daurius.com/ which has a list of my publications indicating my works of research on the Caribbean which contributes to the production of knowledge contained within an alternate discourse that is liberationary which embraces the discourse of Frantz Fanon.

Also by Daurius Figueira

Discourse of Slavery

Massa's White Supremacist Discourse of West Indian Negro Slavery
Deconstructed Volume 1
Massa's White Supremacist Discourse of West Indian Negro Slavery
Deconstructed Volume 2

Frantz Fanon for the 21st Century

Frantz Fanon for the 21st Century Volume 1 Frantz Fanon's Discourse of
Racism and Culture, the Negro and the Arab Deconstructed
Frantz Fanon for the 21st Century Volume 2 Frantz Fanon's Discourse of
Decolonisation and Violence, the Nature of Power and Power Relations of
Neo-colonial African States,
Frantz Fanon for the 21st Century Volume 3 The Algerian Revolution,
Islamic Discourse, the Colonizer and the Discourse of White Supremacy

Standalone

Belize: Human Smuggling, Transnational Organised Crime, Politicians
And Public Servants
Biopower, Racism, State Racism and The Modern/Post Modern North
Atlantic State: Michel Foucault's Genealogy of the Historico-Political
Discourse of Race War Deconstructed

Derek Walcott's Poetry Deconstructed, Its Political and Sociological
Discourse Revealed
Transnational Organized Crime and Drug Trafficking in the Second
Decade of the 21st Century in the Dominican Republic, Suriname,
Venezuela, French Guiana, Martinique and Guadeloupe
The Islamic State and the Muslims of Trinidad and Tobago in the 21st
Century
A Deconstruction of Michel Foucault's 1979 Discourse of Neo-Liberalism
for the 21st Century
A Deconstruction of Qu'ranic Discourse for the 21st Century

About the Author

Daurius Figueira is a researcher, analyst and author located in the anti-Enlightenment and anti-Science discourse/worldview/paradigm specialising in the study of the illicit drug trade, the illicit small arms trade and human smuggling of the Caribbean, Islamic extremism and racism/white supremacy with an emphasis on power relations. You can access his website to experience and download his research papers published online and view his range of books. His website address is: https://www.daurius.com and his blog on the Caribbean is at: https://drugtrade.wordpress.com/

Read more at https://www.daurius.com.